Count It All Joy

Count It All Joy

Grady Wilson

BROADMAN PRESS
Nashville, Tennessee

All inside photos are courtesy of the Billy Graham Evangelistic Association or the Grady Wilson family. BGEA photographers: Russ Busby, Bud Meyer, Äke Lundberg.

Library of Congress Cataloging in Publication Data

Wilson, Grady, 1919-
  Count it all joy.

  Includes index.
  1. Wilson, Grady, 1919-   . 2. Graham, Billy,
1918-   . 3. Evangelists—United States—Biography.
I. Title.
BV3785.W615A35   1984   269'.2'0924 [B]   84-4934
ISBN 0-8054-7214-2

Dedication

To my wife, *Wilma*, and
my daughters,
Nancy Carol and *Connie Jane*,
who have lovingly stood with
me all these years and made
my ministry possible . . .
and to *Billy Graham*
and the Team who have
inspired and uplifted me
in the marvelous ministry
of proclaiming Jesus Christ,
our Lord and Savior

A Personal Word
from Billy Graham

From the very beginning of my ministry Grady and T. W. Wilson have been among my closest associates, not only traveling with me a great deal but also involved in prayer and counseling in most of the decisions I have made in my ministry.

No one could have had more faithful and loyal friends. Everyone who knows Grady loves to hear him tell stories. Next to my father I think he is the best storyteller I have ever known. I think his jokes, exaggerated stories, and wonderful sense of humor have probably helped to keep us balanced as we have traveled the world under such a pressured schedule.

Only when we get to heaven will he realize what he means to me personally, my family, and my ministry. But beyond his storytelling ability, which is unique to Grady, he is also a man with deep dedication to Christ and probably has as much common sense and basic "horse sense" as anyone I know.

At the peak of his ministry he was struck down by serious physical problems. But in the midst of much suffering during the past few years, he has continued to serve the Lord in the ministry of evangelism.

While I have not yet read the finished draft of the book, I am looking forward to it with great anticipation.

BILLY GRAHAM

Preface

My brethren, count it all joy when ye fall into divers temptations (James 1:2, KJV).

My brothers, whenever you have to face trials of many kinds, count yourselves extremely happy (NEB).

"Count it all joy" is one of my favorite expressions from the Bible. That phrase of encouragement represents my heartfelt emotions at this juncture of my life. This book, *Count It All Joy*, covers more than fifty years of my life and ministry for our Lord and Savior Jesus Christ.

The seeds of this volume sprouted in my heart decades ago. Many of my friends have suggested that, because of my sense of humor, this should be a book of funny experiences only—and the book is chock full of them. But that would present a slanted, one-sided picture. Although I consider myself a humorist of sorts, humor and jollity are not really the trademarks of yours truly. My number-one concern is the conversion to Jesus Christ of every person on the face of the earth. My heart goes out to countless millions—and also to defeated, backslidden Christians.

This is my first book, even though I have published scores of sermons and articles for the Billy Graham Evangelistic Association, including *Decision* magazine, then edited by Sherwood Eliot Wirt.[1] I have also recorded numerous tapes and records for the Association, particularly of my reading the Scriptures.

Many cannot think of me without referring to my longtime association and friendship with Billy Graham, whom I first met in October of 1934 at the Mordecai Ham revival campaign in our hometown of Charlotte, North Carolina. Hundreds of people have asked me where I would be and what I would be without Billy. My answer is: certainly my life would be vastly different. Only Cliff Barrows and George Beverly Shea preceded me as Billy's evangelistic Team members. My oldest brother, T. W., and George Wilson (no kin) had served with Billy when he was president of Northwestern Schools in Minneapolis prior to my joining the Graham Team. Even though I was preaching almost three years before Billy entered the ministry, he began a significant evangelistic work as far back as 1943 when he graduated from Wheaton College in Wheaton, Illinois.

Some might comment that I have tried to write a biography of Billy instead of myself—which is not the case. But it still remains that my service for Christ cannot be understood apart from my friendship with Billy. Today there are several associate evangelists on the Team— many who are mentioned in this book—but I was the first "associate evangelist."

T. W. and I have known Billy for a half-century. That's a long, long time. Here is my feeble attempt to chronicle that journey from my teen years in Charlotte to the present. I have included so much about Billy because my life has intertwined and meshed with his. From 1947, when Billy, Cliff, Bev, and I conducted a meeting in Charlotte, we have had a virtually unbroken relationship.

Admittedly, during the last fifteen years I have conducted more and more of my own Crusades and have participated in fewer of Billy's. There are two reasons: the innumerable requests for me to conduct Crusades of my own and occasional illness which, thank God, now seems to be under control. My heart is always with Billy and the Team.

Outside of my own conversion, the most important turning point in my life was meeting a gorgeous girl from Chicago at Wheaton back in 1942. Wilma Hardie and I married in the summer of 1943—a June wedding. Wilma has backed me without reservation—the early pastorates, the weeks (sometimes months) apart in the earlier years of the Graham Crusades, when our daughters, Constance Jane and Nancy Carol, were too young to cart all over the earth, and during the intervening years.

There is a sense in which Billy Graham belongs to the people of the entire world. None of the Team members want to sound possessive. That is not my intention, but the Team members have experienced a God-sent, unique camaraderie. In the early years of the ministry, I would at times fill in for Billy when he was not able to make it. Other Team members have done likewise off and on. Of course, Billy must be terribly sick to miss a preaching engagement.

It is impossible to thank all of those who have lifted up my arms during this ministry. And I hope to live a long time, if Jesus tarries, so I can continue to proclaim the good tidings of the gospel.

Eternal thanks go to the Team members—to George Beverly Shea, to Cliff Barrows, to T. W., all of whom are very close to Billy . . . also to my beloved wife, Wilma, and our two daughters, Nancy Carol and Connie . . . to George Stevens, the Presbyterian evangelist who was preaching when I accepted Christ . . . to Mordecai Ham, the rugged Baptist evangelist, who helped bring me to full commitment during that Charlotte campaign a half-century ago . . . to my parents, Mr. and Mrs. Thomas Wilson, who encouraged me in the Christian walk and reared all of us Wilson kids "in the nurture and admonition of the Lord" . . .

And to Billie Hanks whom I consider "my son in the ministry" . . . and to Allan C. Emery, Jr., president of the Billy Graham Evangelistic Association and chairman of the Executive Committee of the Board . . . and to Bill Mead, another dear friend on the Executive Committee of the BGEA, both of whom gave their blessings to this writing effort. Would to God I could fill a book with a roll call of my Barnabases (Barnabas, who accompanied Paul on his first missionary journey, had a name meaning "encourager").

And to Billy Graham himself, a constant inspiration to me and a man who is truly Christlike. Without his concern and assistance, this book might have "died a-bornin'."

An old preacher once commented that we should "brag on Jesus." That's what I do in these pages. "To God be the glory, great things he hath done." May God receive all the glory, honor, and praise. May this book encourage the Christian and strengthen him/her to a life of victory and fruitfulness. May this book touch those who are not sure they have eternal life.

May you, friend who may not have received Christ into your life, discover him through reading these pages. Also may the drifting Christian, who is sometimes not sure of his salvation, discover a peace that "passeth understanding."

So, this book will mean nothing unless it magnifies our Lord and Savior. My main aim is to weave an amazing tapestry of God's hand in the lives of those whom he has touched.

Count It All Joy sums it all up. Pleasant experiences have come, and I've shouted, "Count it all joy." Bad times have hit, and I've testified, "Count it all joy." Highs have been reached, and I've exulted, "Count it all joy." Lows have also been plumbed. "Count it all joy."

And I pray you will "count it all joy" as you read this book.

GRADY B. WILSON
Charlotte, NC

Introduction

Hanging between life and death after a massive heart attack, I was given virtually no chance to recover. That fateful night in 1977, when I was close to leaving this life, Billy Graham rushed to the hospital.

My doctor remonstrated with Billy that no one was allowed in the intensive-care room. The doctor insisted, "Mr. Graham, just the sight of you might be a shock, and it might be too much on Mr. Wilson's badly damaged heart."

Billy replied, "Doctor, I'm not going to ask you if I can go in and see my longtime friend and associate, Grady Wilson. I'm going in, and I'm going in now. Years ago I was very sick at a hospital. Grady was there beside me, praying with me and standing by me." So, Billy Graham, my close friend for almost a half-century, was with me in those bleak hours when I was clinging to life by a thread.

As I lay on that sick bed, praying when I would regain consciousness, my thoughts swung back to my family—my loving wife, Wilma; our daughters we had nicknamed "Nance" and "Con" (for Nancy and Connie); back to Cliff

Barrows serving as master of ceremonies and music director in countless Billy Graham Crusades around the world; back to George Beverly Shea and his God-given bass-baritone which has endeared him to millions as "America's Beloved Gospel Singer."

My thoughts returned to all of my close associations with Billy. I recalled his serious illness in 1965. Billy was severely hemorrhaging from surgery, a surgery which was a subject of wire services across the globe. Paul Harvey, on his widely-heard radio show, reported that he had talked with me and that I had shared with him the gravity of Billy's condition. The fact is, Billy almost bled to death.

Paul and I had spoken on the telephone, and I gave him the message: "Paul, Billy's lying upstairs now getting a transfusion. He's hemorrhaging badly. I summoned a nurse, and she called for a doctor. Billy's in serious condition."

Paul shocked the national radio audience when he announced: "Ladies and gentlemen, you'd better pray and pray very earnestly for Billy Graham. He's not doing as well as we have been led to believe."

How well I remembered that harrowing wait at the hospital. I stood by Billy, and now he was backing me. My thoughts surged back on me as Billy sat by my bed in that hospital at Manning, South Carolina. Hours before I had gone to my cabin on the Santee-Cooper Reservoir nearby, one of the best fishing spots on earth, I think. With a chain saw I had cut a load of wood for the fireplace and then split it further with an ax-like tool. Horrendous pains had finally struck me, and I had to drag myself back to the cabin. One of my good neighbors had driven me to the hospital.

Although I was in dreadful condition, I couldn't help remembering my life and especially my friendship with

Billy. I had often heard that, when facing impending death, your life passes in review. Perhaps my entire life didn't, but huge segments of it did.

After all, I had been one of Billy Graham's closest associates for years. We had played together, prayed together, and worked together for what seemed a lifetime.

We had laughed together (and loads of those humorous, and even funny, experiences appear in this book). I knew that most of Billy's humor is incidental. He has seldom ever been intentionally funny. Back in our earlier days he had been capable of pulling pranks on his friends, like filling my hat with shaving cream from an aerosol can and like holding hands with my best girl friend during our single days as they sat on a pew while I preached from the pulpit. Still, Billy had nearly always been the straight man in our duo.

We had cried together. People who have only heard him speaking before a massive crowd may miss the tender, sympathetic side of his personality. He preaches with intensity and passion, but he seldom cries in public. Yet, I've seen him on the front lines with severely wounded soldiers in Korea and Vietnam, crying with them. I've seen him crying over the multitudes without Jesus Christ. I've seen him weeping with lepers in a leprosarium.

No one can preach the love of God like he does without that love pouring through his life. No doubt he has preached to more people than anyone in history. His heart is big enough and compassionate enough to love all humankind. John Wesley declared, "The world is my parish." That is true of Billy's ministry.

While recuperating from near-death, I tried to sort out my memories. Billy had challenged me for years, "Grady, you're not getting any younger. Neither am I. It's time you wrote about some of your famous stories." How would I distill so many of these experiences and stories into one book? Not easily, but I would simply do the best I could with the help of God—and just touch some of the humor and pathos I have experienced in my relationship with the Billy Graham Team.

I've had trepidation about it. I've agonized and prayed about it. I am uncomfortably aware that I can never do justice to my lifetime with or without Billy Graham, never scratch the surface about my lovely wife, Wilma, and our darling daughters, Connie and Nancy Carol, never write exactly what I should about our brothers and sisters in Christ throughout the world.

What I'm trying to do, in my own words, is to bare my heart about my life and ministry—and how my life has meshed together with the soul of Christendom's greatest evangelist. Billy would reject those last three words, but I doubt if many would deny it.

It's strange, but I don't recollect the details of our first meeting, though it was at the 1934 Mordecai Ham revival meeting in Charlotte (more later). It was nothing earth-shattering, nothing monumental. Since then we have traveled the world together, though there have also been long separations. For instance, when Billy left for Florida Bible Institute in 1937, I saw him only a few times until I joined him at Wheaton College in 1942. During his public ministry I have been with him nearly all the time—until the late 1960s when I felt called to conduct more Crusades of my own, and my brother, T. W., began traveling with Billy about half the time. Through these decades, if we weren't together in physical presence, we were together through the Holy Spirit.

People have asked me literally thousands of questions about Billy and my relationship to him and the Billy Graham Evangelistic Association. One question most frequently asked is: "Did you have a spiritual premonition of what was going to occur—that Billy Graham would be probably the greatest evangelist in modern history, and that you would be serving by his side?" To which I have always answered honestly, "Of course not. In my wildest dreams I had never envisioned it."

They have also asked me, "Grady, where would you be if you hadn't met Billy Graham?" I've replied, "I don't know, but I'd be somewhere serving Jesus Christ." Back in the late 1930s and early 1940s, those who watched Billy, T. W., and me didn't know who would do what. I was the first of the three to accept the call and to begin preaching. In those days Billy would come hear me preach.

After his graduation from Wheaton, Billy pastored a Baptist church in the suburbs of Chicago. Then he became the first full-time employee of the newly organized Youth for Christ International, later becoming its vice-president. Actually, the first person to join Billy's Team was George Beverly Shea when Bev sang for Billy on "Songs in the Night," a popular radio program emanating from Chicago (1943). The second member to join Billy was Cliff Barrows whom Billy met at the Ben Lippen Conference Center in Western North Carolina (1945). During that time I was serving churches and preaching my share of evangelistic meetings. In 1947 Billy became president of Northwestern Schools in Minneapolis. There Billy made friends like George Wilson, to this day business manager of the BGEA, and Luverne Gustavson, Billy's secretary for years.

During vacation periods and semester breaks at Northwestern, Billy would conduct evangelistic meetings with Cliff and Bev at his side. He asked me to join him in the late 40s to help out in his early Crusades. I would preach at all kinds of meetings he couldn't make, helping with the arrangements and giving counsel here and there. If Billy had a sore throat or had to fly back to Northwestern for an emergency, I would step into his shoes for a night or two.

For all practical purposes I joined Billy's Team in 1947 at the Charlotte Crusade, still serving in the pastorate until the official founding of the Billy Graham Evangelistic Association in 1950. The Charlotte meeting was a turning point in my life. Since that time we have personally seen and felt the power of God as millions of people have flooded the aisles and responded to the simple invitation, "Receive Jesus Christ as your personal Savior."

In early 1952 Billy passed through an agonizing period. The Team conducted a major Crusade in the nation's capital. The Crusade was in the national news day after day. Billy made the momentous decision to resign from Northwestern and enter full-time evangelism. The Team, consisting of Bev, Cliff, and me, was ready. In 1950 Billy had invited T. W. to join us, but T. W. felt God had called him into an evangelistic ministry of his own.

As you realize, Billy has authored a number of books. And many authors have written books about him. In books, magazines, and newspapers, you have read about Billy, his family, and the Team members and their families. Part of the accounts in this book you will either have heard or read. Yet, some of what you will read here is being presented to the public for the first time.

You'll read about the Grahams and Wilsons from the year 1934 up until now: our days selling Fuller Brushes from door to door; our college life; our families; our calling to preach. You'll read about the beginning of the Billy Graham Crusades, our ins and outs, the highs and lows, the triumphs and tragedies, the hilarious and the heartbreaking.

The writer of Proverbs wrote, "And there is a friend that sticketh closer than a brother." Billy Graham has been closer than a brother to me. Outside of our own flesh and blood, a few of us like Cliff Barrows, Bev Shea, George Wilson, T. W., and I are closer than any other friends could possibly be.

Billy is a loyal friend to many. He never forgets a friend, or even a small kindness done for him twenty, thirty, forty, and more years ago.

From time to time many others have traveled with him on his world tours—to help with reservations, hotel and travel arrangements, or even in research for his sermons. Jim Moore, Lee Fisher, Paul Maddox, Doug Judson, and others come to mind as those who have given invaluable behind-the-scenes help to Billy. Sometimes we would travel as a threesome or even as a whole group.

I've been with Billy in the proverbial ups and downs. There have been more downs than you would realize. Several chapters will candidly reveal the discouragements we have often faced.

Evangelism has always had its detractors. There is the accusation that our ministry appeals to "the herd instinct," that there is not a personal touch, that a large percentage of the converts do not "stick." Yet, we have always emphasized one-on-one witnessing for Christ. Most of those who respond to Billy's invitation have been dealt with at one time or another. A counselor talks with each person who comes forward in a meeting. Then, there is intensive follow-up. Through surveys conducted we have found that most of the converts in a Crusade do indeed "stick." Always before us is the New Testament concept that people must ultimately respond to Christ in personal faith.

Because of our close-knit relationship, whatever hurts Billy hurts the other Team members and me. Really, that should be true of any interaction among Christians. When Billy is stuck, we bleed, too.

Billy has been attacked for various reasons—some out of jealousy, some sincere. Years ago he was misunderstood because he believed in integrating the races, misunderstood because he had compassion for the poor, and now misunderstood for his emphasis on peace during the heated nuclear buildup. Sometimes he has been attacked for his connections with presidents, royalty, and other world luminaries. But Billy Graham is also the friend of the "average citizen" or "common folks," as most of us label ourselves. He is totally devoid of arrogance and pride.

Public figures have all kinds of legends and myths repeated about them. Billy has had more than his quota, and it's according to who's looking at him.

People have tried to lump the BGEA with unsavory stereotypes of evangelism, especially in our early days. They accused us of being flamboyant and flashy, hypocritical Elmer-Gantry types. That ilk of criticism has now virtually disappeared.

Almost nonexistent today is criticism of the BGEA's financial dealings. The Association has striven for absolute, bedrock honesty, and I'll touch on that in this volume.

I still accompany Billy and the Team to some of the Crusades. In addition I accept offers for my own Crusades and revival meetings. You've often heard the expression, "I'd rather burn out than rust out." That holds true for us.

Billy has asked me repeatedly, "Grady, why has God set us apart for this ministry?" He has aired this wonder to crowds in our Crusades on every continent. He has emphasized and reemphasized, "If God removed his hand from me, I couldn't continue. I'd fall flat on my face." And any truly called servant of the Master would concur with that sentiment.

All of us are awfully human. That's the basic premise of the gospel we preach. All of us are sinners. We have faults, "warts and all." Because Billy is painfully aware of his humanity, he stays close to his Lord in spiritual discipline and prayer.

Readers and reviewers will be asking, "How can you be objective doing a book, in part about your relationship with your closest friend?" A valid question. No, I can't be altogether objective. Through the years various people have primed me, pumped me, cajoled me—requesting that I help dig up this or that to hurt Billy. "Tell it like it is," they have urged.

As best I can, I'm telling it like it is. If I had a son—and I don't—I would want him to be Christlike first; second, I would want him to be like Billy Graham. Believe me, I've tried to find fault from time to time. Most any friends critique each other. I've looked, maybe not with a jaundiced eye, but I've looked. I've known thousands of godly men and women during my ministry. They read like a Christian "hall of fame," but Billy Graham is the best, most-devoted Christian I've ever known!

Many years ago one of our Team members left us. He tried desperately to make Billy look bad, but it simply didn't work. Yes, Billy has foibles. Don't we all? He has flaws, and he's the first to admit them.

I've seen Billy perturbed or upset just a few times, and then only after an outright lie or innuendo about the ministry had appeared in the media. And I've never heard a foul word escape from his lips. It has been often noted that "a person who doesn't have any temper isn't worth much." Billy has a temper, but he keeps it in check.

As this book is released I have known Billy Graham almost a half-century. And our ministry for Christ becomes more wonderful every day. It reminds me of that chorus we used to sing in our early evangelistic meetings:

> Every day with Jesus Is sweeter than the day before;
> Every day with Jesus, I love Him more and more.[1]

George Beverly Shea, who has been with Billy since 1943, often sings "How Great Thou Art." I can hear the uplifting strains:

> O Lord my God! When I in awesome wonder
> Consider all the worlds thy hands have made,
> I see the stars, I hear the rolling thunder,
> Thy pow'r thro'out the universe displayed,
>
> Then sings my soul, my Savior God to thee;
> How great thou art, how great thou art!
> Then sings my soul, my Savior God to thee;
> How great thou art, how great thou art![2]

As I reflect on my life and these years with my friend Billy Graham and the Billy Graham Evangelistic Association—fellowshipping together, sharing together, preaching together, witnessing together—I must exclaim, "O Lord my God! How great thou art!"

Contents

Count It All Joy

1
Just as I Am . . . and Was

Just as I am, without one plea,
But that thy blood was shed for me,
And that thou bidd'st me come to thee,
O Lamb of God, I come! I come!
—Charlotte Elliott

Millions of people in the Billy Graham Crusades have responded to the plaintive, touching poetry of that old invitation hymn, "Just As I Am." Cliff Barrows and the musicians have played and sung that hymn in at least 90 percent of all our Crusade services. Those words sort of sum up my life—and the life of anyone who has answered "yes" to Jesus Christ.

If you're my age, or even a few years younger, you have probably heard the poem-song, "Love's Old Sweet Song," which began:

Once in the dear dead days beyond recall,
When on the world the mist began to fall.
—G. Clifton Bingham

Within recent years my mind has begun to roll back to "the dear days." They're not dead to me, though—yet sometimes almost beyond recall, but those days keep coming back like the proverbial song.

Charlotte, North Carolina, in the early and mid-1930s was much like any city in America, recovering from the throes of the Great Depression. People found in Charlotte

29

what they wanted to find, even as they do today. Charlotte was considered a highly respectable city, but it had a seamy side even then. Bootleggers in their souped-up cars were prospering. At the same time the churches in the community were flourishing, at least on the surface. Yet, a lazy kind of malaise had set in.

My parents, Mr. and Mrs. Thomas Wilson, had six of us kids—T. W., David, Charles, Helen, Edward, and me. I guess you hear this from many people my age: my parents believed in hard work and honest sweat, particularly my dad. For years he sustained the family with a heating and plumbing business.

The Charlotte News once quoted my dad's philosophy: "We didn't send them to church. We took them—and stayed with them."[1] Our parents were awfully good to us. They believed in a balance between work and play. Yet, they were also firm in their commitments or threats. Dad never backed away; he would keep his word, and that ensured our usually good behavior.

Back in those days, when they disciplined us, my parents would explain, "Grady, we're doing this because we love you." I'd reply, "That's sure hard for me to believe!" They'd answer, "Well, it hurts us more than it does you." We then retorted, "Well, it must be killing you!"

Daddy also confessed in that interview: "If Grady would do anything wrong and he'd think I'd whip him, he'd come up and say he was sorry and he'd never do it again. He'd look so pitiful I couldn't whip him."[2] I was a real politician in those days—and maybe a bit of a con man.

The public is often jaded. People want to be teased and

tantalized about prominent personalities. Certain tabloid newspapers and magazines have thrived on scintillating articles about "celebrities." Who's divorcing whom. Who's on dope. Who's having an affair. It seems to sell magazines, papers, and products.

Many people dote on sensationalism—dope addiction, alcoholism, unclean habits. Sometimes they have been titillated by Christian personalities who have been rescued from lives of deep sin—lurid life-styles.

Now I hate to disappoint you, but our family didn't go through experiences like that—neither did Billy's. I'm not being self-righteous about it, but I'm not going to fabricate my earlier life for the sake of racy press. I never spent a night in jail, except to preach there. As teenagers my brothers and I were often so mischievous that maybe a night or two in jail might have wised us up!

You can count on it that hundreds of writers have tried their hardest to dredge up filth on Billy and the Team. We are the first to admit we are sinners. That's right: sinners! But we are sinners saved by the "amazing grace" of God. The best person in Charlotte or Minneapolis or Bangor or Palm Beach or Ypsilanti or Denver is no more and no less than a sinner saved by Jesus Christ.

In Chapter 2, I deal with how Billy and I first met almost fifty years ago. He was called Billy Frank by his parents. His father, William Franklin, Sr., had a reasonably successful dairy business out in the country from Charlotte. (Charlotte has grown so much it's now in the city limits.)

My brothers and I had rather ordinary boyhoods—so did Billy Graham. Our sister Helen did her feminine share to keep her unruly brothers straight. At the time I was shy outside of the family circle. I suppose that's why I was a cutup—I wanted to overpower my bashfulness.

Nearly every kid goes through a rebellious stage. That's

part and parcel of growing up. It was no different with the Wilson kids. I could double my brothers in foolishness and pranks. But we didn't sow any wild oats, so we didn't have to pray for crop failure!

Of course, reams of material have been written about Billy Graham's boyhood, much of it apocryphal. When Billy and I finally met, we became fast friends. There was a chemistry there. Billy also hit it off with T. W., who is Billy's associate at the Montreat office. I suppose Billy and I have always complemented each other. He was tall, around six feet two, even then. I was short. He was more serious, even though that seriousness was tinctured with brattiness. I was a joker from the word go.

Sometimes I would sneak around and smoke "rabbit tobacco." I also indulged in two of the strongest cigarettes in the world, Home Runs and Picayunes. Man, were they pungent!

Billy's dad once decided to teach an indelible lesson to Billy and Catherine. (Make no mistake about it—he was always teaching their other siblings, Melvin and Jean, too.) Although Mr. Graham was a staunch Christian of Presbyterian persuasion, he used his own form of shock therapy with Billy and Catherine. Upon the repeal of Prohibition during President Roosevelt's first term, beer was declared legal once again. Mr. Graham bought two bottles of beer and made Billy and Catherine take a sip. He wanted them to realize how bad it tasted and instructed them never to drink it. That might backfire with our kids today, but Billy and Catherine never again touched the stuff. I can barely recall tasting the mess, and I always felt it belonged in the swill or the sewer.

Teenagers are perennially active and restless. What an understatement! I found all kinds of pastimes when I wasn't working for and with my father and brothers.

Of course, my knowledge of Billy during the period before I met him is secondhand. Later I became far more of an outdoorsman than he. Billy worked hard on the farm, rising every morning at 3 o'clock during his high-school years and milking between fifteen to twenty cows before going to school. I was interested in hunting and fishing and had more time for those pursuits.

At that time I aspired to become a game warden for North Carolina or a U.S. Forest Service ranger. I envisioned myself wearing one of those Smokey Bear outfits and overseeing my vast forest domain. Preaching was the farthest thought from my mind.

Incidentally, Billy, like many youths of that day, wanted to become a major-league baseball player. After he became established as an evangelist, many books and articles touted him as "a major-league prospect who gave up a promising career in baseball to preach the gospel." Hardly. As I've heard Billy tell it, he had far more desire than ability. At the age of ten he had shaken hands with the immortal Babe Ruth. That fact was blown out of proportion in accounts about Billy's athletic prowess.

I've heard that he was "a pretty fair country ball-player"—but never big-league material. By his own admission he had to struggle for a position as first baseman on Sharon High's team. He was passing fair, to hear him tell it, in throwing, running, and fielding, but his hitting was weak. He desperately wanted to play pro ball, but God knew best. If Billy had been blessed with more baseball skills, it could have changed the history of modern-day Christianity.

My friends and I engaged in the usual Huck Finn-Tom Sawyer adventures—with a vengeance. We fished and hunted in the then-unpolluted area streams and rivers and in the verdant, luxuriant woods. There was nothing like going out in a boat on a lazy, hazy summer afternoon. My friends, my brothers, and I might have returned home empty-handed, but all of the sweat was worth the experience. And there was the bone-chilling, but nonetheless worthwhile, trip to the duck blinds in the fall and winter; tramping through the woods amid the autumn hues of gold, red, silver, and brown. And once in a while, the boat capsized, leaving us waterlogged.

Even though I hunted, my father had taught us respect for life. My brothers and I obeyed all of the game and fish rules, and we never hunted for the sake of killing. My outdoorsman proclivities have carried over to this day. While reminiscing and putting together this book, I spent days at my cabin on the Santee-Cooper Reservoir near Manning, South Carolina. To me it's one of the most picturesque places on the East Coast, with the profusion of palmettos and hanging moss.

Due to my massive heart attacks I've had to curtail my outdoor activities, but fishing is still one of the most relaxing habits in the world, whether or not you catch anything as long as you aren't fishing during church services! You heard about the deacon/elder/steward/vestryman who caught a twenty-three-pound bass but couldn't brag about it because he caught it during his church's morning service! I've hunted and fished around the globe, but I've never fished for piranhas, barracudas, hammerhead sharks, great white whales, or electric eels—at least not intentionally!

After meeting Billy I can recall visiting his dad's farm only once. I was enrolled at Central High in Charlotte; Billy attended Sharon High School out in the country. When I met him Sam Paxton, Winston Covington, and others were his close friends. Most of his social life revolved around Sharon.

For a time Billy, sometimes with me, would set up what we called rabbit boxes. The rabbits would enter the boxes for a morsel of carrot or lettuce, and the lid would close shut. I often carried the rabbits home. Billy did, too, and our mothers would cook them. Sometimes Billy or I would make a little fire and cook the rabbit, eating it out in the field.

I shall never forget when Billy had a brand-new gun. We found no rabbits as we were hunting, but one of the boxes had a rabbit in it. Billy let the rabbit out. He stood there and Billy shot him. Billy says, "My conscience has bothered me ever since, and that is the last time I can recall killing anything."

There were other hobbies, though, that we shared, especially later on. One of them was golf. In those early days, golf was considered a sport of the well-to-do. In the early 1950s Billy and I followed the golf heroes of the day in the press and on radio—players like Gene Sarazen, Sam Snead, Ben Hogan, Byron Nelson, and later Arnold Palmer and Jack Nicklaus. Now I'm not going to bore you with those hackneyed golf jokes. If you're a golfer, you've heard them all, anyway.

As a teenager I occasionally borrowed old clubs and balls and practiced driving and putting in a field or on a vacant lot. Billy never played a game of golf or hit a golf ball until he was at Florida Bible Institute which was near the Temple Terrace Country Club. He often caddied for fifty cents a round. He learned to hit the ball cross-handed and for years played with that style. He finally changed but declares, "My game didn't improve much after I changed."

Neither Billy nor I play golf these days, but we have pleasant memories. Two or three times we were plain malicious with each other. During our earlier Crusade days, we developed the occasional habit of stomping on each other's golf balls. Billy stomped on mine more than once, especially if it was in a muddy, slushy lie. I would in turn stomp on his, sometimes burying it in the ground. We never fought but came close to it.

I became a fair golfer by the mid-1950s. Billy, though, was usually a few strokes better. He might have come closer to being a pro golfer than a baseballer.

In golf we finally learned the rules of etiquette, but we accidentally hit each other on occasions. Once again, it's a wonder we weren't killed before we did learn the rudiments of golf protocol. We would tee off, and often the one who teed off first would walk down the fairway. That's one way to end up with a golf ball sticking in your mouth or ear. It reminds me of several golfing politicians we've played with. They've spent more time with their shots in the crowd than on the fairway itself! No names mentioned here. And I'm sure their liability insurance policies are sky-high. Anyway, I still wince when I think about being hit by one of Billy's errant shots.

Once when Billy was in Louisville for a Crusade, George Harris of *Time* magazine was with us for an interview. George decided to follow Billy and me out to the golf course one afternoon. I was, as usual, giving Billy a hard time, razzing him and resorting to my old annoyance of stepping on his ball. When Billy's back was turned, with my foot I ground his ball into the mire.

George seriously inquired, "Grady, why do you give Billy such a rough time on the golf course?"

"George," I shot back, "if the Lord God Almighty will keep Billy anointed, I'll try to keep him humble!" With that George almost fell out. He blurted out, "Well, you seem to be doing a pretty good job of it."

Like most teenage boys I was kindly disposed toward girls—so was Billy! While in high school Billy and I and our girl friends double-dated only once or twice together. By the time we reached Bob Jones College, where about all you could do was sit and look at a girl, we double-dated several times.

For over thirty years now, writers have gone into detail about Billy's girl friends during his high school and college days. I'm going to spare you all of those details and names. Yes, Billy was popular with girls, though shy. Tall, magnetic, intense. Steely blue eyes, wavy golden hair, he was an answer to "a maiden's prayer."

After Billy became a Christian in late 1934, his tastes changed—and that should be true of every born-again Christian. Some of his worldly girl friends were terribly disappointed. They didn't share Billy's newfound faith and tried to dissuade him from his stand. They tried to drive a wedge between him and his new Christian friends, including me. They probably considered us fanatics at the time.

Billy fell in love once or twice during those high school days, though I think it was really puppy love. I, too, had my own little crushes. Did I ever! I remember one girl from across the city of Charlotte Billy started going with while attending a religious conference in the mountains of North Carolina. Billy realized that he had to break up with her if he were to remain a committed Christian. He certainly hated to part with that girl, but I have to hand it to him. He did it!

Yes, Billy and I enjoyed the company of girls, but both of us were bashful. Billy recalls that he kissed only two girls before he entered college. That ought to demolish the myth that he kissed all the girls. There was virtually no intimacy with the girls. Billy comments, "Grady was one of the most bashful boys I had ever been around when it came to girls. I seriously doubt if he ever kissed a girl before he went to college."

It sounds old-fashioned by the customs of today, but Billy and I never touched a girl in the wrong way. We kept ourselves clean and pure. The strange phenomenon occurring today is a return to sexual purity after the "swinging" decades of the 1960s and 1970s. The current scare concerning herpes and AIDS is also taking its toll. It pays to live a sexually clean life. Many in our society are discovering that truth the hard way.

There is an intense excitement about saving yourself for that honeymoon night. Today many young couples have nothing to look forward to—*if* they marry they've already done it all. With no anticipation left, they often end up in the divorce courts. Paul wisely advised, "Flee youthful lusts" (2 Tim. 2:22).

We tried never to abuse our parents' trust. After Billy accepted Christ he never smoked, drank, danced, or attended a motion picture.

Standards were strict in Christian homes back then— no smoking, no dancing, no drinking, no fast driving, no "petting," no "picture shows." They were a dime or fifteen cents then. Billy didn't go to shows, but I did sometimes. I would sit in a dark corner of the theater and pray that no one would rat on me. I'd snuggle up with a box of popcorn or a candy bar and live those rough-and-tumble adventures with Tom Mix, Tim McCoy, Johnny Mack Brown, and Gene Autry.

Billy recalls driving his dad's snazzy little 1934 Plymouth around Charlotte. He had a penchant for speed but kept it in check. To his recollection he never raced the car but once. Some chroniclers have painted Billy as a reckless speed demon, driving forty-five or fifty MPH in fifteen or twenty MPH zones. Not so.

It's a blessing, though, that I grew out of my prankster days. Someone would have eventually beaten my friends and me to death, or maybe we would have laughed ourselves to death. I've been a gagster all too often. Yes, I believe in one sense that God called me to help Billy laugh and relax, even during his most strenuous periods of duress and pressure. Back then I had to learn through experience. I found all too vividly that practical joking can boomerang.

Money was hard to come by. I was around seventeen when I decided to buy my first pair of glasses. The optometrist charged me thirteen precious bucks. To me that was like draining Fort Knox. I was sporting my new specs at a Christian young people's club and also had a surprise in my hand—one of those metal buzzers that gives another person a jolt when you shake hands.

Heh! Heh! I decided to shake hands with a young lady who was often the recipient of our tomfoolishness. I hadn't considered that, although she always screamed and jumped when we put a grasshopper down her back, she was rather proficient with karate (and we didn't know what to call it then). I pressed my buzzer into her little palm. Whammo! She leaped high into the air. She came down like a lioness, pummeling me, scratching me, and hitting me right across my nose which happened to have my brand-new glasses resting on its bridge. You guessed it. There lay the fragments of my steel-framed specs on the concrete sidewalk, lenses shattered into smithereens. I wanted to cry. The young lady later apologized, but it didn't buy back my thirteen-dollar glasses. You live and learn.

I was wild about the Tarzan movies, first starring Buster Crabbe, former Olympic swimmer, and later Johnny Weismuller, also an Olympic gold-medal winner. As late as our early Crusades, Billy and I would trade Western novels by Zane Grey. What 1930s kid didn't try to imitate the Tarzan yell? We did. Billy's mother said that he would swing on the vines near the house and nearly drive the family batty.

However, Billy never even saw a Tarzan movie until they began to appear on TV. From 1934 until about 1946 Billy never saw a motion picture. He felt it was a sin and kept strictly to that code. He did read the Tarzan and Western books.

Scores of authors and journalists have tried to analyze Billy's early years. Most of them have concluded that there was nothing spectacular about his youth—and certainly nothing exciting and unusual about mine. Neither Billy nor I were brilliant in school. If you've stayed with me this far, you'll recognize that he and I were often distracted. We were average students at the time, although both of us, by discipline and intensive study, have sharpened our intellectual skills.

When we finally met, both of us were in a drifting stage. It happens to most teenagers. The teenage years are sometimes happy—and ours were relatively joyful— but they are also confusing and nerve-wracking, not just for the teenagers but for their parents and kinfolk as well!

Face it: there was nothing extraordinary that would have commended us to the gospel ministry, certainly not to a ministry which has covered every continent on the globe and which has reached millions of persons with that gospel. We were "just plain folks," as Uncle Dave Macon used to sing on Nashville's "Grand Ole Opry."

2
Sunday, Ham, Billy, and Me

I—and every Christian, for that matter—owe a debt to mass evangelism, and it's a story which goes back to 1923 for me. Mass evangelism was going strong across our land, and thousands of inquirers were "hitting the sawdust trail." One now-anonymous journalist coined the term "sawdust trail," because sawdust was often poured on the dirt floors of the tents and "tabernacles" where large-scale revivals were conducted.

There were detractors, sometimes vicious in their attacks. Sinclair Lewis, noted novelist, shocked the nation with his book, *Elmer Gantry* (which was made into a movie three-and-a-half decades later). Gantry was portrayed as an evangelistic con man and bed-hopping charlatan.

The year 1923 was the heyday of the "flapper," "The Charleston," bathtub gin, and F. Scott Fitzgerald. Babe Ruth had become known as "The Sultan of Swat." It was the middle of "The Roaring Twenties."

William Ashley Sunday, called "Billy," was the most celebrated evangelist of that day. The fact is, *Elmer Gantry* was actually written as a diatribe against him and other evangelists. I've never knocked Sunday, and you'll soon understand why.

Around the turn of the twentieth century, Sunday was a baseball player with the Chicago White Stockings (now Sox). One night he was on the seamy side of Chicago doing the town. He became fascinated with the preaching he heard coming from the Pacific Garden Mission. Even though half-drunk, he dropped in on the service and was converted to Christ. He accepted a new contract and a new Manager.

He soon gave up baseball for a career with the YMCA. Later, he became an associate with Evangelist J. Wilbur Chapman, who is still best known for his rousing hymn, "One Day." By 1910 Sunday had a full-blown ministry which began spreading to the major cities of the nation—Boston, Philadelphia, Chicago, New York.

Sunday was a combination acrobat, entertainer, and preacher in the pulpit. He was flamboyant, and that's an understatement. His mannerisms and electrifying style were imitated by preachers all over the nation. His showmanship could sustain the interest of people from all walks of life.

According to an early biographer, during Sunday's invitations, more people came to Jesus laughing than crying. Sunday came up with expressions that are still quoted in pulpits today:

> God must have had a sense of humor, seeing he made the parrot, the monkey, and some of you people.

> Going to church doesn't make you a Christian any more than rolling a wheelbarrow into a garage makes it an automobile.

His "Sundayisms" were, and are, legion.

A sermon from Sunday was a display of pulpit

pyrotechnics. He would pull off his coat, roll up his sleeves to "fight the devil," break a chair, tear hymnbooks, smash water pitchers and glasses, and snap his suspenders. None of that, of course, enamoured him with the press or those who were cynical of evangelical Christianity.

By his death in 1935 Sunday had largely been vindicated to the rank and file of Americans. He had a still-to-be-evaluated influence on American Christianity. Until Billy Graham arose on the scene, Sunday in this century and D. L. Moody in the latter part of the nineteenth century were considered the two most influential evangelists of modern times.

Why all of this about Billy Sunday who died a half-century ago? Because, if it were not for Sunday's ministry, I—and perhaps even Billy Graham—would not be performing the ministry we are today.

In 1923 Sunday was invited by a group of ministers and laymen to carry on a revival meeting in Charlotte. As always, there was a certain amount of opposition. There invariably is when the gospel is preached. It makes the forces of hell angry as stirred-up hornets. Sunday came and delivered a blow to the devil, sure enough. And guess who was among the converts? My dad! But that Sunday campaign (as his meetings were called) was to have a lasting impression on Charlotte—and on the world.

During that revival a number of Christian men, both older Christians and "babes in Christ," formed a Billy Sunday Laymen's Evangelistic Club. In more recent years the name was changed to the CBMC—Charlotte Business Men's Committee. It is still functioning to this day and has a ministry in the area.

My family was Presbyterian, and Billy had an Associate Reformed Presbyterian background. Most of my readers realize that Billy and I are Christians first and Baptists second (since young adulthood). I was reared in the Caldwell Memorial Presbyterian Church, a mainline Presbyterian congregation. It was affiliated with the Southern Presbyterians at the time. I had been sprinkled and dedicated as a child and learned the Catechism. My family was faithful, and my parents insisted that I make it every time the doors were opened. Like many youth, though, I was confused and tended to wander in my heart, if not outwardly.

The Grahams attended the Chalmers Memorial Associate Reformed Presbyterian Church, which was rather staid and traditional. Instead of regular hymns and Gospel songs they sang—really chanted—the Psalms, much like many old Scottish churches do today.

When I was eleven years old, I made a profession of faith in Christ as Lord and Savior. George P. Stevens from Canada was preaching. My mother received Christ in the same meeting. I remember how emotionally moved I was as Dr. Stevens preached on the text, "How shall I go up to my father, and the lad be not with me?" (Gen. 44:34). I was painfully aware that "the lad" was I. I was missing from the family of God, and I fully believe that I was adopted into God's household that night.

As I stepped out from the pew where I was sitting, a second cousin of mine, an officer in the church, came down, put his arms around me, patted me on the back, and said, "God bless you, Grady. We'll be praying for you." And that was it. That was all the counseling in the Christian life I ever had. In retrospect, I know that Jesus entered my heart. I was saved. I was born again. I was headed for heaven. But like multiplied thousands of Christians, I had remained a child in the faith. I wanted to grow, to do better, but I didn't understand how.

Billy had not gone down front in a revival meeting. He had come up as a "good church member." He went to church out of obligation to his parents and their teachings. He admits that at the ages of fifteen and sixteen he had a cynical, show-me streak. Nobody would pull a fast one on him. A contradiction in his life was his forced foolishness, like showing off, and his periods of deep seriousness.

An age-old criticism of mass evangelism is: "The converts don't last." I know one that did—my dad. He agreed with many of the laymen and ministers of Charlotte. Charlotte—a religious, pious, churchgoing town— needed a genuine movement of God, a revival in the New Testament sense.

In 1934 a local group of businessmen held an all-day prayer meeting to discuss inviting Dr. Mordecai Ham to Charlotte. The men were from the Christian Men's Club. The Depression had set in, and thousands of people were personally depressed. There was an I-don't-care attitude everywhere. The local ministerial association was not hepped up over the idea of a city-wide crusade or revival meeting, but those laymen were determined to sponsor a revival anyway. Most of them had been closely associated with the awakening under Billy Sunday eleven years before.

Vernon Patterson, the leader of the group, later prayed that "out of Charlotte the Lord would raise up someone to preach the Gospel to the ends of the earth."[1] What a prophetic prayer that was! The Christian Men's Club decided to invite the evangelistic team of Mordecai Fowler

Ham and his singer, Walter Ramsay.

Ham not only was endowed with biblical first and last names (Mordecai from the Book of Esther and Ham from the Book of Genesis), but he was hard preaching and sin fighting. Ham could "whup you up one side and down the other," and then rub salt into your wounds.

Ham was well educated, well read, and a perfect Southern gentleman. He had been pastor of the First Baptist Church of Oklahoma City. He was a great story-teller, a tremendous student of the Bible, and an ardent Prohibitionist. Even though Prohibition (the Volstead Act) was repealed in 1933, most areas of the nation, especially the South, were legally dry. Of course, bootleggers prospered. In Charlotte they were making the moolah hand over fist.

Ham and Ramsay opened the campaign in September of 1934. Opposition was rabid. First of all, many of the pastors were not happy with his coming, and the newspapers were not sympathetic. It appeared that Ham's opponents worked overtime to make him look bad, pulling several stunts in an attempt to run him out of town. For instance (and there were more instances), a reporter even allegedly tried to hire a prostitute in an effort to sneak her into his room. It became tragic but almost ludicrous. It's amazing what hardened people will do in opposition to a man of God. And I believe that Mordecai Ham, for all his faults, was a man of God. He wasn't everyone's cup of tea as a preacher, but who is?

Parenthetically, as much as Billy is loved and respected around the world, there are still those who dislike him and his preaching. A recent Gallup Poll showed that 78 percent of Americans approve of Billy with only 6 percent disapproving (with the rest undecided). But Billy still has his severe critics. Look what happened to Jeremiah, who was sawn asunder by his own brethren. Think of John the Baptist who was decapitated in prison at Machaerus. And our own Lord and Savior Jesus Christ!

Billy is often concerned about the words of Jesus, "Woe unto you when all men shall speak well of you." He has been kicked from all sides, but he has also had his share of adulation, which he basically dislikes. He has often commented when someone gives him a flowery introduction: "I feel like falling through the floor."

So, a few preachers worked Ham over. Some reporters gouged him. The worldly crowd ripped him—and the more they slashed him, the more the campaign prospered. It lasted eleven weeks! Jesus warned of the hostility of the world. He declared, "I am sending you out as sheep among wolves." As Ruth Graham has often put it, "What could be more dangerous?"

The strange part about it is the Frank Graham family didn't attend the first few weeks. For a time their pastor was cool toward Ham and the meeting. The tabernacle, built of raw pine and steel, was a "fer piece" from their home. I didn't attend until the second week.

With all of that free publicity Ham became the talk of the town, creating a sensation when he publicly stated there was widespread fornication going on at Central High School. Maybe there was, but I wasn't a part of it! One smart aleck student, who claimed to be an atheist, threatened, "We're going out tonight to attack old man Ham from Kentucky, who has indicted every young person in Charlotte of sin and immorality." Many students marched on the tabernacle and demonstrated. Of course, the newspapers focused on the story.

Billy and I still did not know each other. We had a totally

different set of friends. We attended different high schools. I lived in the heart of the city, and he lived out in the country on a farm.

I was restless and not satisfied with my life for I hadn't grown in the Christian faith, I felt. As I later learned, Billy was the vice-president of the youth group in his church. He probably shouldn't have been since he had no assurance of his relationship to God.

I was curious about "old man Ham" as we heard the rumors flying. What kind of old fogey was he? What kind of bluenose party pooper? Maybe my friends and I would go out to the tabernacle and laugh or poke fun. Or sit there and snicker with sardonic grins on our faces.

Yet, Ham was preaching truths we had heard in our own churches. Maybe he was preaching those doctrines more forcefully and potently, but I could make no claim that I hadn't heard the gospel in my church.

Billy's folks finally started going to the Ham meeting, and they were not able to stay away once they started. My folks, including me, were going, too. More than all else, though, I wanted to find out what was going on. "What's happening?" as they express it today.

On my first night there I had an overawed feeling. Several thousand people were present, the largest crowd I'd ever seen in person. Ham stuck his index finger out and aimed it right at me, shouting, "There are some young men back yonder who need Jesus Christ!"

There I was—a backslider, out of God's will for my life. There was Billy somewhere in the audience—a church member but not assured of his salvation either.

One night, after arriving home, Billy had a fitful, almost sleepless night. He brooded about his eternal destiny, and Dr. Ham's entreaties rang in his mind. Billy was burdened abut his life and became painfully aware of his sins, especially his failure to build his life around God.

I was doing my own agonizing, sorting out my experiences. Yes, I had trusted Christ under George Stevens's preaching four years before. I was a Christian but a miserable one. That's the common feeling the misdirected Christian suffers. David expressed agony of spirit when he wrote about the "roaring in my bones." He begged God "to restore a right spirit within."

> Have mercy upon me, O God, according to thy lovingkindness: according unto the multitude of thy tender mercies blot out my transgressions. Wash me thoroughly from mine iniquity, and cleanse me from my sin. For I acknowledge my transgressions: and my sin is ever before me. Against thee, thee only I have sinned, and done this evil in thy sight: that thou mightest be justified when thou speakest, and be clear when thou judgest.
> Create in me a clean heart, O God; and renew a right spirit within me.
> Restore unto me the joy of thy salvation; and uphold me with thy free spirit. Then will I teach transgressors thy ways and sinners shall be converted unto thee
> (Ps. 51:1-4,10,12-13).

I suffered late into the night. The following day high school dragged by. I was obsessed with one thought: *I must straighten myself out with God.* I was filled with disturbing emotions, placed there by the Holy Spirit. I was aching for peace within. I later found out that Billy, whom I hadn't yet met, was going through a similar experience. It's not surprising that decades later Billy wrote a best-selling book, *Peace with God*, which is still in print.

Then, after school I replayed Ham's appeal of the night before, turned it over and over in my mind as I limped through my chores. Ham had kept back nothing, and I could understand why many people hated him—and why they would hate anyone who preached the whole truth. He had preached on mankind's flagrant sin against God, God's judgment on sinners, heaven and hell, the imminent second coming of Christ, and the sacrificial blood of the cross—subjects the world calls "foolishness."

The night I met Billy Graham, according to his memory, we were both in the choir and sat next to each other. I don't recall now, but I'm sure Billy smelled of cows and the barn. No doubt we were both timid.

Before meeting Billy I remember standing around outside, not wanting to enter the tabernacle. But one grand Presbyterian elder, one of the CBMC brethren, grabbed me by the arm and commanded, "Hey, I think I can crowd you on the back row of the choir." Oh brother, that was the last place I wanted to be. That elder ushered me up to a seat. I felt that thousands of eyes were focused on me, watching my every move and looking at no one else. I had no idea what paranoid meant, but I was!

Billy recalls that he attended the Sunday before with his cousin Crook Stafford. Billy heard the announcement for more choir members and felt he could escape Ham's pointing finger by sitting in the choir.

Every human being has a rendezvous with God, whether or not he wants it. God had done his work in my life and then in Billy Graham's. Billy later confessed that he knew he *had* to make his profession of faith in Jesus Christ. Even though Billy had never talked with Dr. Ham, and thousands of people were present, he felt that the evangelist was cognizant of his presence and was preaching straight to him: "But God commendeth his love toward us, in that, while we were yet sinners, Christ died for us" (Rom. 5:8).

Billy and I sat side by side with Crook Stafford and Al McMakin, who managed Frank Graham's dairy. Ham pressed the claims of Christ. We wrestled with our decisions—mine for a deeper commitment, Billy's to settle the matter of his salvation. We weighed all the pros and cons, as every lost and drifting person does. *What will it cost? What will I have to do? What will I have to give up? Can I hold out? What will I do about my so-called friends?*

Then the time for the invitation arrived. The crowd stood to its feet as Ramsay led in the singing of that old invitation hymn which is now the hallmark of a Billy Graham Crusade: "Just as I am, without one plea, But that thy blood was shed for me." People began streaming down the aisles, some standing down front, others kneeling in the sawdust in front of the platform.

I wrestled, not with flesh and blood, but with the forces of hell. The crowd and choir sang several verses of that poignant hymn. We stayed rooted into our places far up in the choir loft. Then Ramsay began singing, "Almost Persuaded," a song which tugs at heartstrings and which has often been used in the Crusades.

> "Almost persuaded" now to believe;
> "Almost persuaded" Christ to receive;
> Seems now some soul to say, "Go Spirit, go Thy way,
> Some more convenient day,
> On Thee I'll call."[2]

I bolted for the aisle and was met by a layman in front of the platform. I responded to commit myself totally to Christ—to lay aside the impediments that had defeated me in my Christian walk. Billy settled his decision another night during the same meeting, and made his "calling and election sure," in the words of the apostle Peter. Billy looks back to that revival meeting as the time he truly received Christ as the Lord, Master, and Savior of his life.

Several of the laymen shook my hand, slapped me on the back, and gave me sincere "God-bless-you" congratulations. That week Billy and I met Dr. Ham for a brief moment. He shook our hands and commended us for our decisions.

The assurance of my salvation surged through my life. There were no ringing bells, no flashes of lightning, no electric charges up and down my spine, but there was assurance, "blessed assurance."

Too long I had drifted as a young Christian, playing with my faith and not counting for Christ. I was no longer content to exist as a young believer. I wanted to live my faith for the Master. It's miserable not knowing for sure, once and for all, that you are a child of God, a genuine disciple for Jesus.

Many groups teach that you can't know in this life. That's an unstable belief. I've heard many sincere people pray, "Lord, save us at last in heaven." The peace of God flooded my heart. I could testify with Paul, "I know whom I have believed, and am persuaded that he is able to keep that which I have committed unto him against that day" [the judgment seat of Christ] (2 Tim. 1:12b).

I knew I had passed from death unto life. I did not want to leave that tabernacle without the surety of salvation. That was an indescribably joyous night and a pivotal turning point in my life—and a few nights later in Billy's. That's why through these years of my ministry I have given an invitation, not only for salvation but also for the assurance of salvation. It is not enough to think so, hope so, or maybe so. That's why the majority of Christians are defeated. They spend so much time worrying about their own spiritual condition that they don't have time to help others.

I think about John Wesley, who had been an Anglican priest and missionary, and the fact that he was dogged by doubts and fears. Then he experienced the assurance of his salvation at Aldersgate, in which God calmed his doubts and Wesley felt "strangely warmed" within his heart. It is not enough to evangelize. We must assist Christians in having a sense of constant security in the Lord.

We should never assume that because a person is a church member, a leader, or even a minister that he has a full-fledged faith. Many a church leader is inwardly shaky and beset by gnawing fears. Many are not sure where they stand with God.

People shook hands with me then, as they did when I made my profession of faith in Brother Stevens's revival meeting. But that was it. There was no counseling and follow-up on my decision, and none on Billy's. There was "God bless you. We're proud of you." We were given no practical helps in following Christ.

That's why the Billy Graham Evangelistic Association has striven, almost from its inception, to have a strong follow-up program. Every inquirer coming forward in a Crusade is counseled by a trained counselor-personal worker. The counselor prays with the inquirer, trying to answer any difficulties and questions. The inquirer is given a packet of helps which will aid him in the Christian life. His name is then referred to a Bible-believing, gospel-preaching church nearest to his home.

Next to the plight of the unsaved person, the saddest situation is the Christian who remains a babe and never grows or advances in his faith. I have known people who have been Christians for decades but are still spiritual children. What a deadweight pulling down the cause of Christ!

Personal contact is important, and Billy and I surely could have stood more of it when we were new Christians. I realize that personal contact is not to be mini-mized. Yet, people can be confronted through radio, television, the printed page, and from the pulpit. No doubt thousands have been converted through reading a booklet or tract. St. Augustine came to receive Christ when he spied a tract which invited, "Take and Read." He did and his life was transformed by the power of the Savior.

People find Christ through different approaches—per-sonal confrontation, listening to Gospel sermons, reading literature, seeing advertisements for Crusades and other religious meetings. The Savior is the same. The salvation is the same. The methods are different.

These previous paragraphs are not a digression. They relate to where Billy, T. W., and I found ourselves. We were committed to Christ. We were saturated with youth-ful enthusiasm. A sense of aimlessness was gone. We wanted to do for the Lord, but we didn't know how. A long road was ahead of us.

3
Fuller Brushes and
Hell Hole Swamp

And that road would lead Billy Graham and T. W. Wilson, both sixteen, and Grady Wilson, fifteen, down many alleys, back roads, and detours. We were saved by Christ, but there was no follow-up and virtually no training in the Christian life.

"Boys will be boys," so the expression goes. T. W. and I were still boys but somewhat changed from our old habits. We pranked but not like we used to. Before God changed us we would grease the streetcar tracks with petroleum jelly, a rather malicious pastime. And we'd soap windows on Halloween, move lawn furniture, and turn over trash cans. In those days you could turn the car ignition on and off and create loud backfiring. We loved to do that at night and early in the morning.

Before our conversion there was a neighborhood kid who egged T. W. and me into downright thievery. A broken-down soft-drink truck was at the service station next door to our house. The three of us formed relays. The kid would throw me a cold drink and I would pass it on to T. W. He in turn would pitch the bottle under the house. We made away with five or six cases of that cola.

That was the only time I ever stole and I wasn't a Christian then.

Fuller Brushes helped mold Billy, T. W., and me. Yes, Fuller Brushes. If you could sell from door to door, you could do most anything. In the summer of 1936 Albert McMakin, regional manager of the Fuller Brush Company and Billy's neighbor, enlisted several of us to sell brushes around home and in South Carolina. I honestly believe that experience more than all else helped us to start overcoming our bashfulness and shyness. We knew we had to produce—and we did. We combined our selling with our witnessing for Christ. We would gain an entree into a home, sell our brushes, and give away our faith.

T. W. and Billy stayed out awfully late several nights. Albert and I would become extremely concerned. We would remain at the boarding house, get down on our knees, and pray for their safe return.

At other times Billy would make an appointment and carry Albert with him to close the deal. The rest of us became jealous because we thought Albert was unduly assisting him, and Billy was the sales leader that summer.

I remember that song of the 1950s, "The Things We Did Last Summer." Now that kind of selling is practically a thing of the past. Back then you could get into 90 percent of the homes and make a sale in 30 to 50 percent of them.

It seemed the day wasn't complete unless T. W. and I had pulled at least one practical joke on each other. We kidded, and some of us short-sheeted each other. We made life miserable for each other and enjoyed every minute of it. In Hartsville, South Carolina, I fell out of a boat and almost drowned. And at the boarding house we'd often put a fellow's hat in his chair and he'd sit on it. Or we'd pull a guy's chair out from under him when he was ready to sit down and eat. But that wasn't really funny, 'cause he could've broken his back.

One night we encountered some roughnecks on the streets of Lancaster. Through the years I've been able to recognize guys who are aching for a fight. There's a universal language. Squinty eyes, curled lips with a snarl, a strutting walk, hands closed into fists. Those guys eyed us as Billy and I were walking down the street. Billy was quickly gaining bravado. He said out loud, "Grady, did you bring your gun along?" I replied, "Buddy, we're OK. Go ahead." Those fellows took it to mean that we had our guns—they left us alone.

Although Billy still looked rather skinny, he began to assert himself. At supper one night a fellow let out an "expletive" not deleted. Billy jumped up from the supper table and challenged him, "Sir, you'll not talk about my Lord like that." To which the curser answered, "I'll say anything I _____ please." Riled, Billy said, "No sir, not around me you won't." The guy was ready to hit Billy, and the entire Fuller Brush crew stood to their feet and said, "We agree with Billy, and we're ready to stand for him and the Lord." The guy weasled out of it and ate his supper in silence.

Around 1950 Billy and I were called to the Fuller Brush Company and given a special citation for our contribution to the success of the company.

Back in high school I became the president of a Christian club. From my work with the Christian Life Service Band I began receiving invitations to preach at small Baptist churches in the country. I also witnessed in jail and on street corners. It seemed the Lord called me to the ministry by laying me on the hearts of those Baptist folks.

I loved, and still do, the Presbyterian denomination. As an infant I had been sprinkled at Caldwell Memorial Presbyterian Church. I entered the Catechism class when I was eleven and finished at twelve. But, because of their high educational standards, the Presbyterians wouldn't have me on a dare. I was raw and untutored—I had a zeal but maybe it wasn't according to knowledge, yet Baptists gave me opportunity after opportunity to preach. There I was, still a Presbyterian, and those Baptists were willingly listening to me and inviting me back. Can you understand the debt I owe to those Southern Baptists who were willing to give a teenaged Calvinist a chance? When no one else would hear me—and later this was also the case with Billy—they would.

I cannot remember where my first sermon was preached, but my first revival was at the Eighteenth Street Mission in Charlotte (which has been a church for many years now). Billy and one of my girl friends were sitting on the front row one night. To keep time I had borrowed Billy's pocket watch. What a night! I was preaching on "God's Four Questions," a sermon I had also borrowed from an unknown preacher. I kept winding and rewinding the watch until it went "boing" and the stem broke. Billy claims that at the end of an hour I announced, "And now let's move on to the second question."

As I preached all over Mecklenburg County, Billy was my chauffeur because I didn't have a car. And believe it or not, he was impressed with my preaching. Billy would accompany me to the Girl's Industrial Home, which was a name for the home for unwed mothers. I didn't have any better sense than to preach to them from John 8 about the woman taken in adultery. I had amazing tact in those days! I must've preached on that a half-dozen times before the matron called me aside and insisted, "Brother Grady, please don't preach on that anymore. These young ladies are rather sensitive."

And I'd visit the jail in Charlotte and Billy would go along, and guess what? I'd preach to them from Acts 16 about Paul and Silas being in jail. That wasn't too well received, either. One time at the jail our good friend Jimmie Johnson invited Billy to testify, and Billy put his foot squarely into his mouth. He announced to the men behind bars, "I'm glad to see so many of you *out* this afternoon."

Jimmie, a twenty-five-year-old evangelist from Alabama, was preaching in the area and would have a significant impact on our young lives. In fact, the first time Billy witnessed to a group was at Jimmie's insistence. Billy went with Jimmie to a jail service at Monroe, North Carolina. Jimmie unexpectedly called on Billy to testify, saying, "Here's a fellow who knows what it means to be saved. He's gonna tell you what Jesus Christ has done in his life." Billy was petrified and during his brief testimony twisted the hem of his coat until it looked like a rope. Jimmie insists that Billy handled his words remarkably well.

Jimmie was a graduate of Bob Jones College in Cleveland, Tennessee (now Bob Jones University in Greenville, South Carolina). Our parents were sold on Jimmie and his ministry and felt that Bob Jones was the school for us. My older brother, T. W., had already enrolled, and we entered in September of 1936.

Although converted, Billy and I hadn't lost our identity and we still loved to cut up. No one could accuse us of a long-faced Christianity. Billy and I started at Bob Jones with a bang. The rules were restrictive and tight, and we really didn't fit in.

On the campus they had "New Talent Night," so the

freshmen could exhibit their talents. Billy and I, though we couldn't carry a tune, decided we'd sing a chorus entitled "Just Inside the Eastern Gate." Before the entire student body we were called on to sing a duet. I stood before that crowd—and no Billy. Still no Billy. I cleared my throat and sang "Just Inside the Eastern Gate" as a solo. T. W. was sitting on the front row and kicked me on the foot. "Sit down, you nut, you're making an idiot of yourself. I'm so embarrassed that I wish I was inside the Eastern Gate right now!" When I returned to my pew I found Billy hiding underneath it.

Both Billy and I contracted colds and were put into the infirmary. There were strict rules everywhere. We were supposed to lie there like zombies. One night we smuggled crackers and peanut butter into our infirmary room. We were eating away when the orderly came back. Billy hid the crackers under the covers, and I tended to the peanut butter. Billy slept with crumbs and I with gooey peanut butter. We also got into trouble for showing Mickey Mouse cartoons at the infirmary.

I was working hard to flunk out, I guess. Some of us—not Billy—hit each other with pies, and I'd sneak black pepper out of the kitchen and put it under sleeping guys' noses. During Bible conference time many of the male students had to sleep in the gym to make room for the visitors. I graciously put toads on their feet.

Billy was taking his lumps in class. I wasn't having as much trouble with my subjects. After our infirmary stay Billy returned to general mathematics and couldn't understand the gap between calculus and analytical geometry. One day he stood to his feet, asking the professor, "Dr., is it possible to resign from this class?" "Yes," came the answer, "but you'll have to take an F." "I'll take it," said Billy, walking out of the class.

Billy stayed ill with flu and bronchitis nearly all the time and had trouble concentrating. Loud, emotional praying bothered him, especially when he was trying to study. One night the guys in an adjoining room were praying so loud that Billy knocked on the wall and yelled, "Hey, God's not deaf!"

Billy and his roommate, Wendell Phillips, had heard about Florida Bible Institute at Temple Terrace near Tampa and were intrigued. They decided at least to finish the semester at Bob Jones.

I want to nail down a point here. Dr. Bob Jones, Sr., founder and then president of the college, was in many respects a tremendous Christian leader, but he was also a rigid patriarch who tried to tell his students what to think, what to do, and how to act. And somehow he could "sniff out" the slightest hint of what he called disloyalty to the school.

Dr. Bob was famous for calling in his students if he sensed their attitudes were changing. Billy and Wendell were summoned to Dr. Bob's office. He'd heard that Billy and Wendell were thinking of changing schools. Dr. Bob sternly warned, "If you leave here, the chances are you'll never be heard of. You'll be buried somewhere out in the sticks." How wrong Dr. Bob was. He gave that same speech to numerous students who are now spiritually and materially successful. Wendell later became a millionaire building contractor. Bill Mead, a multimillionaire and former president of the American Bakers Association, was also one of many who heard Dr. Bob's warning of doom and oblivion.

In January of 1937 the Grahams drove Billy down to the Florida Bible Institute (now Trinity College at Dunedin, Florida). They were warmly greeted by the dean, Rev.

John Minder, who Billy calls "my father in the ministry." Wendell had also enrolled a semester earlier. Dr. W. T. Watson was the president of Florida Bible Institute and also made an abiding imprint on Billy's life.

During the Easter break of 1937 Dean Minder carried Billy with him to visit Rev. Cecil Underwood, a Baptist preacher and interior decorator. The three of them went to a church at Bostwick, Florida, where Cecil was supposed to preach. Cecil graciously asked John to preach, with John replying, "No, Billy's going to preach tonight." Billy was terrified but entered the pulpit, preaching all of the material he could think of in ten minutes. T. W., Billy, and I were discovering that the providence of God moves through human instrumentality.

I was left behind at BJC while Billy and Wendell were basking in the Florida sunshine. I was making average or better grades there and actively participating in college functions—but I thought to myself, silly sophomore that I was, *The Lord's coming back soon. I don't need any more education. I want to win the world, and I'm tied down in school.*

I had accepted the call to preach in 1936. Preaching all over the two Carolinas and East Tennessee, I had now logged plenty of experience in Baptist churches. The pastors and laymen who had hosted me often asked why I didn't go ahead and officially align myself with the Baptist camp. They were asking penetrating questions.

Early in 1938 Billy was having an inward turmoil. He was so intent on becoming a preacher that he enlisted anyone who would help or listen. He would ask friends to go over his notes with him before he preached. I have no idea how many hundreds of sermons he's shared with me before he's preached them. He has always been scrupulously concerned about his homiletical points. He would involve Miss Brunette Brock, Dr. Watson's secretary, to help, and sometimes she'd even type Billy's notes or visit the churches where he preached.

As the greats of evangelism would preach at FBI, Billy became more restless and uneasy. He, like I, burned with "a divine discontent." At night his favorite spot for meditation and talking with the Lord (often out loud) was the Temple Terrace Golf Course. He would also practice his sermons on the cypress trees and stumps and the birds and animals.

One night on that golf course, and maybe that's why he has loved golf courses to this day, he dedicated his life to preaching the gospel, feeling he was not intellectually brilliant and prepared. He made a decision that every servant of God must: "Lord here I am. I'm at your disposal. Lord, if you want me to preach, I'll do it." God was doing the preparing.

In 1938 I was baptized by immersion at a Southern Baptist Church near Huntersville, North Carolina. Rev. Richard (Dick) Brothers had a profound influence on my life and ministry. A bivocational preacher at Gum Springs, North Carolina, he was an engineer for the Seaboard Railroad. They called him "Happy Dick" Brothers because he would play hymns on his train whistle every afternoon when he'd come through his home town of Hamlet, North Carolina. He'd play "O Happy Day That Fixed My Choice," an old hymn by Philip Doddridge and E. F. Rimbault.

Brother Dick was highly popular and always preached to packed houses. In 1938 I was also ordained to the gospel ministry by Brother Brothers. Some of the ministers who were on the ordination council are still alive today.

My first "parish" was the Bethel Baptist Church in the community called "Hell Hole Swamp," South Carolina. It was eighteen miles east of Moncks Corner near the little town of Bethera. Why such an awful name? I found that the community received its nickname because moonshiners were making more illegal whiskey in Berkeley County than all the rest of the counties put together. Then they would ship that stuff all over the two Carolinas and into Charlotte. We'd read about it in the Charlotte newspapers.

As a boy I'd often seen the Charlotte police pour barrels of 'shine into a storm sewer. Then, down the street where the sewer emptied into Sugar Creek, I'd seen old men stand there and try to catch a hatful of that Berkeley County rotgut.

The moonshiners would often threaten me, warning me not to preach against moonshine or moonshiners. I remembered back to the time T. W. and his BJC friend, Henry Schum, had gone into Hell Hole Swamp to evangelize those folks. T. W. and Henry were run out of the community.

That happened after T. W. preached on "The Biggest Sinner in Hell Hole Swamp." He virtually called the man by name. T. W. declared, "The biggest sinner here has 500 head of cattle. The biggest sinner has several women he's running around with." Everybody knew who he was preaching about.

In Hell Hole Swamp, there was plenty of trouble brewing. Folks in the sin business were soon after T. W. and Henry's hides. We wanted a "prophetic ministry" everywhere we went, calling "an ace an ace and a spade a spade." But we all too soon found out that you must pay the price for such a ministry.

It's a wonder T. W., Henry, or I got out alive. Being

pastor in Hell Hole Swamp was enough to make a man out of me and to make me more aware of my downright ignorance and the corresponding necessity for more education.

4
Providential Preparation

God knew exactly what he was doing in our lives. God, in his grand providence, uses both circumstances and people. We had often heard the expression, "Father knows best." Yes, the Heavenly Father knows best.

While Billy was at Florida Bible Institute and I was at Bob Jones College and in the pastorate, we always kept up with each other, either through cards, letters, phone calls, or personal visits. Our visits were usually in the summer around Charlotte.

Billy had plunged himself into preparation for preaching God's Word. And the all-knowing Father was fashioning me. I returned to Bob Jones in 1938 with a new determination and a zest for learning. Digging and studying was not easy for me. I'd rather converse any day with another person than bury myself in a book, but I applied myself at BJC.

Dr. Bob, Sr., wanted to influence every aspect of his students' lives, even to the extent of forming the Gospel Fellowship Association. He wanted to control all of the worthy ministerial students. Before being ordained by Rev. Dick Brothers, I had explained the situation to Dr.

Bob. Because of my new Baptist orientation, I wanted to associate myself with staunch Baptists, and I wanted the proper credentials which would allow me to minister in Baptist congregations. At the time, any departure from Dr. Bob's fiats incurred his displeasure. "Dr. Bob, please understand," I confided in him. "I want a Baptist church to ordain me. I deeply appreciate you, and my moving in the Baptist direction has nothing to do with you."

About the same time he had fallen out with several Bob Jones graduates, including Fred Brown, Henry Grube, and Jimmie Johnson. Those men were already out in the ministry and were effective evangelists.

During the 1939-1940 school year Dr. Bob was upset about me. He remarked to me, "I don't think you're a loyal student. And I hear you've been fishing with Jimmie Johnson down in Florida. I know you've talked about me. Tell me, what did Jimmie Johnson say about me?"

I replied, "Dr. Bob, I can't do that. That would be gossip." I wasn't about to share confidences and rat on a friend.

He answered, flustered, "You let me decide whether it's gossip or loyalty." He then summarily made me resign the offices I had on campus—right there on the spot. And he put me "on campus," which meant I would not be allowed to leave the campus until the end of the school year. There I was, about two-and-a-half months before graduation and at wit's end corner.

It was the early spring of 1940 when I walked into Dr. Bob Jones, Jr.'s, office. I asked, "Dr. Bob, is it possible for someone to resign from a college?" He answered, "Grady, it's possible, but it's certainly not wise. You'll regret it as long as you live." I said, "I am now willing to resign as a member of the student body." He sounded like his daddy when he came back with: "You're going to regret this all the days of your life."

For months I had been committed to preach two meetings at the Central Baptist Church of Decatur, Alabama, where Dr. John Cowell was the pastor. Since I had been put "on campus"—and that decision was binding—resigning was the only way I could preach that Sunday.

In the meantime Billy had left the Florida Bible Institute for Wheaton College in Wheaton, Illinois, not far from Chicago. I was somewhat amazed that Wheaton had accepted him because Billy had undergone academic problems while he was at Bob Jones for most of one semester. And I had heard that, because of its high standards, Wheaton had turned down many potential students. Unlike BJC, Wheaton was fully accredited.

After preaching in Decatur I had driven down to Kosciusko to hear my brother, T. W., preach a revival. T. W. became fighting mad when he heard what Bob, Sr., and Jr., had done to me.

One night in Charlotte I had prayed until 11 o'clock. I besought the Lord, "If you want me to have an education, work it out, dear Lord. If you don't I'll try to preach without it." I left my petitions at the throne of grace and went to bed.

At midnight, of all times, the phone rang. On the line was Dr. Harold Strathern, then the executive director with the R. G. LeTourneau Foundation, then in Toccoa, Georgia (now Longview, Texas). His wife, Dorothy, had sung for Dr. Torrey Johnson at Bible Town USA. Dr. Strathern asked if he could come out to the house.

God does move "in mysterious ways his wonders to perform." Vernon Patterson, explained Dr. Strathern, had recently talked with Mr. R. G. LeTourneau, the famous Christian industrialist and president of his own heavy-equipment company and also LeTourneau Tech, which specializes in training technical missionaries and full-time Christian servants. Patterson was and is an outstanding Christian layman in Charlotte whom Billy, T. W., and I had known for a long time. Mr. Patterson, you will recall, years before had prayed that God would raise up from Charlotte a messenger to carry the Gospel to the ends of the earth.

In talking with Mr. LeTourneau, Mr. Patterson had mentioned in passing my unfortunate treatment at Bob Jones and the fact I was out of school without a diploma. LeTourneau had been giving Dr. Bob $2,000 a month for the BJC ministerial loan fund and had recently asked Dr. Bob for a report.

Then, Dr. Strathern announced, "Mr. LeTourneau wants to pay your way through school, anywhere you want to go—Oxford, Cambridge, Yale, Harvard." Of course, I knew I couldn't make it in any of those institutions. He continued, "Mr. LeTourneau will pick up all of the bills." I broke down and cried like a baby. "I'd just gotten through praying," I exclaimed, "and God has given his answer through you and Mr. LeTourneau!"

"I'd like to go to Wheaton, if possible, but I understand it has terribly high standards." Dr. Strathern reassured me: "Never mind, Mr. LeTourneau and Dr. Edman, the president, are good friends." I found out that LeTourneau helped support Wheaton, too. When the U.S. government would allow it, he gave 90 percent (not 10 or 20 or 30) of everything he made to the Lord's work.

The very next day I received a call from none other than Dr. V. Raymond Edman, Wheaton's president. He reported, "I've just talked with Mr. R. G. LeTourneau and your close friend, Billy Graham, has just been in my office. He's a campus leader here. On their word we'll take you anytime you can get here."

Dr. Strathern gave me a check for my transportation and I headed out on the Greyhound bus. From that day forward I never laid eyes on a bill for my educational expenses there.

You can imagine that Mr. LeTourneau and I became fast friends. He later flew me all over the country to speak for him, and he'd attend Crusades and revivals at his own expense to give his testimony. Years later I performed his son Ted's wedding to Joyce on the TV program from New York, "Bride and Groom." And I preached Mr. LeTourneau's funeral in Longview, Texas. Only eternity will reveal his impact on Christian causes and ministries around the globe.

Parenthetically, Mr. LeTourneau gave financial help to Billy and Cliff Barrows when they were preaching all over England after World War II. Billy at that time had never asked anyone for money, but Youth for Christ had run out of funds for Billy's evangelistic tour of Great Britain, and invitations to preach were coming in from throughout the British Isles. Billy and Cliff wrote Mr. LeTourneau for $7,000, quite a sizeable sum for those days. They fell on their knees and prayed that God would touch Mr. LeTourneau's heart and pocketbook. He did. Mr. LeTourneau later testified, "That's the only time I ever gave somebody money the first time they asked for it."

This is my autobiography, and my life is difficult to report without references to Billy, but here I will keep them to a minimum. At least I want to make you aware of where Billy was during this pivotal juncture of my ministry.

In 1939 Billy became a Southern Baptist. He was conducting one of his first evangelistic meetings at Palatka,

Florida, for Rev. Cecil Underwood. During that time he was baptized by immersion in Silver Lake near Palatka. Billy was later ordained in the Peniel Baptist Church of St. John's Baptist Association. A number of the clergy participated in the ordination. Dr. Woodrow Flynn, who became a lifelong friend of Billy's, preached the ordination sermon.

As Billy was beginning to achieve some of his goals, God singled out a young woman to become his companion and helpmeet. Ruth McCue Bell was the daughter of Dr. and Mrs. L. Nelson Bell who had served as medical missionaries in North China. In spite of civil war and then the Japanese invasion, Dr. Bell, a skilled surgeon, had erected an effective missionary hospital.

When Ruth and Billy met there was a strong attraction, but God had to work out a seeming conflict of interest. Ruth had felt compelled to become a missionary to Western China and then planned, God willing, to pioneer as a missionary to Tibet. Billy, though, hadn't felt the call to missions, although he was open if God gave the nod.

In the spring of 1941 her parents returned on furlough, and they too fell in love with Billy. "Bill," as Ruth has always called him, popped the question in the summer of 1941. It was to be a two-year engagement.

Billy, Ruth, my date, and I double-dated in the area. We would attend services, concerts, and Christian events all around Wheaton and Chicago.

Dr. Edman was receiving invitations to fill pulpits in the area, many of which he couldn't accept. Normally, when students saw a blue slip in their mailboxes, it meant trouble. Fortunately, when I got a blue slip it meant an invitation to preach. Dr. Edman, bless him, kept me busy every Sunday morning and night. He did the same for Billy who was a student officer with good grades in the

80s and 90s, a far cry from his earlier schooling. Billy had learned to discipline himself in study and was willing to burn the midnight oil.

At that time there was a student church at Wheaton called The Tabernacle ("The Tab"). Dr. Edman had served as its pastor, also teaching history at Wheaton, when he was called to become interim president of the college after Dr. Oliver Buswell left. Several candidates were considered for "The Tab" when Dr. Edman left, but Billy was called in June of 1941.

The church was more or less of Swedish evangelical background, and a number of the Wheaton faculty members were on the church's board. Dr. Russell Mixter, one of Wheaton's outstanding professors, was chairman of the board; Dr. Gordon Clark, head of Wheaton's philosophy department, was the Sunday School teacher.

Billy remained pastor there until his graduation in 1943. He received a salary of $15 a week, which helped him through college. In those days, it cost only $600 per school year for room, board, tuition, fees, and incidentals at Wheaton.

And our old buddy—and he was really old to us, thirty-year-old Jimmie Johnson—entered Wheaton about that time, even though he had previously graduated from Bob Jones. He decided to enter Wheaton for a degree that would be recognized, since Wheaton was accredited and Bob Jones was not. He roomed on the same floor in the same house with Billy (which happened to be the home of Ken Hansen, later the founder, president, and then chairman of the board of Service Master). He also became a driving force in the Chicago Crusades, a leader in the development of the Billy Graham Center at Wheaton, and an influential member of the Wheaton Board of trustees.

We were having the time of our lives. On the annual

"Senior Sneak," I met Wilma Hardie. When I saw her my heart registered 9 on the Richter Scale! (See my chapter on "Dolly Pet.") Wilma and I will celebrate another anniversary soon. We were married on June 5, 1943. Billy and Ruth's nuptials followed ours. The date: August 13 (Friday the 13th), 1943.

Throughout my final year at Wheaton I reminded Billy how we had entered college at the same time and I had dropped out an entire year—and yet I was still finishing a semester ahead of him. Even though he had picked up a solid Bible background in Florida, he was able to transfer only a few credits to Wheaton. Of course, I had spent almost four years of virtual "down time" at Bob Jones.

At Wheaton I had to take some extra courses, part of them in the graduate school. In January of 1943 I graduated with Wheaton's first midyear graduating class. Billy graduated in June of 1943. It now seemed that Billy and I were moving in different directions.

After graduation and marriage Billy accepted a call to the First Baptist Church of Western Springs, Illinois, a high middle-class suburb of Chicago. After Wilma and I tied the knot and honeymooned we moved to our church fields in South Carolina—two pastorates at the same time, the Friendship Baptist Church in Charleston and the Immanuel Baptist Church in Summerville. I then had two half-time churches, which was often the case then. For a time I worked in the shipyards at Charleston; Wilma likewise worked in order to supplement our income. I was bivocational in the fullest sense. I knew of Baptist preachers who had three or four churches and Methodists with six or seven "charges."

Wilma and I settled down with our pastoral duties— visitation, fellowshipping with the members, planning the work, preparation for preaching, conducting funerals, and performing weddings. Still, there was a divine discontent within my heart, where the fires of evangelism burned brightly.

Billy renamed his church at Western Springs "The Village Church." He felt it would give it more appeal in an area where Baptists were scarce. Interestingly, Bob Van Kampen was the chairman of the deacons. Van Kampen would later play an important role on Wheaton's board of trustees and also on the board of trustees of the Billy Graham Evangelistic Association.

Torrey Johnson, inundated with radio broadcasts, his pastorate, and teaching at Northern Baptist Seminary, asked Billy and his church to assume one of the broadcasts, the already popular "Songs in the Night," aired by one of Chicago's most powerful radio stations.

George Beverly Shea, especially known as the host of the American Broadcasting Company's "Club Time" and program director of WMBI (the highly rated radio station of the Moody Bible Institute), was persuaded by Billy to become the soloist for "Songs in the Night." That program spread their appeal throughout the Midwest.

Torrey Johnson formed what he called "Chicagoland's Youth for Christ" in the spring of 1944. He had picked up the idea from layman George Wilson who had conducted a "Youth for Christ" night in the First Baptist Church of Minneapolis. As you may know, George has worked with the BGEA since its inception, but that's another story. For twenty-one consecutive Saturday nights Johnson scheduled the 3,000-seat Orchestra Hall next door to the USO center. For the opening rally Johnson chose Billy as the speaker, and people were amazed when forty-two out of 2,800 came forward during the invitation.

Back in South Carolina I was pastoring my churches, and Wilma was still adjusting to my peculiarities. I was even then receiving more requests for revival meetings than I could possibly handle.

In the fall of 1944 Billy was accepted and commissioned as an army chaplain, but at the last minute became seriously ill and was in bed for six weeks. He had to lay aside his desire for military service. In retrospect we can see the leadership of God even in illness.

Next Billy went full-time with the new Youth for Christ International. In 1945-1946 he preached in nearly every state of the union and all the Canadian provinces. Incidentally, on a cold, snowy night in Chatham, Ontario, Billy met his future brother-in-law, Leighton Ford, then a high-school student and director of the local YFC.

Then Torrey Johnson invited Billy, J. Stratton Shufelt, the Gospel singer, Canadian YFC Evangelist Charles (Chuck) Templeton, and Wesley Hartzell, reporter for the Hearst newspapers, on an evangelistic tour of Europe and Great Britain. The trip was to change Billy's life. It was the beginning of the team of Cliff Barrows and Billy Graham.

In the fall of 1946 Billy returned to England with his own team consisting of Cliff Barrows, whom he had recently met, Cliff's young bride, Billie, and Gavin Hamilton, a Britisher who had transferred to the U.S. Hamilton, who had wide acquaintances among the evangelicals in Britain, set up meetings for the Team throughout the Isles. Billy asked George Wilson to accompany them for a short time and to handle the finances.

While in England, Billy was profoundly influenced by many clergy and laity. There he met and came to know a clergyman who later became a lifelong friend, Stephen Olford. Stephen spent considerable time with Billy, especially in Wales, instructing him in the ways of the British churches and British evangelism. Stephen also helped

Billy in the area of victorious Christian living and the meaning of being filled with the Holy Spirit. He deepened Billy's awareness of the Spirit's ministry and the necessity for in-depth Christian living.

Back on the home front Wilma was giving birth to our first child, Nancy Carol. I could have won the prize for "proudest pop" in the Palmetto State. I was performing the functions of the pastoral ministry and loving the work, but a spiritual discontent still probed at my soul. I was a pastor-evangelist but sometimes heavily weighted toward *evangelist*. Nothing thrilled me more than seeing people walk the aisles for Christ. I never liked what is commonly called "administration." Committee meetings could either bore or agitate me.

In the meantime Billy entered another phase of his early ministry—that of a college president. Dr. William Bell Riley, for many years pastor of Minneapolis's First Baptist Church, was president of Northwestern Schools which he founded in 1902. It was an interdenominational, evangelical college and seminary.

Dr. Riley had taken a shine to Billy. On his deathbed Riley had named Billy as his successor to the presidency of Northwestern. In December of 1947 Billy became interim president upon Dr. Riley's death. He then served as president from 1949 until the spring of 1952, when he decided to enter full-time evangelism. I doubt if Billy at that time ever dreamed he would devote the rest of his life to evangelism. He was torn between becoming a Christian educator and an evangelist. I think Ruth's influence tipped the scales toward evangelism.

Billy's tenure at Northwestern was not wasted. The school grew from 700 to 1,200 students under his leadership. Dr. Riley had decided not to build a radio station, even though Loren Bridges and George Wilson had urged him to do so. One of Billy's first actions as president was his OK for them to proceed with the station. It became the foundation of the large and successful Christian network called "The Northwestern Network."

Billy's presidency was providential from the standpoint of the personnel there who would later shape the Billy Graham Evangelistic Association. First and foremost was George Wilson, business manager at Northwestern who was already functioning as part-time business manager of the Association. Then there was Luverne Gustavson who had served as Dr. Riley's secretary. She became Billy's secretary and was to remain with the Team for fourteen years. She was actually the secretary for the entire Team through one of the most historic periods of our ministry. When she gave advice and counsel, we always listened because of her vast experience and ability.

Another pivotal person who came from Northwestern was Jerry Beaven who was registrar of the school. He asked Billy if he could help in the 1950 New England meetings. At the time Billy was not sure of Jerry's ability, but Jerry displayed tremendous organizational skills in the early years of the Association.

And there was Bill Berntsen, one of the best Christian musicians in the world, I feel. He joined the Team from time to time as our organist. Today, Bill is the president of a greatly revived, successful, and fully accredited Northwestern College in Roseville, Minnesota.

Billy wanted a person he could trust—someone from the South who would be a friend and confidant—to stay at the school while he was away raising funds, speaking to the alumni, or preaching. Billy chose my older brother,

T. W., to assume the position of vice-president.

As a pastor I was increasingly torn between pastoring and evangelizing in revival meetings. With gratitude I accepted as many engagements as I could, but there was always the gnawing guilt that I might be neglecting my "church field," the Baptist term for parish.

Although Billy and I were not often together during those years after graduation from Wheaton, we continued to stay in touch. And I was thrilled by Billy's ever-expanding ministry as evangelist and college president.

If I've heard it once, I've heard it a thousand times, "Did you think during those days of preparation that Billy would do what he's done?" I'd have to qualify my answer. Somehow I recognized the potential within him but certainly didn't dream he would become perhaps the most listened-to evangelist in the history of Christendom—and that multiplied millions would respond to his proclamation of the gospel.

Only a few intuitive people felt he would have an especially useful future in the kingdom of God. Many have asked me, "How do you describe Billy's success?" I must reply, "There's no human way possible. God singled him out, and the fact is: certain insightful Christians like Watson, Underwood, Minder, Edman, and Bell, his father-in-law, were used by the Holy Spirit to pave the way.

And if it hadn't been for those little Baptist churches that put up with me, and for brethren in Christ like Dick Brothers and R. G. LeTourneau, I haven't the faintest idea where I'd be today.

There is the recollection that while I was pastoring in "Hell Hole Swamp," Billy was working with John Minder at Tampa Gospel Tabernacle and was also preaching on the streets, in front of bars, in missions, in trailer parks, and in jails. And we had to have guts to stick it out. To this day I could never understand how anybody could preach without an urgent sense of calling from God's Spirit.

It humbles me to remember that Billy has always appreciated my preaching. I accepted the call to preach before he did, and he gave me enthusiastic support.

Many folks might have thought T. W. or I would "go farther" than Billy. During our early ministries Billy thought so. Billy felt that T. W. and I had genuine gifts of preaching. I may have sensed a gift occasionally, but I also suffered from deep feelings of inferiority. I never felt that I did well, no matter the response to the invitation.

Through the years, in characteristic lack of ego, Billy has repeatedly declared that many preachers can out-preach him. He claims that Ruth, his wife, is far more conversant with the Bible than he. To this day he some-times becomes quite tense before he preaches. The tre-mendous responsibility of preaching the gospel, and the awesome fact that we are dealing with eternal matters, is a responsibility that those who do not preach can never understand.

Billy admits that the Lord has granted him an ability to communicate and to give the invitation for people to receive Christ. In my judgment this is the gift of the "evangelist."

My lack of seminary training would have disqualified me in many denominations and institutions. Billy at-tended three schools but never a seminary. I attended two. Both of us have several honorary degrees. Billy strongly considered seminary during his days of ministry with Youth for Christ.

But there is only one way to describe our ministry—a miracle of God's grace. In the words of that stately old hymn by Ernest W. Shurtleff:

> Lead on, O King eternal,
> The day of march has come;
> Henceforth in fields of conquest
> Thy tents shall be our home:
> Thro' days of preparation
> Thy grace has made us strong,
> And now, O King Eternal,
> We lift our battle song.

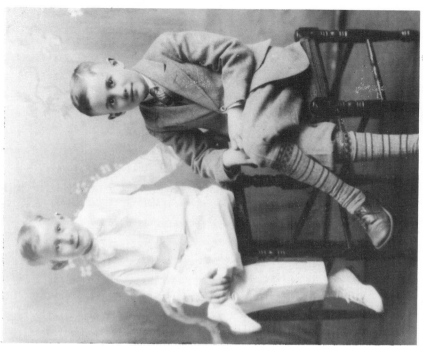

One of our few childhood pictures—T. W., my oldest brother on the right, and yours truly

Gospel Tent Meeting

Continues

MAY 10th - 23rd   7:30 Nightly

700 Block E. 36th St.   No. Charlotte

- Features -

SPECIAL MUSIC

GOOD GOSPEL SINGING

TIMELY TOPICS

OLD TIME GOSPEL

in

STIRRING MESSAGES

With

GRADY WILSON

SUCCESSFUL YOUNG EVANGELIST

Sponsored By CHARLOTTE CHRISTIAN MEN'S CLUB

and COOPERATING CHURCHES

COME - WORK - PRAY

BRING YOUR FAMILY AND FRIENDS

1936

My first revival meeting was in 1936, sponsored by the Charlotte Christian Men's Club.

(GW)

My first sermon on radio in 1937

— *Union Revival* —

FEBRUARY 14th — MARCH 7th

North Lawrence, Ohio

Services at the

Methodist & U. B. Churches

Services Nightly at 7:45

Speakers —

REV. M. W. RAFELD
REV. DON WINTERS
REV. GRADY WILSON

— SPECIAL MUSIC EACH SERVICE —
U R INVITED

REV. GRADY WILSON
Charlotte, N. C.

(GW)

A poster from a union revival in 1944

(Karmen-Winger Photo, Oak Park, IL)

Happy day! Our wedding party in 1943—left to right: Chet Terpstra, Jean Stone, Don Austin, Minnie Lawrence, Grady, Wilma, Jimmie Johnson, best man; Helen Wilson, maid of honor; Billy, and Mary Ludvik.

(GW)

Wilma Hardie Wilson in 1947, the year I entered evangelistic work with Billy Graham

Pastor Han, Bob Pierce of World Vision, Billy, and I in Seoul, Korea, 1951

The "Charge of the Wilson Brigade" at Hardin-Simmons University, also in 1951—left to right: Cliff Barrows, me, George Wilson behind me, Billy, and Dr. Rupert Richardson, the president of Hardin-Simmons

(GW)

"The world's best male quartet" singing at First Baptist, Asheville, NC—left to right: me, Tedd Smith, Cliff Barrows, and Bev Shea

(GW)

Bev and I inspect Harringay Arena in London before a Crusade service, 1954.

Billy summoning me to support a point—London, 1954

A shot of our group during the All-Scotland Crusade

Dr. Modecai Ham and I years after the 1934 Charlotte campaign in which Billy received Christ and I rededicated my life

My publicity photo shot during the 1957 New York Crusade—part of the Madison Square Garden crowd was in the background.

Billy speaking while I listened at William Jewell College's Achievement Day dinner in 1959

Conducting our family altar sometime in the early 50s—Connie on my lap, Wilma, and Nancy Carol

Whispering to President and Mrs. Lyndon Johnson at a Crusade service in Houston's Astrodome, 1966

Trading funny stories with President Johnson at the Little White House in Johnson City, Texas

(GW)

The three women in my life—Wilma and Connie, seated, and Nancy Carol (standing) around 1964

Billy and I on a fishing trip in 1959—even though "fishing for men" comes first, every Christian ought to withdraw for relaxation.

A group of friends fishing near Miami (1961)—left to right—Don Hustad, Cliff Barrows, Joe Blinco, James Rainwater, our host; me, and Bev Shea

A radio interview with ETBC student announcer, John Peden, and John Nance, director of religious activities

With General George H. (Hank) Wilson and his staff at Dobbins Air Force Base in Georgia

(BGEA Photo,

Billy introducing me on nationwide television, 1963

(GW)

Excuse my expression. Here I was speaking to a huge crowd at the Pentagon for a pre-Christmas program.

Billy, Ruth Graham, and I with Rev. Sidney Helwig at services in Montego Bay, Jamaica, 1965

Dr. John Brown, Jr., bestowed honorary doctorates on Cliff Barrows and me on behalf of John Brown University.

Talking with a young man who received Christ in a Crusade I conducted on Taiwan

Preaching in my own Crusade at Lexington, KY

With John Bolten, Christian businessman and financier from Germany

Billy, T. W., and yours truly "in fine fettle"

5
The Birth of the Crusades

If you're interested in Billy, you may have read articles or books about him or by him. You've probably consumed scores of press releases from the wire services, editorials, and magazine articles. You've read his syndicated column, "My Answer."

Maybe you've read books like *Billy Graham: The Authorized Biography*[1] and *Billy Graham: Evangelist to the World*,[2] both by John Pollock. So, I'm not going to give you all the minute details about the BGEA. I want to share personal glimpses and highlights from my ministry of which a part was with Billy Graham.

First there was Billy, of course. God had abundantly blessed him in the pastorate, as president of Northwestern Schools in Minneapolis, and as vice-president of Youth for Christ International.

Early in his ministry invitations for revival meetings poured in. I have mentioned how Billy had represented Youth for Christ, along with a team of other Americans, up and down the British Isles. The meetings had an impact in spite of small-scale opposition.

We actually had our first real Crusade together in

November of 1947 at our hometown. It was an honor to be coming home, and we tried not to think of Jesus' expression concerning, "A prophet is not without honour, but in his own country" (Mark 6:4).

We held forth at the old City Armory which seated 2,800 to 3,000 people. Gil Dodds, the famous American long-distance runner and a grand Christian, showed up in his track outfit and ran clear around that arena several times. That was the Youth for Christ pattern we used for attracting youth. I doubt if we would do exactly the same today.

Gil then came to the platform to give his Christian testimony. We had 50 to 100 people making decisions per night, with total inquiries between 1,500 and 2,000. Back then we had a three-week budget of $12,000, tiny by today's standards.

We left Charlotte with a good taste in our mouths. Crusades at Augusta, Georgia; Modesto, California; Miami, Baltimore, and Altoona, Pennsylvania, were lined up for us.

In the late 1940s an organization called Christ for Greater Los Angeles was conducting interdenominational revivals in the area. Evangelists like Merv Rosell and Jack Shuler had preached and done reasonably well.

CGLA's directors put their heads together and extended an invitation to a young evangelist named Angel Martinez, a graduate of Baylor University and Southern Baptist Theological Seminary. Angel was—and still is—dynamic, handsome, and well versed in the Bible. He has memorized the entire New Testament and huge portions of the Old!

After soul-searching, Martinez answered no, responding that he was basically interested in church revivals, mostly in Baptist churches. Martinez is to this day one of the most powerful evangelists in America. Who at the time was aware of that no's significance?

So CGLA contacted Billy, and he answered in the affirmative. All of the plans were in motion. We prepared well for the LA meeting which was conducted in a giant tent we called "The Canvas Cathedral." Although the meeting was to last only two weeks, many of the cooperating ministers begged Billy to stay longer. I had to leave LA in the middle of the meeting to conduct my own revival in Park Rapids, Minnesota. While I was gone, miracles were occurring in The Canvas Cathedral.

Yet, there was still an undercurrent of opposition. After the third week an affluent, prominent minister came to Billy and complained, "Billy, if you extend this meeting, I'll not only pray that God will take his blessing off this Crusade—but off your ministry!" To this day that splendid man is embarrassed by the encounter.

Dr. Louis Evans, Sr., pastor of the First Presbyterian Church in Hollywood, and Dr. Bob Shuler, pastor of the Trinity Methodist Church, were among the well-known pastors who supported us. Dr. Evans's son, Louis, Jr., married the actress, Colleen Townsend. Dr. Evans, Jr., has recently been in the headlines because President Ronald Reagan has attended his church, the National Presbyterian Church in Washington, D.C.

The critical minister's church leaders had become disillusioned because their pastor wouldn't participate in the Crusade for the last four or five weeks. Billy, out of the bigness of his heart, asked that minister on closing night to pronounce the benediction, publicly thanking him for all he had meant to the Crusade, even though the man hadn't attended in weeks.

For some reason, no doubt of divine origin, William

Randolph Hearst, the most powerful newspaper tycoon in America at that time, liked Billy. He heard about the meeting through a maid who had attended. In an editorial meeting with his staff, he issued a directive: "Puff Graham." In newspaper parlance that meant to "hype" him—give him all-out coverage and do it as favorably as possible. We couldn't have bought that kind of publicity for millions of dollars.

Many celebrities were among the 5,000 who walked the aisles during the extended eight weeks. That added publicity to the already swelling tide. Lou Zamperini, former Olympic runner, had performed with the matchless Jesse Owens at the 1936 Olympiad in Berlin. To spite Hitler, Lou had climbed atop the Reichstag and planted the flag of the good old U.S.A.

During World War II he spent forty-two days on a life raft in the Pacific and then underwent a harrowing stay in a Japanese POW camp. Depressed following his wartime experiences and on the brink of alcoholism, Lou was converted at The Canvas Cathedral. His life was transformed, and he began to pray for the conversion of his former Japanese captors whom he had once hated. He found that Christ causes a reversal of form in the human heart.

Then there was the now-famous Stuart Hamblen, a radio celebrity and country songwriter in Hollywood. We now recognize him for his songs, "This Old House" and "It Is No Secret." Stuart was friendly, good-natured, but what we'd call "gross" today. He was a confirmed alcoholic and almost flaunted it.

His wife, Suzy, was a Christian. One night that darling came to the prayer tent. She confided in desperation, "I think I'll die if Stuart doesn't accept Christ." She reported how Stuart had gambled away $148,000 that year alone.

As quickly as El Lobo, his leading race horse, had won it, that quickly Stuart had lost it.

Stuart, like I did back in 1934, thought the evangelist was pointing straight at him. Disturbed and distraught, Stuart declared that Billy was singling out all of his sins. That night after the service Suzy stayed on her knees petitioning the Lord for Stuart.

He was so under conviction that he headed out to the Sierras to hunt mountain lions. About halfway into the mountains he ran into a blizzard. He later felt that God sent the snow. "I dreaded it," he reported, "but there was a compulsion for me to return to the meeting." He called us at the Langham Hotel, one block off Wilshire Boulevard, at 4 AM.

Stuart and Suzy came to our hotel suite. Old Stuart was broken up and crying as Billy said, "We've been praying for you for weeks. This is an answer to our prayers and to Suzy's."

"Listen, Billy, I know all about what you're reading me from the Bible. My father's a Methodist preacher in Abilene, Texas. But I need prayer. Pray for me."

By this time Wilma and Ruth had joined us. We went around in a circle and prayed for Stuart. He came crawling across the carpet and put his arms around petite Suzy. He prayed, "Oh God, thank you for this little woman. She has prayed me into the arms of Jesus Christ." Then he continued, "Dear God, I've tried to telephone you before, but I never made connections. Somehow I know that I have you on the line now. Please have mercy on this hell-raising sinner from Texas and please save him. For Jesus' sake. Amen."

Then he called Dr. Louis Evans, Sr., Suzy's pastor. It was 6 AM. "Doc, your sermons have finally paid off, and your prayers have been answered. I've been saved here in

Billy Graham's room this morning." Next he buzzed Roy Rogers, one of his old hunting partners, and thanked him. "Roy, your prayers have done it. All of your witnessing to me has gotten through." Roy and Dale Evans, who had starred together in a number of movies, had only recently married.

The legendary John (Duke) Wayne was a close friend of the Hamblens. One night Duke and Stuart were talking like they often did. Duke had heard about the change in Stuart and that he hadn't had a drink in a month. Duke asked him, "Stuart, have you wanted one?"

"No, Duke," he replied. "It is no secret what God can do." Wayne then gave Hamblen an inspiration. "Well, why don't you write a song about 'It's no secret what God can do'?" Hamblen did that immediately. The second verse and the chorus move me deeply.

> There is no night for in His light you'll never walk alone
> Always feel at home wherever you may roam.
> There is no power can conquer you
> while God is on your side.
> Just take Him at His promise.
> Don't run away and hide.
>
> It is no secret what God can do.
> What He's done for others,
> He'll do for you.
> With arms wide open,
> He'll pardon you.
> It is no secret what God can do.[3]

Jim Vaus was once the wiretap and bugging man for the late, notorious Mickey Cohen, a gangland leader in LA. While he was working for Cohen, he had also been a double agent for the Los Angeles Police Department.

Then Jim was converted at The Canvas Cathedral. The day following his profession of faith Jim was supposed to carry electronic devices for the mob to St. Louis. An opposing agent got wind that Vaus was coming to "St. Louie," and they planned to greet him with a machine gun upon his arrival.

But coming from the tent the night before, Jim stopped and called Mickey. He explained, "Mick, I've decided not to make the trip to St. Louis. I've been saved in the Billy Graham meeting at the big tent in downtown LA." Mickey replied, "OK, Jim, good luck. I hope you make it."

In the eight weeks Billy was in LA, an average of 1,000 professions of faith were recorded for Christ each week. The meeting's results were far beyond our expectations.

Billy has gone to the Los Angeles-Hollywood area a number of times since.[2] He has conducted Crusades in the Hollywood Bowl, the twenty-fifth anniversary of The Canvas Cathedral (1964), the Rose Bowl at Pasadena, the American Legion Stadium in Hollywood, the Anaheim Stadium, and in the Los Angeles Coliseum where we had our largest California crowd.

In the Los Angeles Coliseum there is now a bronze plaque stating that it was the largest crowd in the history of that facility—156,000. It was not an estimated count since the people came through turnstiles. After the Coliseum was jammed, and the entire playing area was covered with people, the officials then ordered the gates open—and around 25,000 more squeezed in somewhere! To this day, many times when a football game is played, the public address announcer will say, "This is one of the largest crowds in history, except for the Billy Graham Crusade."

Hundreds of people had asked, "Who is this Billy Graham? Billy who? What's the deal here?" They were beginning to find out who he was. The entire team, Billy, Cliff, Bev, others, and I realized it was God's doing—and that we'd better not tamper with his plans.

Jesus emphasized, "No man, having put his hand to the plough, and looking back, is fit for the kingdom of God" (Luke 9:62). The team had put its hand to the plow, and there was no turning back. God had validated the ministry of the Team. It was not our ministry—it was God's.

One of the highlights of our early ministry was the "New England Tour," which started at Boston in the fall of 1949. Honestly, what we experienced in Boston and New England was the closest to genuine revival I have beheld in my lifetime.

In Boston we opened the meeting in the historic Park Street Congregational Church where Dr. Harold Ockenga was pastor. The church was located right on the Boston Common.

The opening night of what was to have been a week of meetings in one church, far more people were outside than inside. We decided to move the following night to Mechanics Hall which seated 7,500. Later, the crowds outgrew the hall, and we relocated to the Boston Garden which accommodated 16,000. At least 50,000 were present in the rain for the closing service on Boston Common several weeks later.

Billy had a sore throat one night, and I had to sub for him. Dr. Ockenga was dumbfounded. He didn't know what to think of a country boy with a Southern drawl far more pronounced than Billy's. He also couldn't understand how God could honor my homespun humor. Many people responded to my message on being born again, for which we praised God.

At the Boston Garden, Dr. Wade Freeman, the secretary of evangelism for the Baptist General Convention of Texas, attended, along with two young preachers,

Howard Butt, Jr., from Texas and Jack Robinson, former Olympic basketball player and All American at Baylor. Dr. Freeman, a saint of God, burst into tears and exulted, "Grady, I've come from a big state just to see God do big things in what we have known as 'the graveyard of evangelism.'"

Then we moved to Columbia, South Carolina, for our meeting in the Township Auditorium. Toward the end of the Crusade I had to pinch hit for Billy again one night. Just as many came down front when I preached. Now I'm sure that wouldn't have continued if the people had thought Billy wasn't coming back.

The distinguished Henry Luce became fascinated with Billy's ministry. Luce was the publisher and owner of *Time, Life,* and *Fortune* magazines. Luce had been born in China to Presbyterian missionary parents—sounds like Ruth Graham. Luce came down for the Crusade and then spent the night at the governor's mansion, where he and Billy talked earnestly into the wee hours of the morning. The following day Luce instructed a team of *Life* reporters and photographers to cover the Crusade.

Life did a prominent spread of pictures declaring "A NEW EVANGELIST ARRIVES ON THE AMERICAN SCENE." Then *Look* magazine picked up on the Graham story, and an incredible chain had developed.

Willis Haymaker, who had known Billy's parents from about 1935 and later Billy, joined us in Columbia as our advance man and stayed with us for years. He'd had ample and effective experience in setting up evangelistic campaigns for Bob Jones, Gipsy Smith, and other evangelists. An organizational genius, Willis named our meetings or revivals "Crusades," and that stuck.

Since South Carolina is sort of my second home, I recall the towns where we conducted one-night Crusades—

Columbia, of course, Newberry, Greenville, Anderson, Clemson, Spartanburg, Walterboro, Charleston, Sumter, and Lancaster. Jimmy Burns, former U.S. secretary of state, was with us at Spartanburg. We rented the University of South Carolina stadium for a climactic rally. In the morning paper there was a panoramic picture of the empty stadium. The caption stated, in essence, "Billy Graham predicts this stadium will be filled this afternoon, but the weatherman predicts rain all day long! We'll see who's right."

It rained torrentially until time for the service, when the skies cleared. Forty thousand people were there, overflowing the stadium, and both Secretary Jimmy Burns and then-Governor Strom Thurmond were present. Both were bald and had their heads blistered.

Then we returned to receptive New England, our itinerary including Woodstock, Vermont; Concord, New Hampshire, Houlton, Maine, near the Canadian border; Burlington, Vermont; and Fall River, Massachusetts. New Englanders often have the reputation for being reserved and noncommittal, but the gospel can excite people anywhere. Many of my closest friends are New Englanders.

Portland, Oregon, marked another turning point for us. Earlier in Boston, Billy had called us to our knees about going into radio more than our local broadcasts from the Crusade cities. The great Dr. Walter A. Maier of *The Lutheran Hour* had died unexpectedly, and Billy advised, "Boys, let's pray that somebody will step into Dr. Maier's place in calling America back to revival and repentance." Little did we realize that Billy would be God's choice.

Billy said, "I wouldn't dare go on nationwide radio without praying about it." Walter Bennett and Fred Dienert of the Walter Bennett Advertising Agency had continued to contact Billy about the possibilities of radio on the American Broadcasting Company. They showed up in Portland.

On the spot Billy prayed for $25,000. That's like $100,000 or more today. That night Billy announced to the crowd, "Grady Wilson and members of the Team will be in the Team room tonight after the service is over, and if you feel we ought to go on the air coast to coast, come by and give us your commitment and encouragement. Send us a check or cash contribution. Everyone of you will receive a receipt." That night we were handed $23,500 in cash, checks, and pledges.

Bennett and Dienert indicated that was enough. "Not for me," Billy insisted. "The devil could give me $23,500." Bone tired we returned to the hotel. I picked up the mail. There were three envelopes with Billy's name on them. Would you believe that in those envelopes was the total of $1,500? We had our answer.

Ruth Graham suggested we call the program *The Hour of Decision*. It has stuck for almost thirty-five years.

I was responsible for keeping that $25,000 with me! I hid it under my shirts in a dresser drawer. The following day, with a shoe box for my bank bag, I tried to deposit it in a Portland bank. They informed me, "You'll have to deposit it in your own name, Mr. Wilson. And if you do, you'll have to pay income tax on it."

So, I inquired about whether I could deposit it in the name of "The Billy Graham Radio Fund." "Not unless you are incorporated to have a charter," came the response. Back to my room with the box. Back in my drawer under the shirts.

Naturally, Billy inquired about the money. "Billy, I carried it to the bank, but they wouldn't accept it without putting it in my name." Billy burst out, "Well, Grady, you didn't leave it upstairs in your shirt drawer, did you?" "Yep," I nodded, "that's exactly where I put it." "Do something about it now," nervously urged Billy.

George Wilson, with the necessary legal papers, flew in from Minneapolis. Within a matter of hours, "The Billy Graham Evangelistic Association" was chartered, and Frank Phillips, the Crusade chairman, and I were able to deposit the contents of that shoe box in the bank!

You've often heard that "the course of true love never runs smoothly." Neither does the course of genuine evangelism. The Lord was performing miracles to further our outreach, but the devil's forces were arrayed against us.

6
Not All Sweetness and Light

Throughout our ministry we have found that when the power of God is mighty, the forces of hell make tumultuous waves. Criticisms of our work are treated in many chapters of this book, but here I'll detail a few. All criticism is not bad; some can end up being helpful in the long run. Admittedly, many criticisms have been slanted and a few vicious. Perhaps some have stemmed from that green-eyed monster, jealousy. Though Billy Graham might deny it, he has a tendency to look on the good side of everybody.

Thinking back to our first meetings in the late 40s and early 50s, I'd have to admit that we haven't changed our approaches too much. We've never used gimmicks. We don't believe in hucksterism. Billy hasn't modernized his message except, as you know, to inject current events. He reads constantly—books, magazines, newspapers—but most of all the Word of God. Naturally, this has brought about maturity and growth.

In those days we were accused of setting the gospel back fifty years. We especially heard that in England and Australia.

During our meetings of 1949-1951 we were criticized about our handling of finances. When we started our evangelistic work, the worst image of so-called "mass evangelism" was still rather strong in the minds of Americans. For example, at that time all evangelists without exception took up "love offerings." These were usually collected toward the end of evangelistic campaigns and given to the evangelist for his personal travel and living expenses. Some evangelists before us had received huge amounts of money; others nearly starved. Bob Jones, Sr., declared during the 30s: "I'm the highest-paid evangelist in the world." Until the Atlanta Crusade of 1950 we too were on a love-offering basis.

A campaign at Modesto, California (Cliff's hometown), in 1949 was an early turning point for the fledgling Team of Graham, Barrows, Shea, and Wilson. Billy instructed all of us, "Boys, let's go to our rooms and write down all of the criticisms of mass evangelism. Don't hold anything back. Then let's meet for evaluation and prayer this afternoon."

All of us agreed that the number-one pet peeve was the handling of finances. We also listed sensationalism, over-emotionalism, becoming controversial, and the image of being antiintellectual and antichurch. And there was the matter of virtually no follow-up. That very day we determined not to be guilty of those charges, and the Team set out to make necessary changes and adjustments.

At the Atlanta Crusade in 1950 we had a love offering. The final night a newspaper photographer asked the head usher if he could shoot pictures of his duties. The usher, totally innocent, agreed, "Well, OK, but tonight my main responsibility is to carry the love offering back to the ushers' room." So, the photographer shot pictures of the head usher lugging two giant moneybags in his arms.

The same paper came to the Biltmore Hotel the following morning and asked to make pictures of Billy's departure from the city. The picture came out with Billy waving his hat in the air. Along with it, side by side, was the photo of the usher with the moneybags.

Billy was concerned about that because he has never had an impure motive about money. He could have named his price in many other areas, as I will relate later on.

Billy next decided to contact Dr. Jesse Bader, then head of evangelism for the National Council of Churches, to talk about the money situation. Dr. Bader, a truly Spirit-motivated man, advised Billy to cut out the love offerings. He counseled, "Billy, I think you ought to go on an annual salary, you and the Team. Form a board of businessmen who understand finances and let them handle the funds. Organize into a nonprofit evangelistic organization. Don't even give your critics a chance to slam you. You could make a historic decision and change the course of American evangelism."

"Dr. Bader," Billy inquired, "what would be a fair salary for me?" Dr. Bader suggested $15,000 per year and Billy concurred. Many pastors were making more than that in 1950.

Billy, in consultation with Cliff and sometimes one or two others of us, chose twenty-five sound, solid Christian businessmen and women for the board. Today the executive committee of the board (of which no paid employee is a member) meets approximately every six weeks. They handle all the finances. I seriously doubt if there has ever been a Christian organization in which finances have been handled with such integrity.

During the Portland Crusade, when Billy was given a

love offering, Ruth back in Montreat was writing that she desperately needed to pay the bills. Yet, Billy wrote a generous check to Dawson Trotman of the Navigators. Dawson, working with our follow-up program, made a plea for financial aid to help his organization.

I scolded Billy severely: "The idea of you writing that big check when Ruth is barely surviving and paying the bills back home!" I should have known that Billy was earnest and naïve. He is probably the most unselfish man on earth. He'll give you his cloak *and* his coat, in accordance with the Scriptures.

In addition to our image about money, we had to work on the charges of sensationalism. I never felt we were sensational but that we projected a sane, sensible presentation of the Gospel. I guess it's according to your perspective. Billy would request that people not be carried away lest we be misunderstood. But now many of our younger people insist on clapping for anything and everything. I think this annoys Billy, but he accepts it as a part of the younger generation. Whenever a person gives an appealing testimony or even leads in a moving prayer, the young people often clap and cheer.

I've mentioned the early jesting about our clothes. One magazine called Billy "Gabriel in Gabardine." He had purchased a light green gabardine suit on sale.

About two years later I thought a certain gentleman was making me a gift of a canary-yellow suit. It had saddle stitching and white pearl buttons. It was attire for a movie star or entertainer, but it was a gift, so I didn't want to hurt the "giver's" feelings. I wore that brilliant suit the first night in the Hollywood Bowl. Billy embarrassed me. He said, "Ladies and gentlemen, I'll have to apologize for this bright, canary-yellow suit Grady's wearing." The crowd applauded for my suit! I felt like a fat ministerial canary—all caged in. After the service scores of people complimented me on my apparel.

Earlier that day Cliff Barrows shot a fountain pen right onto my suit. I virtually cried. It's the only time I ever actually became angry with Cliff. I heatedly complained, "Cliff, this suit cost over $200!" The "ink" later evaporated, and I found out that Cliff's spouse, Billie, and Ruth had bought a trick pen in a novelty store. To make a sad ending, Wilma cried when she received the bill for my "gift" suit! I did, too.

After many accusations of being flamboyant, Billy moved in the other direction—almost too conservative in his attire and self-conscious about the cost. The average preacher, believe it or not, probably spends as much or more on clothes than Billy or me. Billy shops places like J. C. Penney, Sears, and K-Mart.

The last time we were in Detroit, Billy was talking to our faithful friend, Stan Kresge of K-Mart. Billy unwisely began showing Stan the suit he was wearing. "Stan," he inquired, "how do you like this suit? Isn't it beautiful? I got it at Sears across the street." Kresge, looking hurt, mildly retorted, "Billy, you'd have done much better if you'd bought it at K-Mart!" I groaned, "Good grief, Billy, you can say all the wrong things!"

Not all sweetness and light were the misunderstandings over our publicity in the early days. When we were in the 1950 Atlanta Crusade, an unfortunate goof occurred, and it was totally beyond our control. Dr. Louie D. Newton, the revered pastor of the Druid Hills Baptist Church and one-time president of the Southern Baptist

Convention and the Baptist World Alliance, suspected many men of the cloth. As a layman he had been a newspaperman.

One night on the platform Tedd Smith, our pianist, turned to me and anxiously reported, "Tell Billy that I received a phone call in my hotel room from Dr. Louie D. Newton. Dr. Newton said some crazy man had said he was coming here tonight to try and kill Billy Graham. So tell Billy to be careful and to keep his eyes open."

I soothed Tedd: "Don't worry about it." I leaned over to Billy and gave him the unnerving message. "Billy, if you see someone coming down one of those aisles, you look at me and I'll lead you to an exit. Follow me out."

Billy asked for "every head bowed, every eye closed." He announced (and I wish he hadn't done it), "Ladies and gentlemen, I want you to be in special prayer tonight. One of our Team members, Tedd Smith, received a phone call a little while ago from Dr. Louie D. Newton. Dr. Newton reported that some man had called his office and told him he was coming over here tonight to try and kill me. So I want all of you to be alerted."

The crowd began buzzing. Billy prayed sincerely, "Oh God, protect us tonight and give us safety and give everybody in the audience protection. May the Spirit of God take the message and drive it into the hearts of the people." Nothing bad happened.

The following morning one Atlanta paper quoted Dr. Newton as saying that had been the biggest publicity hoax he had ever heard of. Dr. Newton hadn't called Tedd; the caller was an imposter. Newton felt that it was a newspaper put-up job for publicity on the part of Billy Graham. That embarrassed all of us. The following night Billy publicly apologized to Dr. Newton. How were we to know it was someone imitating Dr. Newton's voice? Tedd

Smith had never before heard Dr. Newton. The press carried only a tiny squib about the apology.

Many years ago the papers showed pictures of the same people coming down for the invitation each night. What the media didn't understand is that we asked the counselors (in the early years called "personal workers") to move forward as soon as the inquirers started coming down. Yes, the same people walk to the front because they are trained counselors to deal with those making decisions.

We learned early to match up inquirers with counselors. We'd rather have a man with a boy or man, a woman with a girl or a woman, senior citizens with senior citizens, and the like. We have specially trained people to counsel with children under twelve years of age. On our staff we maintain regular experts in children's counseling.

Actually, the first full-scale follow-up was in the Memphis Crusade of 1951. Dawson Trotman, founder of the Navigators, headed up the original program, and capable men like Lorne Sanny helped him. Dawson had worked with men in the service around the world and had already tested out a Scripture memorization program and a counseling philosophy. Billy had enlisted Dawson to spearhead the program of conservation of the inquirers.

During our Crusades we do not call those who respond "converts" but rather "inquirers," because all do not come forward for conversion. Many step out for rededication, dedication to full-time Christian service, and for the assurance of salvation.

Billy used to tell the story of the Methodist evangelist, Sam Jones. A drunk staggered up to him and belched, "Mr. Jones, I'm one of your converts." Jones answered in his inimitable manner, "You look like one of *my* converts.

It's plain to see you're not one of the Lord's." That's the reason Billy shys away from the word *convert*. After a person has been established over the years, he can be identified as a convert. Of course, we pray that every inquirer is sincere and that every person making a profession of faith means it.

Incidentally, we have on file tens of thousands of letters from inquirers who were converted years ago, stating they are still following the Lord faithfully over a decade or more after the Crusade in which they responded. There are thousands in the ministry or on the mission field. Once as I was speaking to the Southern Baptist Evangelistic Conference in Texas, the secretary of evangelism asked all of the ministers who had been converted in the Billy Graham ministry to stand. Hundreds rose to their feet.

Charlie Riggs, who lives in Nashville, for years now has directed our follow-up. Charlie is energetic, enterprising, and quietly determined. In Chapter 9 I give you more details about Charlie.

One of Satan's favorite lies is that the inquirers do not "stick" or "hold out." But that has been proven untrue by multiplied thousands of people whose testimonies are recorded in our headquarters at Minneapolis. Recently I was conducting a Crusade in Texas and among those present one night was the former postmaster-general under President Lyndon Johnson, Marvin Watson. We also heard the thrilling testimony of a man named Bunny Martin, "The Yo Yo King of the World," who publicly testified that over thirty years before, while a student at Howard Payne College in Brownwood, Texas, he had accepted Christ under my personal ministry. Yes, we feel that the majority of the inquirers have "hung in there" for Christ.

One prominent Southern politician used to comment, "It's all right to talk about me, good or bad, 'cause when you do, you're leaving somebody else alone." No, it's not all sweetness and light. Misunderstandings, though many times innocent, can hurt the cause of Christ. Unfair, unjust criticism is damaging. Intentional, outright innuendos and deliberate lies are often accepted as truth by those who want to find fault and believe the worst.

We had determined at our Modesto prayer meeting to "abstain from all appearance of evil" (1 Thess. 5:22). Through careful planning and perspiration, under the leadership of the Spirit, we set out to live down the stereotypes of mass evangelism.

7

It Is Marvelous in Our Eyes

Amazement is the noun which sums up the subsequent history of the Billy Graham Evangelistic Association. As we moved into the 1950s and beyond, the Lord would perform a ministry beyond our imagination. It has humbled us all. God directed us "from victory unto victory," and we were often breathless with the majesty and wonder of God's providential plans. Billy has always been careful to give God the glory. He has repeatedly quoted the prophecy of the Old Testament, later repeated in the New:

> Did ye never read in the scriptures, The stone which the builders rejected, the same is become the head of the corner; this is the Lord's doing, and it is marvelous in our eyes? (Matt. 21:42).

We have kept that before us. "This is the Lord's doing, and it is marvelous in our eyes."

I have participated in over four hundred Crusades with the team and have conducted a like number of my own. All I can do is gasp in awe at what God has done in the years I have known Billy and in the period we have labored together—with Cliff, Bev, and the others—as an evangelistic Team. "I stand amazed in the presence of Jesus the Nazarene."

Outside of a twenty-volume work I could not possibly cover the scope of God's purposes in the Crusades. All I can do is touch a few of the highlights. In addition I have sprinkled scores of references to various Crusades throughout these pages.

Early in the ministry the team branched out into motion pictures, joining the radio program, *The Hour of Decision.* Our first motion picture was *The Portland Crusade* in 1950 with Dick Ross as the producer. Through the creative eyes of Dick we began to understand what Christian motion pictures could do. Dick previously had been a radio producer and director for the Mutual Broadcasting Company. He had also worked a year with Bob Pierce producing a film on China.

Mr. Texas was actually the first dramatic motion picture we produced, premiering at the end of the Hollywood Bowl Crusade in October of that year. It starred Redd Harper and Cyndy Walker. Twenty-five thousand people were present, with 500 responding to the invitation. It has been number three on the popularity list of all the Billy Graham films.

In 1951 "Billy Graham Films" was incorporated under the laws of the state of Maryland. Our first distributor was Walter Smyth who had his offices on Connecticut Avenue in Washington, D.C. Dick Ross worked out of various studios. Three or four years later the BGEA built its own studios in Burbank, California. Our production company is directly across the street from the Disney studios, a short distance from Warner Brothers, and a few blocks from NBC. Years later the company name was changed to World Wide Pictures.

As a result of the Houston Crusade in 1951, *Oiltown, U.S.A.* was produced. It concerned the conversion of a Houston oil magnate. Admittedly, it was far more polished than our previous ventures.

As I have explained, our first full-fledged, follow-up program was set up by Dawson Trotman for the 1951 Crusade in Shreveport, Louisiana. Throughout the years the system has been constantly refined. We do not feel there is any foolproof follow-up method. The great agent in follow-up is the Holy Spirit. We have done our best and have utilized the talents, dedication, and brains of the finest preachers and theologians around the world.

In 1952 Billy broke into print with his syndicated column, "My Answer," which still runs in hundreds of magazines and newspapers. In 1953 his first major book, *Peace with God*, was released. Ruth, herself a talented writer, helped Billy finish the manuscript. Many books have subsequently followed, including *World Aflame, The Holy Spirit, How to Be Born Again, Angels, Till Armageddon,* and *Approaching Hoofbeats: The Four Horsemen of the Apocalypse.*

During the six-week Washington Crusade of 1952 Billy led a service on the steps of the United States Capitol. During that Crusade, the parents of Pat Robertson (of "The 700 Club" and the Christian Broadcasting Network) were active. Pat's father was Senator Willis Robertson of Virginia who helped introduce Billy to the political scene in Washington. So, Billy began to have many opportunities to meet with congressmen, senators, and cabinet members. During that period he made many friends who were later to become presidents and leaders of the government.

Congress had passed an act authorizing the service at which Billy read Abraham Lincoln's proclamation for a day of national humiliation and prayer. He then preached a short, uncomplicated message about returning to God, the Bible, and the church. Sam Rayburn, the speaker of the House, declared before the crowd, "This country needs a revival, and I believe Billy Graham is bringing it to us."

At the Chattanooga Crusade in 1953 a special wooden building to seat 15,000 was built at Warner Park. In most of the cities we entered in those days we had to erect our own building. Willis Haymaker was responsible not only for setting up our Crusades, but also for supervision of building construction. The buildings had to meet all fire laws, codes, and regulations, plus be located in an area where people could park. It was not an easy assignment, but somehow it was done in cities like Detroit, Albuquerque, Greensboro, and others.

The most memorable fact about "Choo Choo City" was its being the first racially integrated Crusade in the Deep South. Throughout his ministry Billy has stood for brotherhood and against racism and bigotry, even though he grew up in a Southern culture. In this Crusade he made a bit of history. He saw blacks being seated in the rear, as hundreds of them were attending the services each night. They were being held back by ropes.

One night he saw the ushers putting up the ropes. He walked back and physically pulled down the ropes, saying, "There will be no more ropes as long as I'm preaching." This caused considerable consternation on the committee, even division. But Billy stood his ground. Some Team members at that time were not so sure Billy was right, but the intervening years have proven he was more than right.

Later that year, we had to face the same problem in

Dallas, but again Billy insisted on no segregation. While he did not insist on integration, he did not want the crowd to be forced into segregation. The black leaders of the South deeply appreciated and hailed what was then a courageous step. However, we found that the black people would still sit in the rear or in the places they were accustomed to in an auditorium or stadium. Interesting them to move in among the whites, even after the Supreme Court decision of 1954, was difficult.

People have asked me through the years, "Which have been the greatest Crusades?" That's almost impossible to answer because everyone has been distinctive unto itself. Although massive crowds are impressive, big doesn't necessarily mean best. Even those Crusades which seemed disappointing still made a lasting impact.

The British revival meetings Billy and Cliff conducted in 1946 and 1947 marked a milestone. (Of course, I was not yet a member of Billy's team.) That extensive campaign brought them together and taught them a tremendous amount about methods we use in our Crusades today. During that time Billy learned a great deal about the Anglican world, the Plymouth Brethren, the Methodists, the Baptists, and the Church Free Council that would often back Billy and Cliff in those meetings.

The next turning point, which I deal with in another chapter, was the Los Angeles Crusade under The Canvas Cathedral in 1949. It was supposed to last three weeks and was extended to eight. That Crusade gave the team national, even international, attention.

Next would probably be the Far Eastern trip Billy and I made with Bob Pierce, which opened our eyes to world missions and the pressing needs of other countries. After that trip we were never exactly the same. We were

haunted by world need, a world by and large without
Jesus Christ and his redemption. We were beginning to
become world evangelists.

Another turning point was the London Crusade of
1954. That became international news. According to media authorities Billy had more press coverage during that
period than any other human being in the world, including President Eisenhower.

The fifth major juncture probably was the sixteen-week
New York Crusade. That campaign gave Billy national
attention on a scale he had never before experienced. It
also presented him with the backing of many influential
denominational leaders, because the Crusade in 1957 was
sponsored by the Protestant Council of Churches. This
also put Billy into contact with many leaders who were on
the fringes of evangelicalism. That Crusade was the
longest in duration. We had run for twelve weeks in the
1954 London Crusade.

In many respects the first London Crusade was perhaps the most miraculous. As I explain all over this book,
in London we had to overcome and confront all kinds of
barriers—public relations difficulties even before we set
foot on British soil, our coming with "American evangelism," and an insulation against the gospel.

I honestly doubt if we ever preached in as many
different locales as we did in London—in Hyde Park
where people debate and harangue for hours, at the
Surrey Ship Docks where we saw thousands of workers
come to Christ, in shops and shopping areas, at pubs, and
in breweries.

Some of the converts were members of the staff at
Buckingham Palace. The captain of the Queen's elite
guards gave up his position to become a missionary to the
East Side. The head buyer for the exclusive Harrod's of

London responded to Christ, influencing many because she was highly respected in fashion and also an excellent speaker. Joan Winmill, the acclaimed actress, gave her heart to Christ. She virtually played her own story in the World Wide production, *Souls in Conflict*. She married Bill Brown, now president of World Wide Pictures, in 1955.

As usual there was the *unusual*. I preached at the Tower of London for five days. A one-eyed man attended and kept asking me, "What about reincarnation?" One day he changed his tack to, "Why hasn't Christianity solved the world's problems? It has been around for 2,000 years."

A little missioner from the London City Mission answered him out loud: "Sir, soap has been in the world for more than 2,000 years, and why is your shirt collar still dirty?" I wish I'd thought of that! I picked up on that— "Why don't you go home and apply some soap to your collar and some Christianity to your life."

We were trying to be as inconspicuous as possible to avoid undue criticism. One afternoon when Billy was terribly busy, a vicar came from the country and demanded to speak with him. The cleric insisted, "I must see Mr. Graham," to which I replied, "I'm sorry but you can't. Perhaps another day."

"What are you Yanks doing here, anyway?" he queried. He then added, "I want you to go back where you came from." I answered, "We're here because a thousand clergymen invited us."

"Well, I wasn't one of them," he countered.

"We're not going back," I explained, "until God does what he wants to do in our lives."

"I hope that's tomorrow," he shot back.

I said, "I can promise you it's not going to be that soon. By the way it's not costing you a pence. We're paying our own expenses."

"I don't care about that," he retorted. "You came over here on the *Queen Mary*. It's a big, expensive ship. I suppose you came first class. Have you Yanks never read where the Lord Jesus Christ rode into Jerusalem on an ass?"

"Oh yes, I've read that many times every year, especially on Palm Sunday. But," I went on, "if you'll show me an ass that can swim the Atlantic Ocean, I want to buy him tomorrow and I'll pay for him in pure gold!"

With that he jumped up in a huff and left. At least I gave him an answer.

In Hyde Park there was a prominent clergyman who used to speak every Sunday afternoon. Ruth would sneak into the crowd to hear him. One day when she was there someone asked that clergyman what he thought of Billy and the Team. He was most emphatic that we ought to go home. "I don't like any of those Americans," he railed. "They're overdressed. They're overfed. And they're *over here*." He received a loud roar of "Hear! Hear!" which means approval in England.

Yet, we were confronted with only two hecklers during the entire three months at the Harringay Arena. I recall when Billy was preaching in John Brown's Shipyard. A boy about twelve was down front listening intently. The boy's father came along and slapped the little fellow at least fifteen feet in front of the workers. Billy responded, "Jesus Christ loves that man and that boy. He loves them both and can meet their needs as well." Out loud the man cursed Billy and dragged the boy out of the crowd.

I was preaching at a brewery when one bloke yelled, "Why don't you Yanks go back to America? I attended last night and Graham said, 'Any of you can come, but it'll cost you two bob [shillings] to hear me preach.'"

Brazenly I answered, "That's a lie. I've been there every

night. Mr. Graham has never charged anyone anywhere to come hear him preach. Furthermore, if you'll promise to go hear Mr. Graham tonight I'll give you two bob out of my pocket." His mates raucously urged him on, but he wouldn't take me up on it.

May 22, 1954, was the last day of the London Crusade. At Wembley Stadium, Billy preached to the largest religious crowd in the history of the nation—120,000. It is almost impossible to believe that three hours earlier he had preached to 65,000 across the city at White City Stadium, and it was raining at both services! As far as we know that 120,000 is still the record crowd for any event at Wembley Stadium. On the same day Bob Benninghof, an engineer assigned to us, arranged for the Team to utilize land lines for a radio hookup of all the Isles, with the exception of Southern Ireland.

Billy was invited back for the Wembley Stadium Crusade in May of 1955. In many respects our second visit was too short, for it rained nearly the entire week. The newspapers had been on strike, and there was little media exposure compared to the year before. Few leading dignitaries of the Church of England attended. And the new Prime Minister, Anthony Eden, had called for a national election. Yet, the smallest crowd numbered 50,000, the largest, 90,000. Some of the greatest names in Britain came forward to accept Christ in mud over their ankles.

Then Billy and Ruth visited with the Queen Mother and Princess Margaret at Clarence House. Billy also preached to the Royal Family at Windsor the following Sunday. I can still see the number-one headline in Monday morning's *London Express*: BILLY AT THE PALACE.

In 1966 we returned for a Crusade in Earl's Court, the biggest indoor meeting place in London. Thirty-four thousand per service packed the Court and an adjoining annex for the month we were there. Closed-circuit television enabled us to carry the message throughout Britain and all over Europe, and many other doors in Europe were opened through the electronic medium.

Billy is loved as well as hated. Lee Fisher, who is now retired from the Team, was on a London subway train. He noticed a man reading a newspaper which headlined: BILLY IS BACK IN ENGLAND. The man, with gritted teeth, mumbled to himself again and again, "I hate Billy Graham. I hate Billy Graham. I hate . . . "

In my estimation one of the most marvelous Crusades was in Paris (1955). France, of course, is traditionally secular with a flavor of Roman Catholicism, but we understood that no more than 5 to 10 percent of the people ever attended mass. Evangelicals were miniscule in number.

Our Parisian Crusade was in the Veledrome d'Iver, a bicycle racing arena seating 9,000. It was overflowing for every service. Because of the response, we decided to make an evangelistic tour of France. Leighton Ford, Billy's brother-in-law, preached in Toulouse, I in Moulouse, and T. W. in Nancy. We preached under the Billy Graham Crusade banner, and at the end of each of our meetings Billy would preach the last sermon.

Then we had several special meetings in Switzerland, one in Basel, the hometown of theologian Karl Barth, who had become a friend of the Grahams. Barth predicted to Billy, "Billy, you are coming to my city, and these people will not likely respond. You will not have a corporal's guard attend your meeting." He also suggested that no one, or only a few, would respond to the invitation. Billy went to Basel. Fifteen thousand were in attendance at each service. Hundreds stepped out for Christ nightly, and Barth was pleasantly surprised. I can still see him at that first service sitting under an umbrella as it was raining. To his credit, he came in the rain to hear the gospel.

A few days later Billy visited with Emil Brunner in Zurich. Brunner remarked, in essence, "Mr. Graham, your theology needs sharpening a bit." Billy smiled and said, "I agree." Brunner expressed a liking for Billy's invitation. He pointed out that he was existential enough to believe that every person needs a definite commitment.

In Basel, Billy had a chat with theologian Oscar Cullman. Billy asked him, "Sir, why do you theologians disagree so violently on your theology? One believes one set of tenets. The next believes another. Sir, am I to wait until all the theologians of the world come together?" Cullman answered, "No sir, don't do that. You go on and preach your message as God has directed you. Don't wait for us to be together, because we never will be."

Cullman further acknowledged that Americans preach a simple, uncomplicated gospel. He observed that the German mind wants a system of theology by which they can arrive at certain conclusions.

One unnamed theologian expressed a distaste for Billy's repeatedly saying, "The Bible says. The Bible says." Yet, that was the facet of Billy's presentation Barth liked best. Barth said, "I love to see you hold up the Bible and say, 'The Bible says . . . '" Billy learned that Barth and Brunner were far apart theologically. Of course, extreme fundamentalists called Billy a "liberal" because he was friends with these European theologians, with whom he did not altogether agree. Yet, Billy was learning through all these experiences.

The theologian who probably made the most significant impression on Billy during those days was Dr. James Stuart, professor of New College at the University of Edinburgh. He and Billy used to go out for long walks. They would travel to the west coast of Scotland and spend two or three days at a time together, Billy absorbing all of the help and suggestions he could receive.

Those Crusades in the early and mid-50s sharpened and toughened us. I had never thought of preaching in a brewery. In the States they might run you out of the country if you did—but we have to go where people are. In London one of our Team members was infuriated about preaching in places like the docks or shops. He remarked, "I'm not built that way." So, some of us doubled up, including Don Moomaw, former All-American football player who is President Reagan's adviser at the Bel Air Presbyterian Church in California, and Joe Blinco, the English Methodist evangelist.

When I preached in the streets and had to parry off hecklers, I thought about John Wesley. Kicked out of official pulpits Wesley preached in fields, in the streets, and on the docks.

Joe Blinco was one of the best in dealing with hecklers. One day a fellow interrupted a message with, "Hey, Holy Joe, why are you trying to cram religion down my throat?" Joe quickly retorted, "Mister, if you don't want something crammed down your throat, keep your blooming big mouth shut!" Many accepted Christ in that service. It takes all kinds to reach people for the Lord.

When Joe died of a brain tumor, Billy felt as though someone had cut off his right arm. Joe's practical counsel, advice, love, and encouragement with us as an associate evangelist will always be missed. Ralph Mitchell, who also came to us from England, worked out of our

Minneapolis office and has been a monumental blessing to the ministry.

During our All-Scotland Crusade in 1955 Billy had one of his bouts of laryngitis. I was called on to fill his shoes. Each night we had been having capacity crowds at Kelvin Hall and an overflow hall nearby. People from all over Scotland were commuting in, and the crowds were averaging 30,000. Mr. and Mrs. Maxey Jarman of Nashville and Howard Butt, Jr., of Texas were there to give me support. Mr. Jarman was at the time chairman of the board of Genesco, one of the largest shoe and clothing manufacturers in the world. Howard was a lay preacher and grocery store executive in Texas.

Usually, if Billy has to leave a Crusade and it is announced ahead of time, the crowds and the number responding decline. Along with the team, Jarman and Butt prayed for the power of the Holy Spirit to anoint me. The attendance didn't decline, and we had the same number of responses, 600 to 700 per service, as when Billy preached.

A long time afterward I received a letter from a bonnie lassie who for months had saved her money for the trip to the Glasgow Crusade. She longed to hear Billy. She wrote, "When Mr. Barrows announced that you were going to preach instead of Mr. Graham, I wanted to jump up and curse out loud I was so angry. I said to myself, *They can't do this to me because I've been waiting and saving all these months to hear Billy Graham.* Ten minutes after you began speaking, Mr. Wilson, I knew why I was there. When you gave the invitation I joyfully walked out for Christ. Now I'm so happy I stayed, even though Billy Graham didn't preach that night. I thank God that he used you to move my heart to Jesus."

Such experiences have made it all worthwhile. It was all right if people referred to me as Billy's caddy, his utility infielder. I have a strong sense of calling—to lift up Billy's arms as Joshua and Aaron did for Moses. Billy has had many associates. I am deeply privileged to have been not only the first, but one of the closest of those evangelists.

8
Showers of Blessing

Through these decades we have often cried aloud, "My cup runneth over. Surely goodness and mercy shall follow me all the days of my life: and I will dwell in the house of the Lord for ever."

Wherever the Team preached there was a remarkable stirring of hearts. In the 1950s we conducted Crusades on every continent but South America. After years of invitations we finally went to every country in Latin America except Bolivia.

In 1956 the Team traveled to India and the Far East for the first time. In population, India is still the second-largest nation in the world next to China. The unending masses of humanity were staggering—the vast majority of those 800-million-plus people were those who did not know Christ.

In India, Billy has preached to some of the largest crowds until that time—hundreds of thousands. Billy became keenly conscious that the answer was the enlistment of Indians to carry the message to their own people. Billy soon learned that the people of India will respond to Christ's message. They have an estimated 350 million gods, and they are happy to add Christ to their pantheon. It is relatively easy to get an Indian to make at least a token decision for Christ. This is where so many immature evangelists and young Christian zealots have gone wrong in India. That is why there are so few lasting results. Billy decided early on to change his invitation. He made it so hard that fewer and fewer Indians responded, but those who came forward really meant business in comparison to the first time he went to India. Billy has returned to India three times since 1956 and has experienced gratifying results.

For years the Nationalist Chinese have had open hearts to the gospel, largely through the Christianity of the late Chiang Kai-shek and his family. In Taipei, Taiwan, the stadium was jammed to capacity every service. President Chiang was ill but his son was present. During our trip to Taiwan I conducted a satellite Crusade at Taichung. The pictures of the event looked like a bicycle convention, because thousands of Chinese had ridden their bikes. I couldn't imagine how they could find their bikes, but they did.

Think of it. Thousands of people listening to the gospel, and their chairs were concrete blocks! I had three interpreters—one in Taiwanese, one in Mandarin, and one in Cantonese. We had to alternate the order of interpretation because each group wanted its language interpreted first. Sounds like some of our churches back home, doesn't it? We had thousands of inquirers in spite of the language problem.

Then we moved to Hong Kong. There we had two stadiums back to back with services going simultaneously, one seating 30,000 and the other 20,000. I would give the invitation in the overflow stadium while Billy gave it in the main arena. We've done that frequently in other locales like Australia, Great Britain, and Scotland. If there has been an overflow crowd Billy has sent the other associates and me to lead the invitations. And we've often had closed-circuit TV of Billy's message with us pressing for the decisions in the overflow halls or stadiums.

Back in the states Billy founded *Christianity Today,* an evangelical magazine which is still independently published to this day. What John Pollock wrote in 1966 still holds true in the 1980s:

> *Christianity Today* is disliked by extreme fundamentalists, despised by extreme liberals, and mistrusted by many moderate liberals. But tangible evidence of its growing impact on Christian thinking is the rapid rise of its paid circulation. . . . It has stimulated new writers and thinkers, provided a forum for the sifting of ideas, helped lift evangelicals out of their anti-intellectual mire, and has directed or clarified the theological views of many ministers and laymen who were trudging in a welter of secondhand liberalism.[1]

New York City wasn't called "The Big Apple" in 1957, but it has always been exactly that. A melting pot, a city where "a person can find anything he wants," and a city with a restless, deep-seated hunger for meaning.

References to the Manhattan Crusade are all through this book. Billy had preached to an estimated 2,357,400 people in person at Madison Square Garden, Yankee Stadium (where 100,000 were present in sweltering 105-degree heat), and in Times Square, often called "The Center of the World" (where 160,000 to 200,000 gathered for the closing service on September 1, 1957).

At Yankee Stadium 25,000 were turned away. I believe that was the largest crowd in the history of the stadium.

Even when Pope Paul VI held mass there, that many were not present because so much room was needed for the Pope's huge platforms.

The attendance at Madison Square Garden still holds a record, for we stayed there for sixteen weeks when we had been scheduled for only six. Billy also averaged about three to four times a day preaching. There we also started the national televising of our Crusades, a milestone in our ministry.

Our closing service was held in Times Square. The police blocked off scores of blocks in every direction, the people gathering shoulder to shoulder. Billy's sermon was taken from the marquees of the theaters and was carried live on national television. It seemed that every news cameraman in New York was there. It made front-page headlines not only in America but in many parts of the world.

One of the outstanding converts in New York was Mrs. Cornelius Vanderbilt Whitney, called Eleanor by her friends. Many of her socialite friends accepted Christ as a result of her decision. The decisions influenced by her probably ran into the hundreds, and she has gone abroad sharing Christ, even on safaris in the jungles and cruises in the West Indies and the Mediterranean.

Another convert was Tom Phillips, president of Raytheon Corporation. He later figured prominently in leading Chuck Colson, one-time aide to President Nixon, to the Lord.

For the Yankee Stadium rally President Eisenhower had been invited, but Vice-president Richard Nixon attended in the president's place. President Eisenhower called Billy several times during that Crusade and encouraged him because Billy was appearing on such programs as "Meet the Press," "The Today Show," and others. Walter

Cronkite also interviewed Billy during the Crusade.

At the Yankee Stadium meeting Mr. Nixon remarked to Billy, "Billy, this is a great tribute to you." Billy replied, "Mr. Vice-president, this is God's doing. This is not my crowd. This is not my doing."

Mr. Nixon then observed, "Billy, I believe this is one of the reasons God has blessed your ministry. You always give him credit." After that meeting, when thousands came forward for Christ, the ministers invited Billy for another month. He agreed.

Billy remarked to me, "I don't believe I can make it another day. All of my strength has departed from me. I've preached all the material I can lay my hands on. Yet God wants me here." Billy then agreed to preach for only the night services. With help from the Holy Spirit, Billy's associates, and the prayers of people all over the world, he was able to muster the stamina for the task ahead.

Since that time, now over a quarter-century ago, I don't believe he's ever regained all of his strength. When he mounts the platform, though, it seems that the Holy Spirit gives him a resurgence of vitality and power.

Shortly thereafter we were visiting Southern Baptist Theological Seminary in Louisville. We went golfing that afternoon, and Billy complained to me that he kept seeing weird ridges on the ground. We then flew to the annual meeting of the Baptist General Convention of Texas (Southern Baptists) where Billy preached. Then we flew directly to the Mayo Clinic where they found a difficulty in his left eye.

Once again the doctors advised, "You have to slow down. God's been good to you, but if you keep this up, one day you'll drop dead in the pulpit." (Parenthetically, I thought: *I'd rather drop dead there than anyplace else.*)

The Australian Crusade was coming up, but Billy had to start a week late in Melbourne. Billy promised the doctors he would limit most of his activity to preaching at night, a little swimming, and a few holes of golf. During that Australian Crusade, which lasted six months, Lee Fisher was with us, helping Billy in the preparation of his sermons as well as playing golf as often as possible with Billy, Cliff, me, and the others. This helped Billy keep relaxed. I feel he left the Australian meetings stronger than when he arrived.

The response to the invitation at Melbourne was so astonishing that one night Billy had to stop the thousands of people from streaming down the aisles. The platform was about to collapse from the sheer weight of the people who crowded down front. Billy explained, "There is no more room." He asked the inquirers who could not come down to write the Team for follow-up materials which would help them in their newfound life for Christ.

The Australians and New Zealanders are a likable people with warmth and simplicity. They still have a bit of the adventuresome, pioneering spirit. The Britishers who settled there were made of sturdy stuff. I took to them and they to me.

Strangely enough, this was the only time in my entire ministry I asked a person not to make a public decision. A prominent prelate of the Anglican Church in Australia had been attending every service. I sensed that there was a deep conviction and uneasiness in his life. During the invitation at the final service the choir was singing "Just As I Am." With intensity, that church leader whispered to me, "Mr. Wilson, I want a copy of that song if you can get it for me. It's the most beautiful song I've ever heard." Tears rimmed his eyes as he continued, "I feel I should go forward and recommit myself to Christ. In fact, I am not absolutely sure I am a Christian, yet I want to be."

"Your grace," I counseled, "The press is sensation seeking. You can go forward in your heart." He bowed his head, and I could sense he was praying. I repeat: this was the only time I ever asked a person not to go forward.

Ministering in Australia and New Zealand we had three-and-a-half million in attendance. The results in Melbourne were astonishing enough—over 28,000 decisions with the final attendance at the Melbourne Cricket Club (one site of the 1956 Olympics) reaching 136,000. This site is called the "sacred turf" of the Cricket Ground in Melbourne. It was the first and only time it has ever been opened up as it was that day.

Yet, in Sydney 150,000 showed up for the final rally at the Showground and the adjoining Cricket Ground. The final tally of decisions was 57,000!

In New Zealand I conducted a Crusade at Auckland. Lane Adams preached at Christchurch and Leighton Ford at Wellington. Our entire team was going up and down New Zealand's islands. The average attendance was in the neighborhood of 15,000 per night. When Billy came for the final meeting 60,000 were present. There were more decisions in that one night than we had experienced all the previous week.

Then, as a result of the Australian Crusades, many members of Parliament and mayors of towns and cities were converted. Next, I received an invitation to preach in Perth, Australia, the beautiful "City of Roses." The press, however, did not heap roses upon us. They thought of us, for the most part, as American circus performers or entertainers.

Many of the clergymen came to me and inquired, "Can't you get Mr. Graham to preach about the unbridled debauchery on Anzac Day?" Anzac Day in Australia is similar to Memorial Day in the U.S. It is the "Australian-New Zealand Army Corps Day," a holiday for remembering their war dead. But it has turned into a time to kick up one's heels and throw off all restraints.

One clergyman had advised against saying anything about the excesses of Anzac Day. He remarked, "These blokes need one day a year when they can cavort. And besides, you'd be getting into political matters." Billy wasn't compromising but felt he was being judicious.

One Sunday afternoon I was preaching to a crowd of 15,000 in Perth. In passing I commented, "If your war dead could see the drunkenness I saw in Sydney on Anzac Day, many of those dear veterans who gave their lives for their country would turn over in their graves in absolute shock and horror!"

My comments hit the front pages of almost every Aussie newspaper. Clergymen throughout the land called and wrote me, giving me, as it were, a mighty "Amen." The clergyman who had cautioned against grappling with the subject was upset and called Billy about it. Billy cautioned me about my statement. "Go slow with that. That's mixing in Australian politics. It's embarrassing." What was said was said, and I wasn't the least bit sorry.

Some of the Team members then flew to London. Ruth and Wilma met us there. Our first day there the four of us were strolling through the gorgeous Royal Parks near Buckingham Palace. There in the broad, open daylight, all sorts of people were engaged in various sex acts. Ruth turned to Billy and said, "Bill, it's a tragic day when people will turn the Royal Parks into bedrooms."

So, the following day Billy commented on our shocking stroll through the Royal Parks. Billy stated, "It looked as though your parks have been turned into bedrooms." By the time we went out onto the street the papers already had his observation as a major headline. The press carried cartoons and stories about it for several days. For five days Parliament considered that very matter. The members of Parliament decided to clamp down and weed the immorality out of the parks.

As a result of my 1959 tour of New Zealand I and my own Team were invited back in 1960. We stayed for twenty-six days the second time around. When we arrived a deadly drought had set in. The land was dying, along with the livestock. The mayor of one town attended a luncheon of clergy and civic leaders and had several choice words for me. He said, "I was living in Canada years ago, and the only American evangelist I ever heard of was Aimee Semple McPherson. That lady was a big showman, and she professed to perform miracles. As far as I know the only thing evangelists can do is perform miracles. Before this crowd I'm challenging Mr. Wilson to perform a miracle and bring us some rain."

My opening remarks were, "Mr. Lord Mayor, thank you for this welcome, but I'm not in the rainmaking business. God called me to proclaim his Word. But I'll tell you what I'll do, sir. I'll meet you at any church in this town tonight and have an all-night prayer meeting for rain." I prayed for rain at that luncheon which let out at 2 PM. At 2:30 it began raining and the bottom fell out. The torrential rain lasted all that day, into the night, and throughout the following day.

One of the businessmen from that town phoned me and remarked, "Maybe you should ask the Lord Mayor when he wants you to cut the rain off." The mayor's challenge, my prayer for rain, and the much-needed deluge made all of the papers. The papers declared that

Grady Wilson, an associate evangelist with Billy Graham, was a rainmaker and a performer of miracles. No, God did it. To him be the glory. I was later told that the skeptical mayor began attending church the following Sunday—after an absence of years.

In 1960 the Team toured Africa extensively. We learned long ago that the world situation is so changeable and volatile that we must walk through doors when they are open. In over two decades the climate of that vast continent has changed dramatically. The thrust all across Africa has been to throw off the vestiges of colonialism and to restore local rule. Most every nation in Africa has been wracked by revolution, and many of them are now ruled by despots far worse than those in colonial days. What thrills me as I revise this manuscript is: throughout Africa the Christian faith is spreading like a life-giving stream. The accounts of missionaries cause us to "rejoice with a joy unspeakable and full of glory." Jesus Christ wants to be everyone's Messiah, regardless of origin, skin color, background, and social customs. Christ is for "every kindred, every tribe."

We visited several nations, including Liberia which was originally founded by American blacks. The late Dr. William Tolbert was president and also a strong Baptist pastor. (He was slain in a coup several years ago.) One of our associate evangelists, Howard Jones, preached for many years on the Christian radio station from Monrovia, the capital city.

Opportunities were presented to us in Ghana, Nigeria, Zimbabwe, and many other countries which have since changed their names. For two weeks the Team conducted a Crusade in Lagos, Nigeria. Dr. Ayorinde was chairman of the Crusade which was held out at the race course. Dr.

Ayorinde, a Baptist leader, had tribal scars and slashes on his face. Ten to twelve thousand came out each night to hear the Gospel message.

Then I moved on to Kaduna, Nigeria, where thousands sat on the bare ground to receive the word. Dr. Farrell Runyan, a Southern Baptist missionary, had made all of the Crusade arrangements.

Communicating through translators, no matter how skilled they are, isn't always easy. One night I was giving an illustration about one of my daughters back home in Charlotte. I used the wording, "A thought came home to me." The interpreter looked at me quizzically and asked, "What?" I changed it to: "A thought occurred to me." He replied, "Oh."

I gave an illustration about a highly popular soft drink and the interpreter had trouble with that. Then I pointed to a little boy on the front row. "See that little boy down front. He's drinking that soft drink." Every person there, perhaps ten thousand, stood up, craning their necks to see that boy with the soft drink.

We've had as many as three interpreters on the platform. In Nairobi, Kenya, there were twelve languages or dialects spoken by those attending the Crusades. So, our interpreters had to work from little booths, and we had to divide the crowd into groups according to language. Each group had its own translation coming over a separate speaker system. The counseling materials had to be translated into as many as twenty-five languages and/or dialects. During those times we would have desired Pentecost to repeat itself when the multitude exclaimed, "Every man heard them [the Christians] speak in his own language" (Acts 2:6).

In Africa, Billy was trying to give an illustration about taking his little son, William Franklin (now the Reverend

William Franklin Graham, director of the Samaritan's Purse in Boone, North Carolina), on a stroll in the mountains near Montreat. Billy was trying his hardest to illustrate the incarnation of Jesus. Billy, through the interpreter, explained, "And we accidentally stepped on an ant hill, killing several of the ants. I told my son that there was no way to apologize to those ants without becoming an ant."

The crowd jumped to its feet, yelling "Hallelujah" and "Hurrah." They kept on laughing and applauding. Billy hadn't thought of it, but in that section of Africa there are huge army ants which build giant mounds. They can destroy villages and towns. The crowd totally missed Billy's point and was showing its approval of father and son for killing those ants.

In 1970 Billy conducted "Euro 70" in Dortmund, Germany, and the Crusade employed closed-circuit TV as far north as Oslo, Norway. During that meeting I had the privilege of meeting the wife of Willy Brandt, the chancellor of West Germany and former mayor of West Berlin. She sat beside me on the platform as Billy preached. In English she repeated again and again, "This is marvelous. This is wonderful."

We had a tremendous response all over Germany and the Scandinavian countries. More than 100,000 persons each night watched Billy on closed-circuit TV with a different associate giving the invitation in each location.

One of the most memorable Crusades was the team's 1973 visit to Korea, also touched on in other chapters of this book. The team covered the length and breadth of South Korea. Outside of Seoul I had the privilege of preaching to 400 military leaders. It was an odd scene. They had moved their office chairs out onto a lawn and listened in comfort. Several received Christ, and Billy had them stand during the invitation at the final service in Seoul, where an estimated 1,120,000 were packed into Yoido Plaza.

The largest crowd I've ever preached to was in Pusan where 60,000 came to the closing service. We had averaged 15,000 to 20,000 a night the previous week.

The first crowds Billy had in Yoido Plaza numbered 500,000 to 600,000 and more each night. Korea is becoming a bastion of Christianity. In Seoul alone there are over 2,000 churches, including the two largest churches in the world.

Our school of evangelism in Seoul, directed by Dr. Kenneth L. Chafin, was the largest in our history. Over 9,000 ministers and laypersons participated in that school.

Some prominent evangelical leaders have predicted that one day Christians from the Far East will send missionaries to the Western World. The Koreans' hunger for Christ shames the American believer.

One hundred thousand persons responded to Billy's invitation that last day in Yoido Plaza; multiplied hundreds of thousands made decisions throughout Korea, including the satellite Crusades conducted by John Wesley White (Taegu), Akbar Haqq (Taejon), Howard Jones (Chonju), Ralph Bell (Kwangju), Cliff Barrows (Chunjon), and me (Pusan).

Billy and the Team have experienced countless triumphs, and we have beheld, with profound pain, many tragedies.

Scandinavian people are basically good, robust people but years of a permissive attitude have thrown off restraints. Unfortunately, some of our most violent opposition has occurred in Norway, Sweden, and Denmark. In

1965 we were there with fair results.

Indicative of their response was our preaching in a Copenhagen hosiery factory. One man defiantly drank two bottles of strong drink in front of the crowd which applauded, even though there were signs all around reading: *No alcoholic beverages allowed.*

In one city, dissident students pelted Billy with rotten eggs while he was preaching. He took it in stride and continued preaching. When the Team came back to the states, Bev Shea reported that those radicals were sitting between T. W. and Dr. Bob Evans of the Greater Europe Mission. Bev reported, "Grady, immediately after the service Billy said, 'If Grady had been here, he'd never have allowed this to happen.'"

Many years before at the Forum in Copenhagen, a dreadful tragedy had occurred. Anytime an American performer had appeared, radical students had turned up to interrupt the performance. They heckled and booed, also threatening harm to the performers. On a night Billy was to preach, a group of these "students" entered the Forum. The manager recognized them.

As quickly as possible he intercepted them in the aisle and warned them, "Just a minute. I don't want you people coming in here disturbing the American preacher. This man is sincere, and he's trying to do good in our city." One fellow pushed the manager aside and yelled, "Get out of our way." With that a woman radical reached beneath her skirt, pulled out a vial of acid, and threw it into the manager's face. The man was blinded in both eyes for life.

When Billy and other members of the Team visited that man in the hospital his eyes were bandaged. Billy had a prayer with him, trying to comfort and console him. Billy, choked up, said, "Sir, you have done this in the name of

God and for the glory of God. I thank you from the depths of my heart."

More than likely that acid had been intended for Billy Graham. These years I have thought about how sacrificial that man was, how he was ruined for life because he was trying to protect Billy Graham.

In 1977 the Team returned to Sweden and Denmark. Äke Lundburg, then our Team photographer, is a native of Sweden. He cautioned Billy, "I know you're going to be sick and disappointed, but I am afraid the people here in Sweden will not respond like they do in other countries. I don't look for anyone to come forward the first night or for the first several nights." Billy thanked Äke, saying, "I appreciate your coming to me. We'll simply have to wait on the leading of the Holy Spirit."

The Swedish campaign opened at Gothenburg. Evie Tornquist, that lovely singer of Norwegian extraction, sang a solo and then a duet with Bev Shea. Hearts were being warmed. When the invitation was extended eighty-three came that night. Night after night the decisions doubled, tripled, and quadrupled. The bishop of the state church came in civilian clothes the first couple of nights to "spy out the land." His church was not accustomed to our kind of evangelism. The third night the bishop came in his clerical garb and wanted all of Sweden to know that he was aligned with Billy Graham. He led in the closing prayer of the Crusade.

At the end of the Crusade he begged Billy to return the following year. He enthusiastically promised, "We'll move to the big sports arena and have 50,000 every night."

The late Dr. Robert G. Lee, one of America's most famous preachers, once preached that if he had a thousand heads, and every head had a thousand tongues, and every tongue spoke a thousand different dialects, and if he could speak for eternity, he could never praise Jesus sufficiently.

And that's how the Team feels about preaching "the unsearchable riches" of Christ. We could never conduct enough Crusades, preach enough sermons, touch enough people. And we are frightfully limited. Oh, how I wish we were enabled to preach in ten different Crusades at the same time, to preach in every town on the face of this earth, to answer "yes" to every invitation for a Crusade. How sad it is that Billy and the Team have had to answer "no" to literally hundreds of requests.

My prayer is that we will still be conducting Crusades when Jesus comes back!

9
The Team—Pulling Together

Unless I develop amnesia (a little boy called it "magnesia") I can never forget the early days of the Graham Team. When Billy asked me to assist him at Charlotte in 1947, Cliff and Billie Barrows, George Beverly Shea, and a few others were already ministering with him. Cliff and Billie had helped Billy as he had preached throughout Britain for eighteen months.

After Charlotte the earliest Team consisted of Billy, Cliff, Bev, and me. Over the decades Billy has added a number of associates as the Holy Spirit has led. I wish it were possible for me to write about every Team member in the history of the BGEA, but that would be impossible. Here I can share only a few personal reminiscences.

T. W., my oldest brother, officially joined the Team during the Chicago Crusade in 1962. Years before, T. W. had served as vice-president to Billy at Northwestern Schools. Billy and T. W. have had a close spiritual bond since our teenage and young-adult days around Charlotte. And T. W. had also exerted considerable godly influence over Billy and me during our college careers.

Billy invited T. W. to become his personal assistant, and it necessitated T. W.'s moving to Montreat with his family. Billy needed a reliable person to head up the Montreat office, handling innumerable phone calls, answering mail, and screening requests for Billy's time.

T. W. is an evangelist par excellence. I have found myself wishing that he might conduct a few Crusades of his own part of the time. He has preached to tremendous crowds, and he has an anointed gift of evangelism. He can present an appealing invitation, and he's a far better preacher than I. His son, Jim, is making his mark as an evangelist. Jim has preached on *The Hour of Decision* recently and is in demand for his own meetings.

Billy's close friendship with Cliff Barrows dates back to 1945 when they met at the Ben Lippen Bible Conference in North Carolina. Their personalities clicked, and Cliff, with his bright enthusiasm, has often been the "master of ceremonies" for Crusades, television, radio, and other BGEA engagements. Since its inception he has emceed *The Hour of Decision*. He has a gracious warmth that comes through the air waves.

Cliff is one member of the team who has kept his youth. It almost makes me jealous of him. He's one of the cleanest, most upright men I've ever known. He is faithful to God and his family in every respect. When I look at Cliff I am reminded of Jesus' words about Nathanael, "Behold an Israelite indeed, in whom there is no guile!" (John 1:47).

His wife's real name is Wilma, but her nickname is Billie. One time a friend gave Cliff and me the co-ownership of a boat. I painted "Wilma" (my wife's name) on the side of the bow. Cliff said, "My Billie [his Wilma] would like to have 'Billie' painted on the other side." It was done, of course.

Cliff's adherence to early-morning devotions is remarkable. He has often met with Charlie Riggs and me at 5 or 6 AM. We'd drink coffee or orange juice and share Scripture verses back and forth. We'd even have contests to see who could quote the most verses from memory. Incidentally, I think it's sad that so many Christians are giving up Scripture memorization. After all, the Bible quotes the psalmist's testimony, "Thy word have I hid in mine heart, that I might not sin against thee" (Ps. 119:11).

Way back Cliff played plenty of golf with the team members. Honestly, he couldn't hit the side of a barn with his woods, but he was deadly with his irons. He became so discouraged he quit golf for two years. Then suddenly he decided to play us again and whipped us. We found out that he had been taking private lessons from a pro during that layoff. He's that kind of guy—he wants to do everything well.

Once when we were in Pittsburgh I became fascinated with the chess games Cliff and Billy were playing. Then, in Houston I watched them play until I learned how. I thought to myself, *Now I'll have a chance to beat 'em.* And I began to beat both of them.

One morning I decided to go down to Cliff's room at 7 in the morning. The door wasn't locked, and I walked right in. Cliff looked sheepish, and he had every reason to. There he sat playing chess with Don Rosenburg, one of the greatest chess champions on earth. I chided Cliff, "Cliff, be sure your sins will find you out!" Since then I've never played another chess game with him. Although Cliff has what many call a "laid-back" demeanor, he is intense in what he does.

What other musician could have directed the music for

Crusades all over the globe, leading the choir and congregation in many languages? Cliff Barrows is endowed by God with a personality which excites people into singing praises to God.

Eternity alone will reveal how many people have decided "I'd Rather Have Jesus" while listening to George Beverly Shea sing. His singing lifts me to heaven.

To my knowledge no one has ever even suggested that Bev is not totally sincere. Sincerity and love exude from him. He is a living testimony to the gospel he proclaims in song. Bev is one of the most dedicated men I've ever known, putting most of us to shame. He is truly humble, almost to the point of being self-effacing.

Bev is best known for his song "I'd Rather Have Jesus," which he wrote in 1939. The song has been his testimony through the years. Until 1982 he had his own music company, Chancel, but sold it to another company. In recent years many listeners have closely identified him with "How Great Thou Art."

Many years ago a popular Indian singer, Chief White Feathers, included "I'd Rather Have Jesus" in his repertoire. The story goes that Chief White Feathers sang that moving song for King George VI of England when the King was visiting President Roosevelt. When the song was over the King turned to President Roosevelt and observed, in essence, "Mr. President, the words of that song express the sentiment in my heart. I'd rather have Jesus than to be the king of a vast domain."

The offices in Minneapolis and Montreat have received numerous letters and cards, thanking Bev for that song. One lady testified that she had turned on the gas and intended to commit suicide when she heard that song over the radio:

> Than to be the king of a vast domain
> Or be held in sin's dread sway.
> I'd Rather Have Jesus than anything
> This world affords today.[1]

She arose from where she lay awaiting death, turned off the gas, aired out the house, and fell on her knees, receiving Christ as her Savior.

Bev has always been a strong family man. His late wife, Irma, was a love. She often accompanied Bev on the Crusades, but she remained behind the scenes, praying for and supporting her husband. Irma was not widely recognized as a musician, but she was a graduate of the Juilliard School of Music in New York City. Irma and Bev were as devoted to each other as any couple I've ever seen.

After a debilitating illness in 1978, Irma went home to be with the Lord. Billy conducted her funeral in his old church at Western Springs, Illinois. Bev requested that I conduct the graveside rites at Houghton College, New York, where Irma and Bev had attended.

One of the most moving experiences of my life happened after the benediction at the graveside. Bev reached over and joined hands with his grown children, Ronnie and Elaine. Then Bev, with a voice that is recognized worldwide, sang "Amazing Grace," and the crowd joined in. There must've been 400 people there to pay their respects, and they sang John Newton's old hymn:

> Amazing grace! how sweet the sound,
> That saved a wretch like me!
> I once was lost, but now am found,
> Was blind, but now I see.

And I thought, *Nothing could be more appropriate at the funeral of a radiant Christian than singing hymns of praise to the One who conquered death.*

George M. Wilson, who is now executive vice-president in charge of the office in Minneapolis, first met Billy in 1944. Since then George has figured prominently in Billy's ministry. George had run a Christian book store in Minneapolis and labored enthusiastically in Dr. W. B. Riley's First Baptist Church. As already pointed out, he worked with youth and actually gave Torrey Johnson the inspiration for the founding of Youth for Christ. For years George has served as an energetic, creative business mentor to Billy.

Everybody thinks he's kin to T. W. and me, but he's not. He's the oldest man on the Team with the exception of Bev. George started out the Minneapolis office with a staff of volunteers from Northwestern Schools where he was also business manager when Billy was president.

George has indefatigable energy. He has headed the staff which varies from 500 to 600 workers. He also has a rare sense of humor, sometimes tinctured with practical joking.

George once had a friend in Minneapolis who was printing Christmas cards for various Team members. Cliff was so late with his request for cards that he simply sent a picture of himself and his family—all of them dressed up in red nightgowns. He asked George to pick an appropriate Bible verse and have the printer do the rest. He also sent George an extensive mailing list.

George called me and said, "Tell Cliff that I put on the card: 'Even Solomon in all his glory was not arrayed like one of these'" (Matt. 6:29). I quickly shared that tidbit with Cliff, and he almost fainted. Cliff called George immediately and asked him, "George, why did you do a thing like that?" A few days later Cliff received the real card with the quotation from Isaiah 9:6, "For unto us a child is born, unto us a son is given."

George is "Mr. Can Do It" and "Mr. Can Find It," so one time I asked George to be on the lookout for a little aluminum fishing boat (with outboard motor) for me. I knew he had a knack for finding items at low cost, and I instructed, "Whatever you do, George, let me know. I'm down here in a revival at the First Baptist Church of Jacksonville, North Carolina." George seemed to snicker over the phone.

The following day he sent a special delivery letter to our home in Charlotte. Wilma opened it and it read:

> Dear Grady,
>   The yacht you ordered will be delivered to your home in Charlotte. They will require a down payment of $995 on delivery. Tell Wilma to have the money ready.
>
>   George Wilson

I had a crushing schedule so I didn't arrive at the motel until late in the night. Wilma hadn't been able to reach me by phone, and you might imagine she was frantic. She had sent me a special delivery letter and had scrawled across the face of the envelope: *"Have You Lost Your Mind?"* Inside she had written: "We need a dishwasher. We need a dryer." Etc., etc. The list continued. "Don't you think it's extremely foolish for you to be buying a big yacht when we're going without the necessities of life?"

Man, was I in the doghouse! It tickled George, of course. I called him and implored, "George, whatta you mean? Man, whatcha think you're doing? I'm down here trying to patch up homes, and you're up there in Minneapolis trying to break up a home—mine!"

All kidding aside, God has used George as the "business head" and organizational genius behind Billy's ministry.

When Billy first met Leighton Ford in 1945, there was

an almost instant rapport between the two. Leighton was a high-school student and directed the Chatham, Ontario, Youth for Christ.

Later, Leighton graduated from Wheaton, where he majored in philosophy, and from Columbia Presbyterian Seminary, where he served as president of the senior class. At Wheaton he found his wife-to-be, Jean Graham, Billy's younger sister. Billy was thrilled about the prospects and encouraged Jean to hang on to Leighton, which she did.

Billy performed their wedding ceremony in 1953 at Charlotte. During the ceremony Billy made a cute flub, "Now that Leighton and Jean have exchanged wings— oh, I mean rings!"

Leighton officially joined the team in 1955 as associate evangelist. Leighton has amazing impact on ministers. They gravitate to him. He helped further the Team's policy of working with local ministers many months before the Crusade services.

With his philosophically trained mind, Leighton can reach intellectuals. At the same time he can preach the gospel in language easy enough to be understood by a child. He is highly versatile emotionally and mentally and probably comes as close to 1 Corinthians 9:22 as any Team member: "I am made all things to all men, that I might by all means save some."

Leighton, like most of the associate evangelists, has a solid schedule of his own Crusades. He has a sharp, perceptive mind. He has preached for Billy at Crusades, conferences, and on radio. He is an accomplished author and has written widely, including two best-selling books.

Charlie Riggs directs our counselor training and follow-up programs. He started out with Dawson Trotman, our first follow-up man, who was also the president of the Navigators. Charlie makes his home in Nashville but spends considerable time on the road preparing and following up for the Crusades.

Charlie practices what he preaches. Deeply sincere and dedicated, Charlie is one of the best Scripture memorizers I've ever met. Also, I have never seen him riled or hotheaded in all of these years. He's also one of the best one-on-one soul-winners I've known.

His work is monumental. In Sydney, Australia, he taught 9,500 counselors in one week. He had the main cathedral filled every night. He was preaching to more counselors in one week than many evangelists preach to in an entire year. Charlie's calling is indispensable.

Tedd Smith joined the team as pianist in 1950 and has been with us ever since. A Canadian, he won his first gold medal for music as a nine-year-old. Tedd graduated from the Royal Conservatory of Music at Toronto. Tedd has always totally submerged himself in uplifting music for Christ. He and his wife, Thelma, are two of my favorite people.

He has composed much music for the Billy Graham films. He did the entire musical score for *The Hiding Place*, based on Corrie ten Boom's best-selling true story. He has done scores of concerts across America. Like virtually every successful concert pianist, Tedd practices nearly every day—for hours.

Several years ago the Team was going by train from Frankfurt to Berlin. Officials had informed us that the train would be stopped and searched in the Eastern Zone during the early-morning hours. Tedd was unnerved by the prospect of going through the Russian Occupied Zone. He wanted to leave the train and fly. To calm his nerves and help him sleep I gave him two sleeping pills instead of one. I certainly wanted him to sleep well.

When we reached Berlin the following morning and were met by the U.S. military chaplains, all Tedd would do was open his eyes and fall back into sleep. Cliff Barrows and Walter Smyth literally had to carry Tedd out the end of the railroad car. He woke up later in the day. For a long time Tedd accused T. W. of giving him those pills.

Paul Mickelson came as organist in 1950 and was followed by Don Hustad, who is now on the faculty of Southern Baptist Theological Seminary in Louisville. John Innes is our regular Crusade organist at the present. Dr. Hustad visits with us occasionally, especially in the summer.

Throughout this book I have mentioned Dawson Trotman who pioneered our follow-up program. Billy first met him when Dawson spoke at Wheaton in 1941. Dawson had founded the Navigators, an organization which had started out working with sailors on the West Coast, leading them to Christ, and then guiding them in a program of Scripture memorization through which each convert would use the Word of God in establishing another Christian.

Dawson was an absolute genius at orienting new believers. In 1956 deep sorrow fell on the Team when Dawson was drowned in a boating accident. In 1957 Riggs assumed Dawson's duties at the New York Crusade and has had charge ever since.

Colonel Paul Maddox, who had been an army chaplain in Europe, came as personal assistant to Billy in 1950. He also assisted Billy with the administration at North-western Schools. Paul stayed with us around ten years but stepped down when his wife's health failed. T. W. succeeded him. Billy's personal assistant has to keep up with the whole picture, even to the extent of making sure that Billy rests enough, doesn't overextend himself, and makes his appointments with the doctor.

No one could do justice to the individual and collective talents of the Team members and staff. Jim Mathis directs the Team office in Minneapolis. Several years ago our Team offices were moved to Atlanta, but they are back in Minneapolis now.

You cannot imagine the detailed planning and down-right hard work that are involved in mapping out the Crusades. Every day we thank God for the superlative work of Sterling Huston who is the coordinator for our Crusades in the United States. Dr. Walter Herbert Smyth, who has known Billy since Youth for Christ days, directs our overseas Crusades. Dr. Smyth began with the BGEA in the film distribution office and came into his own as a Crusade director during the Australian and New Zealand Crusades of the late 1950s.

The treasurer of the Billy Graham Evangelistic Association is Joel Aarsvold. He has the dual role of recording secretary and treasurer. The Association handles a tremendous volume of mail which pours in from all over the world, especially during certain seasons and when Billy is on nationwide TV.

Since all of us are limited and life is short, I regret that I have not had more opportunity to fellowship with some of the Team members. Many of them minister in farflung corners of the globe, perhaps coming to the States only once a year. Then their time is compacted with BGEA conferences and preaching.

By now you are aware that, in addition to serving on Billy's Team, I have more than my share of Crusades of my own. Here I'll only skirt the fringes.

In the mid-1960s I formed a new Wilson Team. Years before joining Billy I was conducting numerous revival meetings, even when I was in the pastorate. In the chapter concerning Billie Hanks, Ethel Waters, and other friends, I mentioned several who assisted me in those halcyon days.

The first member I invited aboard for my current Team was Ted Cornell from Wyckoff, New Jersey. Ted is a virtuoso on the piano or organ. He graduated from the prestigious Juilliard School of Music in New York City. At Juilliard, even the students who are barely accepted must be exceptionally gifted. Ted was a fellow student with the well-known concert pianist, Van Cliburn, a native of Shreveport, Louisiana, but often thought of as a Texan.

At first we had something of a communications barrier. Ted simply could not understand my Deep South lingo. He would often turn around and ask, "Pardon me, what did you say?" Deep down inside he must've thought I was a bona fide hick. But it shows you how Christ and his gospel weld different people together. At long last Ted learned to understand my Southernese and I his Yankee talk. To me Ted is as great as any pianist alive or dead.

One day a professor at Juilliard advised him, "Ted, why don't you give up this religious bit and go into the concert stage? You can travel all over giving concerts like Van." (Van, too, is a dedicated Christian.) Ted replied, "Well, sir, you'd have to sit where I sit and see thousands of people coming down those long aisles and taking a stand for Christ before you could really understand my answer to that question." So, Ted has spent these years, not for the encores and plaudits of people, but for the praise of God.

That works in two directions: we praise Him, and He praises us in return. Isn't that amazing? Someday Jesus will say to Ted, and to every Christian, "Well done, thou good and faithful servant; thou hast been faithful over a few things, I will make thee ruler over many things: enter thou into the joy of thy Lord."

Ted is also a composer and arranger and has headed up a choral group in greater New York City. He could spend virtually every night conducting his chorale, but he's chosen to be a part of our evangelistic ministry.

Around 1967 Steve Musto came on with us. Steve has studied under some of the greatest maestros. He has recorded with the Miami Symphony Orchestra, among others. For years he was identified with "The Young People's Church of the Air" and Dr. Percy Crawford, its host and originator. He has appeared numerous times on "The Day of Discovery" with Richard DeHaan from Cypress Gardens, Florida. Steve's wife, Barbara, is also an accomplished soloist, and she and Steve often sing duets together.

Steve is our Cliff Barrows, too, directing the choir and leading the congregational singing, in addition to thrilling our hearts with his solos. He often sings favorites like "The King Is Coming" and "How Great Thou Art." He often, as does Bev Shea, sings with the choir.

Many years ago at Miami International Airport someone asked Billy Graham who he thought was the greatest musical team of all. Without hesitation Billy answered, "Of course, my Team. Next to my own Team it would have to be Steve Musto and Ted Cornell."

Many years ago Grover Maughon, who had been an executive with Sears & Roebuck in Atlanta, came with me at a tremendous cut in salary. His explanation was that he wanted to engage in full-time Christian outreach. He came on voluntarily under the leadership of the Holy Spirit. Grover is my Crusade director and does all the planning and organizational work. In other words, he coordinates all of the Crusades, including preparation, arrangements, organization, and follow-up. Even though he is officially with the BGEA, he spends a considerable amount of time working closely with my Crusades. And sometimes he serves with some of the other associate evangelists. He's my Charlie Riggs, and he doesn't mind my making that comparison.

My Team members are some of the purest, most dedicated personal soul-winners I've ever seen. Ted, Steve, and Grover are sometimes the last folks to leave the meeting place, whether a stadium, colosseum, or church building. They're often there praying and counseling, at times even at midnight or after. They have inspired me. When I finish preaching I'm so weary I have to leave as soon as possible and return to my hotel. I'm drained, exhausted, and usually wringing wet with perspiration, even in the wintertime. I have to change my clothes as soon as possible or come down with the laryngitis or the flu—or both. It's comforting to know you have unstinting help from your associates.

I've preached in my own Crusades around the earth, but 90 percent have been here in the U.S. I've held forth in Lexington, Kentucky; Rome, Georgia; Anchorage, Alaska; as well as in New Zealand, Australia, and all over the world. I hate to omit cities, but there's no way I can begin to list them here.

Ted Cornell will never forget his first Crusade with me back in 1965. It was in Harlan County, Kentucky, and that Crusade would go down in history as my most-publicized and most unusual Crusade. Harlan County at that time (not now) was one of the most violent and crime-infested places in America. People had nicknamed the county "Bloody Harlan." It was a "Phenix City" in its own right. Phenix City had been cleaned up in the late 1950s, but it took the murder of Alabama Attorney General Patterson to awaken the public.

In Harlan County many law enforcement officials had been gunned down. *Life* magazine had given extensive coverage to the crime and violence there.

The Associated Press sent down Sid Moody from headquarters in New York City. There he would give my Crusade special coverage. An associate of Billy Graham was presenting the Prince of Peace to perhaps the most unpeaceful area of the nation.

Our Crusade was also written up in the Army newspaper, *The Stars and Stripes*, both Eastern and Western editions. Coverage was even carried outside the U.S. The AP from the word go thought Harlan County was a weird place to conduct a Crusade, and I admit it was risky.

Back to Ted. You couldn't blame Ted for being nervous and looking over his shoulder. When Ted arrived there he heard about the murders during the heyday of John L. Lewis, founder of the United Mine Workers, who came to the area to organize the coal miners.

It was hard to separate fact from fiction. Those grizzled miners would sit around and talk about a valley or hill where there were "wars." In fact, the local undertaker carried me to the railroad track in the heart of Harlan and pointed out, "Mr. Wilson, I remember picking up thirty-two bodies one morning when the miners got into a battle." Whew!

It took us two or three days to get acquainted with the people around there because many of them didn't "cotton to" outsiders. I mentioned to the crowd one night, "I love home-churned country buttermilk." So the next morning a local dairy farmer pulled up with a pickup truck full of buttermilk in those big cans. "Mr. Wilson," he announced graciously, "we want you and your Team to have plenty of buttermilk while you're here for this meeting."

And overwhelmed, I said, "Brother, that's more butter-milk than I could use in ten months, let alone in ten days. The only person I know who has a large walk-in refriger-ator is the owner of the cafe across the street where we've been taking our meals. Let me go over there and see if he'll let us put this in his 'frig.'" The proprietor agreed to keep the buttermilk for us.

There in Harlan County, our cups ran over with bless-ings—and home-churned buttermilk.

A couple of days after we arrived there, a storekeeper murdered a man at a combination post office-country store not far away. Sid Moody heard I was going out to visit the accused killer and insisted on accompanying me.

On arriving at the store I said, "Well, I heard you had a little excitement here last night." The fellow replied, "Yes sir, some old rascal had been breaking into my store a heap of times during the last month, and I finally got tired of it. So last night I come over here with a double-barreled shotgun loaded with .00 buckshot, and I put a little cot behind the counter. And when that feller busted into my store, I laid him in the floor." And all of that happened in the early days of that Crusade.

Not all of the Crusades are quite that bizarre, but there

is excitement in all of them. I would rather preach than eat, and that's something else!

From time to time I remember all of the Team members, current and past, in my devotions—those from the BGEA and those from my personal Team. One by one I place them before the throne of grace. I call their names and I see their faces and I hear their voices. And I never pray without Billy on my heart.

10
Valleys . . . and Mountaintops

Through the years fellow preachers have commented to our Team, "What a snap. No fuss. No muss. No bother. Everything runs smoothly as silk for the Team. International exposure. Millions of people making decisions in the Crusades. No trouble."

Those who make those comments haven't kept up with the BGEA. Yes, we've had those mountaintop experiences, and they could—and have—filled many volumes by themselves. But we have had our lows, our valleys, and our rough places.

One of our low points in the early ministry was the meeting in Altoona, Pennsylvania. That was shortly before "The Canvas Cathedral" campaign in Los Angeles. In Altoona we found several different ministerial associations at odds with one another. It's disappointing that Christian brethren often have a hard time getting along.

That's also true in many clique-filled local churches: one group against another; factionalism develops; rivalries ensue. The preacher is often on the horns of the dilemma. He sometimes "gets it in the neck," even though the people are often not actually mad with him.

Where there is strife among the groups which invite us, we cannot have a spiritually victorious Crusade. We had come into Altoona from a campaign in the old Baltimore Lyric Theater which had seated only 2,800 people. The meeting there had been sponsored by the Baltimore Youth for Christ.

It was written of Jesus' ministry, "He did not many mighty works there [in Nazareth] because of their unbelief" (Matt. 13:58). No mighty works were done in Altoona. We did have a few hundred responses to the invitation but nothing like we expected.

Another example was during our preparation for the London Crusade in 1954. We were on the *Queen Mary* en route to Britain. Every day we would have long periods of prayer and Bible study as we were bound for the first Crusade that was to usher in worldwide attention for the BGEA.

Our preparaton for the London Crusade had run into a problem. The British home secretary, Fife, had been approached by several members of Parliament who were disturbed over a calendar released by the BGEA in Canada. It stated that British socialism had done more harm than Hitler's bombs had inflicted on England. But this statement had been made by a member of Parliament himself, John Henderson from Scotland, who had been visiting in our Washington, D.C., Crusade when he had addressed the clergy. Even though Henderson made that statement, Billy received credit for it in the calendar.

Billy immediately called Jerry Beaven who was assisting Roy Cattell of the British Evangelical Alliance in setting up the meeting. In the meantime, the newspapers from London were calling on the radio-telephone to the *Queen Mary* out in the middle of the Atlantic. Billy explained to representatives of each newspaper that he was not coming to Britain to dabble in politics, or even to discuss British politics. And he certainly was not going to import Americanism. He was coming to preach the Gospel of Christ.

The captain of the ship had originally alerted him to the public relations flap which was brewing. Terry Ferrer, religion editor of *Newsweek* magazine, also communicated with Billy concerning the matter. Ms. Ferrer was the sister of Mel and José Ferrer, the famous stars of stage, screen, and television. We became concerned, called our prayer group together, and went to prayer. We literally sailed to Britain on our knees!

Dr. Paul Rees, the well-known pastor-Bible teacher, was with us, as was Dr. Wade Freeman from Texas. We prayed around our dinner table in the dining room; then we would pray in Billy's cabin. We prayed as we had never prayed before.

Ms. Ferrer had cautioned us that a member of Parliament had posed the question as to whether we would be allowed to disembark when we reached the Isles. God moves mysteriously. Nothing but a crisis would have focused attention on the London Crusade like this widely reported brouhaha.

A massive wall of protective prayer was built around the Team long before we docked at Southampton. All over the world Christians had read about the threat to God's cause. Multiplied thousands were praying for the London Crusade, and the crisis cemented the British Christians even more closely together.

An appreciative, large crowd welcomed us at Southampton. We spent the night there with an old friend of Billy and Cliff's, Oliver Stott. The following day we headed for London by train. When we arrived at Waterloo Station, thousands had jammed the station. The newspapers headlined it as the largest reception given anyone since Mary Pickford and Douglas Fairbanks arrived over two decades before.

From then on the Harringay Arena was packed virtually every night, in spite of inclement weather during the early days. Through the entire three months the building began to burst at the seams. Some nights we had two services, and Saturdays we often had three services to accommodate the crowds.

A low point was the Syracuse, New York, Crusade of 1955. It followed almost on the heels of London. Billy had to be away a couple of nights, and I tried to fill his shoes. One of Billy's relatives had died, and he was to conduct the funeral in Oklahoma. We also didn't think we were going to meet the financial budget. Toward the end of the Crusade, because offerings were falling short, Billy decided that we would give the special offering (for the worldwide ministry) back to the local committee.

Admittedly, we've been disappointed by a couple of those who joined the organization and then left us, under rather pressing and delicate circumstances.

In the early 1950s—even after God was clearly showing his hand, multiplied thousands were coming to Christ, and the whole evangelical world was being revived— some of our former friends accused us of compromise.

Billy for a time was the president of Northwestern Schools in Minneapolis. He succeeded the late W. B. Riley, who was a leader of the Fundamentalist movement in the early 1900s. Yet, great men like Dr. Bob Jones, Sr., then president of Bob Jones University at Greenville, South Carolina, and Dr. John R. Rice, editor of *The Sword of the Lord*, accused us of compromise. They felt that inviting all who participate in a Crusade to come, no matter what their theological background, was an indication of compromise. What they did not understand was that Billy never compromised his preaching—and never will. If any compromise was done, it was on the part of those who did not believe in his preaching. The compromise was on the other foot.

I speak in love even about those who opposed us. Dr. John R. Rice, now in heaven, was at first one of our staunchest supporters. In 1955 he came to the All-Scotland Crusade. He excitedly testified privately and publicly, "What I'm witnessing in Kelvin Hall [at Glasgow] is of the Spirit of God. I am seeing people smitten with the conviction of the Holy Spirit." He further said, "Nobody, not even Bob Jones, can convince me this is not the work of God."

Yet, within a few months he was attacking Billy's ministry, claiming that Billy was compromising his convictions and the gospel. Rice had accused us of putting the counseling in the hands of a Bible-rejecting ultraliberal, and that simply was not the case.

When we were in Madison Square Garden, I offered, "Dr. Rice, I want you to come over here to see for yourself. I'll send you a round-trip ticket from Chicago to New York." (Dr. Rice's office was then in Wheaton, Illinois.)

He replied, "Grady, I'm convinced that you're compromising." He wouldn't come. Lo and behold, in the next issue of *The Sword of the Lord*, he accused me of offering a "bribe" for him to attend the New York Crusade! Billy has never fought back, and the Team seldom answers unfounded attacks.

Almost two decades later I was about to leave the Charlotte Airport and noticed an elderly gentleman walking around with his hands behind his back. It was Dr. Rice.

"Dr. Rice, this is Grady Wilson."

"Oh yes, Grady," he answered in recognition. "Tell me, please, how are Billy and Ruth Graham?" I answered that they were doing well.

"Oh," he went on. "Thank them for the Christmas card they send me every year." I then slipped my arm around him and said, "Dr. Rice, don't you worry about anything you've written about Billy and the Team. Just remember this—we love you with all of our hearts." I gave him a big hug. His eyes filled with tears and he said, "God bless you, Grady. I appreciate that so much. Be sure to give Billy and Ruth my love."

Not long afterward Billy received a personal letter from Dr. Rice, saying, "Billy, one of these days we need to get together and reminisce about old times." At one time Dr. Rice had devoted quite a bit of energy against our ministry. However, toward the end of his life, he and Billy had several excellent exchanges by telephone and letter. Billy never criticized Dr. Rice and always had tremendous respect and Christian love for him.

Billy and I attended Bob Jones College (now University) when it was located at Cleveland, Tennessee. Billy spent only three months there. I suppose that Dr. Bob Jones, Sr., considered us upstarts, young whippersnappers. Yet, he stood behind our Crusade ministry in the beginning. Dr. Bob himself had been a successful evangelist. He used to write rather lengthy letters to Billy. In the beginning Billy tried to answer him but soon gave up and would merely acknowledge Dr. Jones's long diatribes. Dr. Bob and John R. Rice were close friends and usually saw eye to eye. More than anyone else I think Dr. Bob influenced Dr. John to turn on us. There's no telling how many people were against us because of what they read in Rice's paper. That's in the past. We love Dr. Bob and his family. Likewise for the Rices.

Before the Altoona meeting Billy had attended the World Council of Churches in Amsterdam as an observer representing Youth for Christ. This had become known and Billy was not trying to keep it a secret. One night as Billy walked off of the platform at Altoona, a feisty little preacher confronted him. Like a bantam rooster he was ready to fight. Rolling up his sleeves, he physically threatened to fight Billy.

He fumed, "Mr. Graham, we don't want you in Altoona. I'm ready to fight you and to fight for the faith." Billy, sensing perhaps that the man was influenced by Dr. Carl McIntyre, was ready for the question. The preacher asked heatedly, "What were you doing at the World Council of Churches?" Billy answered, "Well, I was just doing the same thing Dr. Carl McIntyre was doing, sitting in the seats for observers." The little man wilted and dropped his arms, moaning, "Oh, I didn't know Dr. McIntyre was there." With that he dejectedly walked away.

On the other side of the spectrum, we have been flayed by self-admitted liberals who have declared that we were theological morons and that we preached a gospel fifty to a hundred years old. (Hopefully, we preach a gospel two thousand years old!) We have been called obscurantists and other names, some of them understandable, I guess.

Even though I never graduated from Bob Jones, I was crushed when Dr. Bob withdrew his support of our ministry and even asked his students not to pray for the BGEA's work. Likewise, Dr. Rice trenchantly rebuked

Billy for liberalism, both in connection with the London and New York Crusades. Since we were invited by church unions or ministerial associations, and insisted on that kind of support, we recognized that not every individual minister would agree with what Billy preached. But why turn down an opportunity to preach the gospel because we are not able to check out every cooperating preacher's theological pedigree? Billy has always been first and foremost a churchman. He believes in the organized church, never criticizing pastors or the churches. He feels that the best approach is to love them and boost them. Above all, he loves his own denomination, the Southern Baptist Convention. However, he also feels closeness with the Anglican church and, of course, with the Presbyterian church because he was reared a Presbyterian and his wife, Ruth, still belongs to that denomination.

Especially in our early days, many godly, well-intentioned pastors opposed us for various reasons. It was seldom doctrinal. Most of them are now in favor of our work. Some thought our methods were flashy and high-handed. Yet by today's standards they were low-key. Consider the case of the evangelist who drew a crowd by riding a donkey downtown and calling himself "A Jackass for Jesus."

Others felt we were snobbish because they didn't understand the pressures under which Billy was laboring. One denominational president thought Billy had the "big head," because Billy didn't recognize him on a plane. That certainly was not intentional. Later, that marvelous preacher became fast friends with Billy and pulled out all of the stops to promote our ministry.

God has turned around possible low points and worked them out for his glory. Billy has often faced antagonistic groups in public meetings and the circles of academé. In the late 1960s, when the dissent was running wild and when the slogan often was: "Burn, baby, burn," Billy received an invitation to address students of Columbia University. He was invited there by an avowed student atheist whose grandfather was a world-renowned evangelist in the Chicago area. His father is a minister in the Midwest. (The family had been praying for that young man for years.)

He swore and even blasphemed when he came to our hotel room in New York. Dr. Martin Luther King had spoken to the students several months before without incident, but students had already threatened bodily harm to Billy if he appeared on campus that day, or even at the Riverside church. The atmosphere was laden with tension, and the radical organizations were set to frustrate Billy or worse.

Defiant and militant, over a thousand dissidents showed up at the Riverside church. Billy agreed to have lunch with representatives of all those groups. He met with them and tried, as best he could, to answer their questions, many of them loaded. Billy spoke on the resurrection of Jesus Christ.

Preaching on Christ's victory over the grave and life after death, Billy quoted from Winston Churchill, Konrad Adenauer, and other famous world leaders who firmly believed that Christ rose from the dead and that he is alive forevermore. He declared that we have more evidence for the resurrection than for any other single fact in human history. Throughout the message you could've heard a pin drop.

While being escorted from the church, we were surrounded by several New York policemen and a number of friendly students. We felt a strange, awed reverence from many of those young radicals, many of whom were atheists or agnostics. The student leader who had invited us followed us to the police car which awaited us. As Billy and I stepped into the car, he gave us a warm handshake, tears filled his eyes, and he gave us his blessing! "God bless you and thanks for coming." *God bless you* from an avowed atheist! He almost sobbed out, "Billy, the next time you and Grady put up a prayer, you just remember this old boy," and he pointed to his heart.

There have been thousands of high moments I could report. For example, there was the day we left Seoul, Korea, after the closing of the Crusade in 1973. The largest audience in the history of evangelism—1,120,000—was present for the final service in Yoido Plaza. I shall never forget Brother Han, pastor of the largest Presbyterian church in Seoul, pronouncing the benediction. After he had finished, he asked the crowd to wave their handkerchiefs in good-bye to Billy, but most of all in tribute to the Christ whom Billy preaches. As we were heading by helicopter to the airfield at Kimpo, the multitude was still shouting and waving their handkerchiefs.

I have mentioned Billy's tears on the Korean battlefield many years before. He's not an habitual weeper, but when we were airborne, moisture filled his eyes. He said, "I'll never forget this moment as long as I live. God has been here, and he has vindicated his name and his Gospel here in South Korea." Some have estimated that over 100,000 people responded to his invitation at the close of that mammoth service.

October 6, 1974. Billy preached to the largest crowd ever to gather at Maracana Stadium in Rio de Janeiro, Brazil—256,000 were counted as they came through the turnstiles, with thousands outside who could not enter. It was the last day of the Crusade which had already averaged over 100,000 a night until then. *The Guinness Book of World Records* used to state that the biggest crowd ever assembled to hear a single performer was in that stadium for a concert by Frank Sinatra. Anyhow, the largest crowd in the history of that stadium was for that final service. Of course, the largest crowd to hear a single performance or speaker was at the Yoido Plaza service I just mentioned. I intend to write *The Guinness Book of World Records* and have them set it straight.

When Billy preached to that massive crowd at Maracana Stadium, it was estimated that 10 percent of the audience responded to the invitation. There was no way for people to come forward because those on the platform sat in the middle of the soccer field, and the platform was sur-rounded by a moat normally filled with water eight to ten feet deep. I commented to Billy, "You've got a built-in baptistry here." When we arrived Sunday afternoon the moat had been drained for standing room space. We asked why the field was arranged like that, and the officials explained that sometimes the soccer crowds would be so violent, screaming "kill the umpire," that the game officials had to be protected.

Since our early days I have always felt pleased with how Billy has handled himself at press conferences. Reporters want to sell newspapers. It's a fact that sensationalism sells, and many scribes have tried to prime Billy for that kind of material. I think Billy is at his best fielding questions from commentators or reporters. It seems that God gives him wisdom for the occasion—and the right answers.

In the early days of my ministry, some of my young ministerial friends who had gone into evangelism asked me why I was becoming associated with Billy Graham. They sort of sneered. "Grady, how does it feel to be a 'caddy' for Billy?" I brushed that aside. Years later they apologized and exclaimed, "Going with Billy was in the plan of God." And that's absolutely correct!

The Team members and I have walked on the mountain peaks with Billy. And we've been in some of the valleys with him. "I have planted, Apollos watered; but God gave the increase" (1 Cor. 3:6). Every Team member has had his own end of the stick to carry.

> To God be the glory, great things he hath done;
> So loved he the world that he gave us his Son.
> . . . .
> Praise the Lord, praise the Lord,
> Let the earth hear his voice!
> Praise the Lord, praise the Lord,
> Let the people rejoice!
> O come to the Father, thro' Jesus the Son,
> And give him the glory, great things he hath done.
>
> —Fanny J. Crosby

11
"Dolly Pet"

Many unhappily married people have protested, "Hey, you're kidding me. You couldn't have a happy marriage. All these years of the Crusades, being on the road—sometimes in exotic places. C'mon. You and Wilma are putting on a front." You've heard that old saw, "Misery loves company," but Wilma and I don't belong as company to the miserably married.

In my senior year at Wheaton, I kept seeing this lady with long, brownish hair and blue eyes—to me, close to perfection. She had a creamy complexion, too. So, I inquired around and found out her name was Wilma Hardie. I also learned that she was engaged to a Canadian fellow she had gone with almost four years. Back then it simply wasn't polite to break up an engagement. My, times have changed. Today one's engagement would merely serve as a challenge.

I mentioned to some of my classmates, "Fellows, I'd love to date that Wilma Hardie." They cautioned, "She's already engaged. Forget it." I was persistent: "But she's not wearing a ring."

My dreams began to materialize on the "Senior Sneak,"

sort of a senior outing for Wheaton's graduating class. I remarked to a friend, "That Wilma Hardie . . . if she's engaged, who's she engaged to?" I happened to be talking to a fellow whose sister was a close friend of Wilma's. "Well, do you know anything about her?" I queried. "Uh huh, I know that she and her boyfriend just broke up." My heart jumped up into my throat; I wanted to sprout wings and fly, but I tried to act calm and cool. "Oh yeah," I answered, deep inside about to go crazy with excitement.

I asked, "Well, do you think it would be wrong if I asked her for a date?" So, the guy helped me bolster my courage. He egged me on with a dare: "Yeah, Grady, go ahead. Ask her."

With a gigantic lump in my throat and my palms sweating, I found her in the cafeteria. I sidled over to her table, trying to act nonchalant. But I nervously asked, "Look, would you like to take a canoe ride this afternoon?" She responded, "Yes, oh, I'd love to." I couldn't believe it. *A woman who is almost married,* I thought, *is going out with me this afternoon!*

Every man and his brother were trying to date Wilma Hardie. Maybe it was the appeal of "forbidden fruit" because she had the reputation of going steady and being engaged. The Wheaton men probably figured their efforts were futile because of her long-standing courtship, but her Canadian steady had graduated from Wheaton the year before and gone to another school as a teacher.

I can't say I was nervous on that first date with Wilma. I would call it "romantically excited." We engaged in all of the small talk—the college, our favorite subjects, our likes and dislikes, and our hopes for the future—but we also had in-depth spiritual conversation. I also found out Wilma's mother had nicknamed her "Dolly Pet." I called her that for four or five years thereafter. Of course, we didn't even hold hands on that first date.

As we were pulling in the canoe, staring at Wilma from a log was a little green water snake. You'd have thought it was a boa constrictor the way she reacted. I reached down, picked up that snake, and threw it into the bushes. You'd also have thought I was Sir Lancelot. But when Wilma saw the snake, she automatically threw her arms around my neck and embraced me for dear life. I was thankful for that snake! Anyhow, I'd testify that snake was there in the divine purpose of God. No joke.

That also delayed our arrival in the dining room for supper. We were bashful when we walked in. We could hear the hubbub undercurrent and the sighs, the ooohhs, and the ahhs. We felt every senior there was thinking, *Hey, there's something strange going on.*

We could hear the buzzing campaign. You couldn't mistake it. For all those years she had gone with that Canadian guy. All of a sudden, here was Grady Wilson with Wilma Hardie. And I rushed her right then and there, asking her if she would devote the rest of her free time to me. She agreed. Praise the Lord.

Coming back on the Greyhound from Muskegon, Michigan, we nearly had a bad accident. The bus driver had to swerve on the highway to miss an oncoming car, and the bus almost turned over. Fortunately, Wilma fell into my arms once again. Out loud I moaned, "Oh, Lord, protect us." As she patted me on the back, and she was close to me, she whispered, "You see, the Lord answered your prayer." She felt that my little cry for help had kept the bus from turning over, when I realize that many others on that bus were also praying. From there it was the beginning of a long love story.

Wilma was quieter than I, of course. In fact, most folks are. Wilma and I complemented each other. That's the way a relationship should be. She was more refined and cultured than I; I was still a boy in many respects. Though I was preaching the gospel, I was still immature and loved to play jokes on others, even though I didn't try many on Wilma. I was afraid of losing her if I acted foolishly.

I still think she's the prettiest woman in the world, and every husband ought to feel like that about his wife. I've got eyes. I've met hundreds of ladies in many countries. I've looked academically at hundreds of women, but none of them compare with Wilma. Husbands, if you don't have those emotions about your wives, then you ought to ask the Lord's forgiveness.

Wilma and I weren't much into music. Even though it was "The Swing Era," we weren't allowed to dance. A dedicated Christian, according to the evangelical life-style, didn't dance, didn't drink, didn't smoke, and didn't attend "picture shows." Those were taboos at Wheaton.

I was always fond of the very unromantic "On Top of Old Smokie" and "Carolina Moon." Naturally, I also liked "Carolina in the Morning." Wilma also enjoyed songs about the moon—more romantic ones like "Moon Over Miami" and "Shine On, Harvest Moon." The old songs. Of course, in the early 1940s we liked Guy Lombardo and his Royal Canadians, along with his singing brothers, Carmen and Leibert.

Billy had already met and was going with Ruth Bell, the attractive daughter of Dr. and Mrs. L. Nelson Bell, former missionaries to China. They had to return home because of World War II (which actually broke out in China around 1937).

Even though we had rules and regulations at Wheaton, I felt like an uncaged bird when I had arrived there—after the extremely stringent rules of Bob Jones College. The regulations at Wheaton were somewhat more rigid than a secular school but nothing compared to the rules at BJC.

Jimmie Johnson was Billy's suitemate during that time, and they lived down the street from us on campus. Jimmie had a car, a brand-new Oldsmobile 98, but we didn't. Jimmie already had quite a reputation as a preacher-evangelist. We were glad to be Jimmie's friends. Imagine that kind of friendship. He even gave me a set of keys to his car! And Jimmie Johnson is the only man I know of who had two B.A. degrees—one from Bob Jones and one from Wheaton.

Wilma graduated in the class of 1942. She had gone on to business college first and then planned to enter nursing school in Chicago. After kind of a whirlwind romance, Wilma and I were married on June 5, 1943, after I graduated in the class of 1943. The service was conducted at Wilma's church, the Cicero Bible Church in Cicero, Illinois, one of the largest churches at that time.

Dr. William McCarrell, the pastor and also head of the evangelism department of Moody Bible Institute, performed the ceremony. Jimmie Johnson was my best man. There was plenty of confusion since Jimmie hadn't shown up for the rehearsal the night before. The men of the wedding party were Wheaton students who graduated the same year with Billy. Besides that, everybody seemed to be late arriving. That was scary, and I was beside myself. Would somebody think I was standing up Wilma? But Wilma hadn't even arrived; Dr. McCarrell was late; we all were late.

Dr. McCarrell had told me that my cue to kiss the bride would be: "Let us pray." But he didn't tell me he was going to pray three times during the ceremony! In the early part of the ceremony he had an invocation, sort of. He said,

"Let us all pray." When he did, I leaned over and kissed Wilma prematurely.

Jimmie, my best man, stage whispered: "Not now, you moron." I had to lift her veil to kiss her, and I did kiss her. Then when Dr. McCarrell spoke those words, "with all my worldly goods, I thee endow," Jimmie whispered again, "There goes your shotgun and your rod and reel." Some of the wedding party heard that and became tickled.

Finally, Dr. McCarrell came to the genuine kissing place. "Let's bow our heads." Precious few bowed their heads. They wanted to watch. So, I kissed Wilma again. I had already kissed her at least three times—again and again and again. And then Dr. McCarrell again announced, "Let's pray." Can you imagine that? Everybody in that congregation thought we had a kissing disease. But we were married fair and square.

Then Dr. Mc intoned, "I now pronounce you man and wife." This time, after our kissing bout, I hesitated. Dr. Mc nodded at us, instructing, "You may now kiss the bride." I lost track of the kisses.

Ruth and Billy were married around nine weeks later, Friday, August 13, 1943, in the Gaither Chapel at Montreat Presbyterian Assembly.

The Reverend John Minder, who was one of Billy's "fathers in the ministry," helped perform the ceremony, with Dr. Kerr Taylor, a Presbyterian missionary who had been in the Bell's home when Ruth was born in China. Incidentally, Dr. Randy Taylor, pastor of the Myers Park Presbyterian Church in Charlotte, is Kerr Taylor's son.

Parenthetically, though Billy had become a Baptist by then, Ruth has remained a Presbyterian. And, contrary to much thinking, it hasn't seemed to cause them many problems. For years now Billy has belonged to the First Baptist Church of Dallas, pastored by Dr. W. A. Criswell.

The night before Ruth and Billy tied the knot the Bells had a huge Chinese meal complete with garlic, a favorite Chinese seasoning. Many missionaries from China were visiting at Montreat at the same time, and they came to the Bell home for the festivities. When I drove up into the yard of the Bell home, I held my nose and gasped out, "Somebody around here has been eating garlic." Maybe it was to keep the vampires away? I still kid the Grahams about that garlic meal for the missionaries.

I guess my sense of humor was initially tested with Wilma on our Senior Sneak meeting, because I told all kinds of jokes—but never dirty or racist ones. Wilma was quiet and a rather good athlete, for she had participated in women's sports at Wheaton. She had a medal in rifle marksmanship, so I knew to stay in line. I didn't want trouble with Annie Oakley! She could hit the bull's-eye every time, and she had a bronze medal given to her by the athletic department.

On our honeymoon we spent about two weeks in Florida. We got blistered, and I remember that corny joke about: "They thought marriage was bliss, but they got blistered." And then we went back to assume my ministry in South Carolina, at the Friendship Baptist Church in Charleston and the Immanuel Baptist Church in Summerville.

Her parents, of Scottish descent, were Mr. and Mrs. Richard Russell Hardie. Her father, the foreman for a cutting oil factory in Chicago, did most of the talking around home. He was always telling dry jokes from Aberdeen, Scotland.

To live with me, Wilma's had to develop a sense of

humor. I guess opposites attract, and in our case maybe that's true. Wilma has always had a quiet grace, an inward beauty that shines through—a radiance. My radiance came from kidding and teasing, and sometimes I think my face is permanently red because I often blushed as a young adult—and still do.

I'm a hunter and fisherman. I used to golf considerably, but I'm not mechanically inclined. Wilma certainly didn't marry a handyman. I did take a small course in that stuff in high school.

Shortly after we married, I built a little bookshelf. Proud of myself, I put it in one of the closets in our first parsonage. It was loaded down with my theology books, and it must have been *heavy* theology. One day a member of the church came by. Wilma politely helped the lady with her raincoat, opened the closet door to hang it up, and a ton of books fell off my rickety shelves. Without batting an eyelash Wilma remarked, "Grady's not called to be a carpenter."

And there were times, because money was scarce, I'd decide on do-it-yourself auto repair. The car would end up in worse shape after I had finished with it. Then I'd have to pay twice as much to have it straightened out, and Wilma would comment, "Grady's not called to be a mechanic."

Humor and joy fill our lives from morning until evening.

One of my churches was really considered full time. Wilma had been a Methodist, but she decided to become a Baptist on my behalf. She was baptized by Jimmy Morgan at the North Fort Worth Baptist Church. She first belonged to the Methodist Church in Chicago, but because of doctrinal differences her family had gone over to the Cicero Bible Church.

Over the years she has been a faithful minister's wife. I couldn't have asked for more, and I have always included her in our plans, even asking her permission and advice about moves, the Crusades, my travel, and work load. She has truly shared my burdens, the concerns of my heart and ministry, and she has always been concerned about my health.

During my massive heart attacks she stood by me without wavering. With each beat of my damaged heart I thanked the Lord for sending that little green snake and the bus wreck that almost happened. So many people today are breaking up early, and years later they'll be sorry they didn't stay together and hang on through thick and thin. During my last heart attack I don't think she got a wink of sleep for five-and-a-half days. She sat up in a chair right by my bed; she may have dozed intermittently, but she was awake most of the time watching me. The doctor had told her privately that I had very little chance of living. Her prayers and determination did more than anything else to pull me through.

Now, I'd be fibbing if I claimed we never even had adjustments to make, any arguments to patch up when they were over, any difficulties, any differences of opinion. Sam Jones, the crusty Methodist evangelist around the turn of the century, once heard a testimony from an elderly gent in a meeting. The old man testified, "Brethren, my wife and I have been married fifty-five years, and we've never disagreed on anything—never had an argument." Jones came to the platform when the old man sat down and said in his hard-boiled manner: "Thank you, liar!" I couldn't get by with that, but he did. Ruth Graham once observed that if two married people agree totally on everything, then one of them is not necessary. That's true.

My wife is Scottish in background, and I am Scotch-Irish. Most of our disagreements have been over trifles. We've agreed on the basics—the doctrines of Christianity, the handling of finances, the rearing of our two daughters, the fact that God has called us to his ministry. Yes, *us*.

I loved her hairstyle when we met, courted, and then married. It was long and often done up in a bun behind her head. It may have looked matronly, but I adored it. When she'd have her hair cut in the summertime, I'd disagree with that.

I think my greatest disappointment, though, was a trick she played on me. She had gone to the beauty shop one day, and she came in wearing a blond wig. I was crestfallen, but I didn't make a comment. She looked unusual, and I wasn't accustomed to that blond hair. Finally, she couldn't stand it anymore. She said, "What do you think of my hairdo?" I said, "I haven't seen your hairdo, but the wig you have on is unique." We both laughed about it. She thought I would rave and rant.

She's been a blessed wife and an adoring mother to the girls. It's not easy being married to a man who's gone more than half of the time—at least was gone that much from the time the Team was formed until my heart attacks struck me. I'm still gone a considerable amount of the time. I am involved in most of the Crusades in one way or another. Of course, now that the girls are grown, Wilma can travel with me, and that's a blessing. It takes patience for a woman to put up with a traveling man. When I was gone, of course, I ran up a huge phone bill.

It's comforting to know you have a faithful, loving, trusting wife at home. Wilma has stuck with me. This day and time many homes are breaking up because wives are tired of their husbands being gone so much of the time, even if it's for necessary business. She has kept me going. I intend to live my remaining years side by side with Wilma.

12
Wilma, Nancy, and Connie

Since 1944 I have been outnumbered at home. Our oldest daughter, Nancy Carol, joined Wilma and me that year. Constance Jane (Connie) arrived in 1952.

We've nearly always used double names with our girls. Sometimes we called Connie "Con" or "Stance," and Nancy Carol has often been "Nance."

Connie Jane at this writing is single and lives with Wilma and me in Charlotte, where she works as my secretary. She's my second right arm, and she keeps me straight. I'd never meet an appointment if it weren't for her.

Nancy Carol and her husband, Gerald Gardner, are missionaries with the Wycliffe Bible Translators, now stationed in Waxhaw, North Carolina. Both girls attended Hampden-DuBose Academy, founded by Dr. Pierre Du-Bose, a South Carolinian by birth.

"Independent" describes Nancy Carol to a T. Maybe that's why she's a successful missionary. As a child she could be awfully strong-willed, but that's true with many kids. That's often part of growing up. I once wondered if the time would arrive when Nance would listen to anything Wilma and I had to say. She was self-reliant and wanted to make all of her decisions on her own, but all those qualities, used properly, can help qualify a person for the hard knocks of life.

Of course, she would make many decisions without consulting us. We begged and pleaded for her to attend Wheaton College. Now I can see it wasn't right for us to insist that she go to Wheaton. Then we thought her refusal was sheer insubordination.

"You and Mother both graduated from that school, and I don't want to go there," she would remind us. She recalled that all during her academy days she had been known as "Grady Wilson's daughter. You know, he's Billy Graham's associate evangelist." I can recognize now that such would make her feel like a mere extension, having no identity outside her father.

Since she chose her own identity and course in life, she enrolled in Moody Bible Institute in Chicago. Nancy Carol had been a devoted student in the academy and had dedicated herself to becoming a missionary.

While at home one summer Nance wrestled with her educational future. She loved Moody but somehow felt God was leading her to enter BIOLA (the Bible Institute of Los Angeles), also an excellent school for Christian training. She exulted, "Daddy, I want to study nursing and prepare myself for missionary medicine."

BIOLA was the only school we knew of at that time which had a program of study for Christian nurses going to the mission field. I had known Dr. Louis Talbot, then the president of BIOLA, for many years. (Not long ago I met. Dr. J. Richard Chase who was president of BIOLA for sixteen years and is now president of Wheaton College.) We consented. What else could we do, anyhow? I felt that, no matter how busy he was, Dr. Talbot would give her the necessary backing and encouragement. Some of our dearest friends, many of whom we first met in 1949, were there.

Bless her. She did her "thing," attended BIOLA, did her nurse's training at Hollywood Presbyterian Hospital, and finished up in the school of missionary medicine at La Mirada, California. There she was influenced by many marvelous Christian young women.

During that period she made many mission trips into Mexico. Under the supervision of a top dental surgeon she was allowed to pull teeth on various occasions. I surely wouldn't let her practice on me, though! In Mexico she worked in the barrios with disadvantaged Mexicans.

And all the while God was moving to find her a missionary mate. She met Gerald Gardner, who was an aeronautical engineer and pilot, working in engineering at the giant Pac-Aero Company at LA. He first graduated from LeTourneau Tech in Longview, Texas, founded by R. G. LeTourneau, who had profoundly helped my life as a young ministerial student. Gerald had completed his studies at the Pittsburg School of Aeronautical Engineering before working with Pac-Aero. His flight training was completed at LeTourneau, so he was a combination engineer-pilot.

Long before they met Nancy Carol and Gerald had dedicated themselves to missions. There is no doubt God led them together. Maybe you're reading this and saying, "I'm dedicated to serving Christ, but I can't find anybody to go with me." Don't give up. God may well be working out his will for your mate. I don't believe Nancy Carol and

Gerald came together by accident. My finding Wilma was no quirk of fate, either. It was God's doing.

When Gerald felt the call he was employed with Aspen Airways flying the triangle over the Rockies—Colorado Springs to Aspen and back to Denver. He was flying world-famous people into Aspen—senators, congressmen, and entertainers.

Michael, their oldest son, was born when they were living in Denver. While Nance was praying for a daughter, I was praying for another grandson. When their twin boys, John and Paul, were born Nance said over the phone, "Daddy, why did you pray so hard for a grandson? Now you have two more!" Perhaps that shows us the fallacy of praying for boys or girls—simply pray that they'll be healthy and then follow the Lord. After having three straight sons, it was unlikely that girls would follow, but Lorianne and Karyn Christine did.

When the Gardners found that Wycliffe would commission them, Gerald announced his resignation. His manager immediately promoted him, raised his salary, and made him a full-fledged captain, trying to keep him at Aspen. Gerald could do it all—fly and even take an entire plane apart and put it back together.

Gerald answered his boss, "No thank you, sir. I appreciate all of this and the confidence you've shown in me, but we have to do what God has called us to do. Nance and I have been called to the mission field, and we are bound and determined to go."

After their language school, Wycliffe sent the Gardners to Loma Linda, Colombia, which is on a vast prairie adjacent to the Andes Mountains. There they used their skills of flying, medicine, and linguistics to make the gospel available in another tongue.

The Wycliffe Bible Translators are dedicated to translating the Word of God into every language and dialect on the globe. The book, *Two Thousand Tongues to Go*, presents the story of the organization, founded by Cameron Townsend, affectionately known as "Uncle Cam." *Uncle Cam* is another book which gives insight into the work of WBT. The Translators are constantly aware that they still have countless tongues to go before the Bible is made available to every language group.

Thousands of Christians became interested in Wycliffe because of the translators who were killed by Auca Indians in Ecuador in 1953.[1] Two relatives of those translators, Rachel Saint and Elisabeth Elliot, have through their writings made the world aware of the sacrifice involved in carrying God's Word to remote peoples.

Let me digress for a moment. Uncle Cam, when he was over eighty, had just been released from the hospital after surgery. Do you think he was content to rest? No, he got special permission from the Russian government to enter the wastelands of Russia to help a tribe without a written language. In the name of culture and education he did it. You know what was in his heart—to give God's Word to another tribe! I wonder how many people would do that for the cause of atheism.

I well recall my visit with Nancy and Gerald at Loma Linda. When I arrived there was a raging brush fire coming toward the missionary compound where two hundred missionaries and their families lived. I pitched in and helped fight the fire to keep it from burning the entire compound to the ground. The mission director's home was destroyed by fire.

That night we had an informal service in the little chapel. All of us were weeping over the loss of that home. Those servants of God live solely by faith, yet they took up $6,000 in that one service for the mission director. Talk about sacrificial giving, that gesture of love made me feel so inadequate and spiritually poor.

There is deep faith and brotherhood among those missionaries because they share the same Christ, the same hardships, the same total dedication—and that same fellowship should exist among all Christians, "full-time" servants or not.

Most missionaries must pass through a rigorous training program which includes survival training—also how to "make do" with almost nothing. The Gardners, for instance, had to spend the night in the jungles several miles from their compound. They had to eat whatever they found, sleep in sleeping bags, and be exposed to snakes and wild animals. That may sound cruel and harsh, but it's essential. There's no telling what could happen to a family while flying over primitive stretches of jungle, grassland, and areas infested with hostile humans or animals.

Only two weeks after my visit with them I was in New Zealand for a Crusade, and I was to address the Parliament. At two o'clock in the morning Wilma called over oceanic phone. Broken up, she told me that little Paul had died at Loma Linda. I broke down and cried to the Lord, "Lord, why? Paul was the healthiest of the twins. Why did he contract pneumonia and die?" Even though I knew Paul was "safe in the arms of Jesus," I took it hard.

At the Parliament the presiding officer graciously introduced me, explaining I was in a period of grief and strain. One member of Parliament, an outspoken atheist who had vowed to give me a hard time, melted and was most sympathetic, even though she had previously said, "I don't believe in this American evangelism and what you fellows are trying to do."

She came to me after the message and gently comforted me, "God bless you, sir. We're thinking about you, knowing what you've gone through." Even through tragedy God had prepared the hearts of some skeptical people.

Nancy Carol, we understand now, needed an independent disposition for her to make it as a missionary. It's not a place for quitters, limp dishrags, and Caspar Milquetoasts. There is dreadful danger, and that is true of many mission fields today. It's no joke that radicals try to brainwash people into thinking that missionaries are "American agents" or "spies."

I call her my "brave, little missionary." But she was almost sidelined several years before she met Gerald. She "fell in love" (that's what she thought at the time) with a young man who was the son of an evangelistic worker. The young man manifested intense emotional pressures, coming up to me in a Crusade and insisting, "I want Nancy Carol's hand in marriage." I replied, "Well, I think you ought to get to know her a little better." (He had known her for the full time of two weeks!)

He became adamant. "Listen to me, preacher, God deals with me in special ways. God has told me right out of the skies that she is to become my wife."

"Well," I answered, "He hasn't told me that yet." I continued, "Young man, would you give me time to pray about it?" He came back with, "There's nothing to pray about."

To make a long story short, I tried to talk with Nancy

Carol. "Daddy," she protested, "I don't care what you say. I love him and I want to marry him, and that's the way it is!"

"Honey, I honestly don't think this is the man for you. Your mother and I feel very strongly that you ought to wait a while. Finish your education at BIOLA." Maybe I shouldn't have done it, but I asked her to promise not to correspond with the fellow when she returned to school. At first she rebelled. I can understand that now. Mother and Daddy were trying to control her life once again. Couldn't they leave her alone? Couldn't she make her own decision, especially about something as personal and intimate as love?

The very night the young man proposed to her, I had prayer with her, putting my arms around her and cradling her. "Darling," I whispered, "You must remember that God has given you Christian parents to counsel with you and advise you. We're not always wrong. I love you so very much." And I kissed her, but she pouted and sulked.

Back in Charlotte one morning I found the boy's photo at my breakfast plate, staring at me. I knew she was having trouble over the boy. I said, "Honey, I'm going to ask you to lay this aside briefly. We'll pay your way through school, but we'd appreciate your listening to us a little bit. Please give this a period of rest. You've known this fellow only a few weeks. Pray about it. Maybe God has somebody else picked out for you. You go through this semester and promise me that you won't write him or contact him. OK?"

Crushed, she said, "Daddy, I'll go back to BIOLA, and I'll give you my promise." She returned to school.

I have related this incident many times through the years. I can see the raised eyebrows, and many are probably thinking, *He's awfully unfair and hard on his daughter*. I wouldn't recommend that all parents step in like we did. I doubt if many counselors would have agreed with my paternalistic approach, but subsequent events have proved the wisdom of my advice.

The very day that headstrong young man arrived at the Crusade and confronted me, he met another woman he married three months later. We heard that he divorced her only three months after they were wed. He wrecked that young woman's life and badly hurt her parents. Wherever that young man is, though, I pray for him.

Nancy Carol has thanked me no less than a thousand times since then that I cared enough to bare my heartfelt feelings to her. Always with radiance she has shared these words, "Daddy, I know now that God didn't want me to marry that man. Gerald Gardner is the one God chose for me, but if I'd gone ahead and been impulsive, there's no telling where I'd be now." Where she is, is in the center of God's will with the man of her heart.

Variety is the spice of life, and thank God we're all different. Constance (Connie) Jane has an entirely different makeup from Nancy Carol. When she was young we seldom had to reprimand her. All I had to do was look at her, and she would automatically burst into tears. She'd come running to me and apologize tearfully, "Daddy, Daddy, I'm so sorry. I did wrong. I beg your forgiveness. I want to do right. I want to be a Christian girl."

When Uncle Billy (that's what she calls him) was preaching at the Cow Palace in San Francisco, she responded to the invitation. Nancy Carol also went forward under his preaching several years before. So both of our daughters were converted and made their professions of faith when Billy preached.

Even though Connie was a sweet girl, we could see the difference in her life from that moment onward. Every-time she and Nance see us they say, "Momma, Daddy, we love you." They are lamps in our lives.

Connie, until she became my secretary, had done other secretarial work for a couple of years. She's a graduate of the Baptist College in Charleston, South Carolina. Since Connie lives at home with us, she combines her quarters with her office. As unorganized and serendipitous as I am, I'd never make it without her. She has also been sort of a nurse and doctor's aide to me. She has memorized my doctor's instructions and has tried to see that I take my medication on time. She reprimands me sternly when I fail to follow the doctor's orders.

She gives me plenty of pep talks and lectures. I have to keep my weight down. I'm an inveterate eater. I'd balloon out once again if I didn't have Connie and Wilma after me. Before my heart attacks—I'm almost ashamed to admit it—I'd often have a small refrigerator installed in my hotel room, so I could snack all hours of the day and night. And I like everything that's fattening.

This may date the book—'cause she could be married soon—but now she's single. I've often asked, "Honey, does your heart still belong to Daddy?" She'll answer flirtatiously, "Who else?"

When she's around I take a backseat. She has a strange sense of humor, and people have often suggested, "She's a chip off the old block." The fact is, most of the time she jokes more than I do (if that's possible). With that dry sense of humor she's always telling funny jokes and stories.

One time I was in a city-wide meeting at Rome, Georgia, when she was a student at the academy. I called and assured her, "Darling, I don't know whether your mother or I will meet you at the Atlanta Airport, but you can be sure one of us will be right there to meet you." Very dryly she answered, "Daddy, if I don't know which one of you will be there to meet me, how will I know who to look for?" That's Con.

One of our most heartwarming remembrances from her young life happened shortly after she had made her profession of faith. It was Mother's Day, and Con had slept a little late that morning. Wilma said, "Dear, it looks like you'd obey your mother this day of all days. This is the one day in the year that you really ought to do everything you can to please Mother." Wilma sort of chided and rebuked Connie.

What Wilma didn't know is that Connie had been planning a special tribute for mother. Connie had filled her piggy bank with pennies, nickels, and dimes. She had saved $9.99 over the months. On her own the day before, she had called a florist. She asked the florist, "Sir, how many roses can I buy for that much money?"

It touched the heart of that florist; he could tell it was a little girl. "Well, darling," he answered, "I'll just give you two dozen long-stem American Beauty roses for your mother on Mother's Day."

When Wilma and the girls came home from church (I was on the road), the florist showed up with the roses. Wilma was flabbergasted. She read the card on the box: "With all my love to Mother. Connie Jane." Wilma broke down and wept. She threw her arms around Connie Jane and begged, "Please forgive me, dear, that I said even one unkind word to you today."

Nancy Carol, though of a different disposition, knew how to pluck her parents' heartstrings as well. When I returned to Charlotte from the LA meeting of 1949, I would put Nancy Carol on the kitchen table and say to her, "Now, darling, jump into Daddy's arms." Without a moment's hesitation she would leap into my arms because she had implicit faith and trust in me. I've used that illustration hundreds of times around the world. Maybe you thought that was original with your preacher. I've related that simple illustration to mankind's condition, the fact that we must put that same kind of childlike faith in the Lord God Almighty. Oftentimes we ministers tell our children to act like grownups, but Jesus told grownups to become as little children or they wouldn't enter the kingdom. Wasn't that a switch?

And Wilma and I have never felt like overwhelming Con and Nance. I've preached many a sermon dealing with values and discipline in the home, and I've quoted the Scripture repeatedly: "He that spareth the rod hateth his son" (Prov. 13:24). That applies to daughters, too. But the best discipline you can give a child is the right example. I didn't have to spank the girls too often. I didn't like to, either.

We have had more than our share of blush-causing incidents. When I was pastor in Charleston, one morning Nancy Carol had climbed up on the mimeograph machine which was in my office at home. I had to do the bulletins. Does that sound familiar to some of you pastors? Wilma had spent about an hour getting that child ready for Sunday School. Since both Wilma and I taught a Sunday School class, we were in a hurry as usual.

Nancy Carol crawled on that machine and rolled on the roller from her nose to her toes. What was once a crisp, white pinafore was covered with gooey ink. Ink was in her mouth, in her nose, and on her chin; she looked like an escapee from an old-time minstrel show.

Wilma flew into a panic, perspiring and fuming. She finally redressed Nancy Carol and the family rushed to church. Later, one of the ladies called me out of the class. She whispered, "Pastor, may I speak to you for a moment? Pastor, I hate to tell you this. I'm so embarrassed."

Nervously I asked, "What is it, ma'am?" She blurted out, "Er—er—Nancy Carol doesn't have any panties on!" I said, with face red as a beet, "Oh, my soul!" I got somebody to lead the discussion and sped home to put panties on Nance.

That's one for Nance. Now for Con. When Connie was no more than two-and-a-half years old Wilma had taken her to a downtown Charlotte department store. When they entered the plumbing department, Con disappeared. Wilma, like most mothers, was scared to death. She called and searched. No Connie Jane.

In the area of the bathroom displays—complete with bath tub, commode, lavatory, mirror, medicine chest— Wilma saw a laughing crowd gathering. The crowd was laughing like hyenas; people were nudging one another. Then a light bulb flickered in Wilma's head. *Oh, no*, she groaned to herself. She tiptoed and looked over the people's shoulders. There Connie Jean sat—you know where—answering nature's call, and proud as a peacock that she had an appreciative audience for the first time in her life. She thought to herself, *All of these friendly people have come to see me.*

Her Mommy hid behind a pole until the crowd was dispersed. Then she grabbed up the little exhibitionist, took the escalator, and exited the store posthaste.

Our family probably isn't that different from any other Christian unit. We have some peculiarities, of course, because every person is different. Billy's family, for instance, has had oysters for Christmas-morning breakfast for years. That's a tradition Ruth brought over with her missionary parents.

Even though I have often been separated from my wife and daughters we have had considerable togetherness. My friends realize I'm not a superpious soul given to "prissy piosity," but I am extremely tender when it comes to my family's life for Christ. For years our family has had a dedicated family altar. We are committed to family worship. I feel that in a family prayer circle there is an atmosphere conducive to love and spiritual growth. We have hammered out many problems at our family altar.

We've always enjoyed water sports together—boating, water-skiing, swimming. I have taught Wilma, Nance, and Con to water-ski and to fish. I love Charlotte, but I spend about a tenth of my time, when not in revivals or Crusades, fishing or loafing at our reservoir retreat.

I've tried to teach the girls to hunt, but they won't bite. The sight of a snake petrifies them, and they hate those "gallon-nippers" in the South Carolina swamps. Those are swamp mosquitoes, and when they bite you *they nip a gallon of blood*! Wilma wanted to go squirrel hunting with me shortly after we were married since she didn't want to be separated from me, but after she saw the rattlers and donated blood to the nippers, she decided that was carrying togetherness too far. I didn't help, either, by telling her how many rattlesnakes I've stepped on. Not long ago I killed one with twelve rattles and a button.

Everybody needs a place where they can relax and withdraw from the hustle and bustle. Jesus himself withdrew with his disciples. At our cabin the family can draw aside and commune with nature. We meditate, pray, play games, fish, and picnic. Many of the sermons I've preached on *The Hour of Decision* and in the Crusades I have prepared at the cabin. I have also rehearsed the special Bible readings I have done for *The Hour of Decision* and for tapes and records.

The girls have given me strong counsel which has helped salvage my ministry. You cannot imagine the severe strains of our past ministry. Without the women in my life urging me to "stay cool," I could've become explosive about the captious criticisms leveled toward the BGEA.

Through the years I've wanted to write harsh letters in reply to the unfair, unjust critics, to answer in writing those charges which have appeared in writing. I have written scores of letters and signed them. Wilma and the girls have read them, most of the time advising, "Dear, don't send that. It won't do a bit of good." Kindly but forcefully they would calm me down. To this day I still have some of those letters in the bottom of my shirt drawer or down in my file drawer.

I've kept those letters of frustration as a reminder of what could've happened if I'd sent them. You've heard that old proverb about the things you can't bring back— the shot arrow and the word fitfully spoken (or written). By half-cocked responses I could have curtailed or even destroyed my ministry.

Once a famous Scottish cleric was undergoing unspeakably horrible persecution. Someone asked how he was surviving, and he replied, "I will make it, for you see I have a happy home." Thank God for Wilma, Connie, and Nancy Carol and her family.

"For you see I have a happy home."

> God, give us Christian homes!
> Homes where the Bible is loved and taught,
> Homes where the Master's will is sought,
> Homes crowned with beauty thy love hath wrought;
> God, give us Christian homes;
> God, give us Christian Homes![1]

13
Billie, Ethel, and Other Friends

Literally thousands—no exaggeration—of Christians around the world have influenced my life and ministry. No amount of books could do justice to those who have aided me, advised me, helped me, and blessed me. Remorse fills my heart because I am not able to include hundreds of my friends in these pages.

God has sent many young men to assist me in my ministry. Some of them like Dr. Billie Hanks, Jr., have already written books of their own, have gone to the top of the business world, and have excelled in their chosen fields of service.

Billie has often called himself "Grady Wilson's Timothy." Those conversant with the life of Paul will remember his special relationship to young Timothy, his "son in the ministry." I first met Billie in his home, Gleneagles, Scotland, when he was only ten years old. Then we prayed that God would use him someday on a worldwide scale. Our prayers have indeed been answered.

Billie joined my own personal Team when he was a freshman at Baylor University in Waco, Texas. He brought

with him Rev. Herb Shipp, a fellow student from Scotts-
dale, Arizona, to work in my Crusades. Herb was also on
fire for God and had a passion for winning the lost to
Christ. Wherever they found youth and young adults,
they would rap with them, interesting them in coming to
my Crusades and participating in discussion groups
which involved Bible study.

Billie, while a student at Southwestern Baptist Theological Seminary, wrote a column for the newspaper and
formed a Christian youth camp out in the "hill country" of
Texas. His camp has influenced literally thousands of
young people and adults in Christian discipleship training, as well as turning many to Christ in evangelistic
Crusades of his own. I've had missionaries from places
like Sierra Leone, India, Southwest Asia, and Australia
write me about the blessings of Billie's ministry on every
continent. Many schools, colleges, and universities across
America have formed a "Billie Hanks Chair of Evangelism
and Christian Discipleship Training." Recently a businessman from Oklahoma commented, "Billie Hanks has
more ideas than the Christian church could catch up with
in a thousand years."

Several years ago Billie, along with his parents, Freda
and Billie Hanks, Sr., sponsored a special recognition day
for me at the youth ranch near Sweetwater, Texas. For
many months they had laid plans for that occasion. They
invited thousands of my dearest friends from all over the
world. They set aside November 24, 1974, as "Grady
Wilson Day." Hundreds who could not attend sent tele-
grams, cablegrams, letters, cards, and greetings.

Among my dearest friends is Paul Harvey, the famed
speaker, author, lecturer, and commentator. He wrote
simply: "When I die, I want to be with Grady Wilson."

Another friend, a Cardinal in the Catholic Church, wrote: "I should have enjoyed being with you in person at this rally, had it not been for the long distance involved. I do, however, desire to assure you of my spiritual presence on that happy day, thanking God for all your achievements in faithfully proclaiming the Gospel over forty years and praying Him to grant you ever-renewed strength and vigor, so you will be able to continue in the good work for many years to come."

Outstanding businessmen from around the world, like Allan Emery and Bill Mead, either were present among the 4,000 persons there or sent special greetings.

Billy Graham, Ethel Waters, Ted Cornell, Steve Musto, and other members of the Team were with us. Dr. Elwin L. Skiles, who represented Hardin-Simmons University at Abilene, came, bringing along the university choir. The choir sang appropriate numbers for the Sunday afternoon service which was conducted in a massive tent. Dr. Skiles presented me with a ten-gallon Stetson hat and also spoke a word on behalf of Hardin-Simmons where our Team had visited more than two decades before. The Texas secretary of state, representing Governor Dolph Briscoe, made me an honorary citizen of Texas and presented me with an attractive plaque bearing the governor's signature and the state seal of the "Lone Star State." Proudly do I proclaim everywhere that I am an honorary citizen of Texas!

I traveled to Texas thinking I was going on a deer hunt with Robert Carroll who accompanied me. To my utter shock people began appearing from all over the world. And all of that was the super-secret "brainchild" of my "Timothy," Billie Hanks, Jr.! Now in these later years he has become my counselor as well. He has made several trips and many phone calls to help and encourage me following my heart attacks and in planning the writing of this book.

Bill Deans of Charleston, South Carolina, is a dynamic young Christian who has served as a most helpful friend and confidant. Billy and his wife, Hope, are like son and daughter to Wilma and me, and like brother and sister to our daughters, Connie and Nancy.

Other men who have made up my Team have proven prayerful and encouraging, particularly during those trying days of my close encounter with death and open-heart surgery. Grover Maughon, Ted Cornell, and Steve Musto have now been on my Team more than fifteen years. They are extremely gifted and dependable and have drawn crowds to our meetings.

Throughout the years God has sent me other talented and dedicated people with whom to minister. Rev. Arnie Robertson and Ier and Emily Basinger served with me as musicians and were rich blessings. During my college years the Lord opened the door for me to conduct revival meetings. Dr. Jesse Roberts, Dr. J. R. Faulkner, and Rev. L. A. Gable were my song leader-soloists during those formative years of my evangelistic ministry. Many have filled the gap for the Lord and have helped my own Team reach thousands for Christ.

Clif and Ruth Jones, a young couple in the lumber business, had recently moved to South Carolina when Wilma and I had our first daughter, Nancy Carol. Wilma and I were struggling to make ends meet, as most young ministerial couples do. I was pastoring two churches and also working six days a week with Wilma at the Charleston Port of Embarkation. Wilma had worked until shortly before Nancy Carol arrived.

While visiting my little family in the hospital, Clif

commented about how drained and exhausted I was. He asked me why I was killing myself maintaining two churches and working at the Port. The churches were twenty miles apart, and I was directing the Saturday night Youth for Christ rallies which I had founded in Charleston. In addition I was conducting a weekly radio program. It was essential for me to have a car. We had purchased a used jalopie, but we couldn't meet the payments, plus our rent, groceries, and medical expenses, on the meager salaries from the small churches and my Port job. Clif and Ruth insisted on paying the rest of the car notes, so we could give up the Port work and concentrate on the Lord's work.

With the pressure lessened, the anxiety which nearly ruined my health with a duodenal ulcer was also relieved, and the ulcer was cured. These dear friends have been like kinfolks to us, giving their time, counsel, love, and help when we built our home.

And throughout these pages I express thanks to the Team members who have bolstered us with love, prayers, and every type of support. In another chapter I give thanks for the late R. G. LeTourneau, the industrialist and founder of LeTourneau University in Longview, Texas. He stepped in when my early hopes of ministerial education were sagging, paying my way to Wheaton College.

For many years one of my closest friends has been Bill Mead who was at Bob Jones College with me. He is past president of the American Bakers Association and past president of the Board of Directors of the Billy Graham Evangelistic Association. Allan Emery, the current president of the Board, and I have a long-standing friendship going back to our days at Wheaton. His wisdom and counsel continue to be invaluable to me and the entire BGEA.

Only eternity will reveal the impact of these, my friends, for the kingdom of God.

For years *The Reader's Digest* has run a heralded feature entitled "The Most Unforgettable Character I've Met." I have met many unforgettable characters, but the late and great singer, Ethel Waters, qualifies for that designation in my book. Her indomitable spirit, her winsomeness, her genuine love for humanity, and her sweet voice, even when she was dying, were straight from heaven.

At one time music critics agreed she had one of the purest, clearest voices in the entertainment world. She had starred in the movies and on Broadway. When the Team met Ethel, her most recent success had been in the highly-acclaimed Broadway production of *A Member of the Wedding*, adapted from Carson McCullers's book of the same title. I still recall pictures of her rocking young Julie Harris (now of "Knots Landing" on TV) in her lap and singing the immortal song identified with her, "His Eye Is on the Sparrow."

She showed up the first night at our 1957 New York Crusade, and she sat far in the back. By her later admission she was tremendously inspired by Cliff Barrows and the Crusade choir. At the time she was in bad health and her weight had blossomed to 375 pounds or thereabouts. She was suffering from high blood pressure, heart trouble, and diabetes. She was beginning a weight-loss program and finally peeled off over 200 pounds.

I cannot forget that first night she came up to Cliff after the service, almost shouting, "Cliffie boy, if you'll remove one of those armrests up there in that choir, I'll be glad to join your choir. I promise not to miss a night singing in that choir. I'll cancel all my appearances in night clubs and on the stage. I'll be there if you want me." Cliff was awed and by all means he wanted her in the choir.

Then followed her relationship with Billy and the Team which ended only when God called her away in 1977. She and I hit it off from the beginning. Our senses of humor worked a mystique which bound our souls together.

Even though she was not a Team member in an official sense, we considered her one. On five nights during the last eight weeks of the New York Crusade she sang "His Eye Is on the Sparrow." You could hear people on the streets of Manhattan singing or whistling that poignant refrain. She accompanied the Team on many of its major American Crusades. And she often sang for my Team in Wilson meetings.

For her health I tried to dissuade her from making long, strenuous trips, but she would call me and plead, almost in a little-girl voice, "Now, Grade (she always called me that), you're not going to leave me behind, are you?" I felt her going to the Barbados or Alaska was too taxing, but she won out.

When I was about to leave for an Anchorage, Alaska, meeting, she called me from California. "Grade, you're not going to run off without me, are you?" I argued as usual, "Ethel, honey, it's a long way to go. But if you want to go, though, you can go." She came. As a result of her being there, the pastor of the First Baptist Church sold his airplane so he could put us on television every night, thus giving us the potential of reaching 80 percent of Alaska's population through thirty-eight relay stations.

And she had an impact in the Barbados, another place I insisted she bypass because of her health. After a while I learned it did no good for me to answer no. Ethel was determined to go, even if she had to swim. Prior to our arrival there, certain black leaders had come through, seemingly trying to foment unrest against the United States. The first day in the Barbados, one black reporter asked, "Miss Waters, isn't it terrible to live in America where they tolerate bigotry and the ghettos?" She answered no. "I'm an American," she came back, "and proud to be an American. I thank God for America."

The reporters then inquired, "How can you tolerate all that immorality in America?" Ethel was never better, replying, "Don't talk to me about immorality. Anybody in America can become whatever they want to be. I was born in a ghetto, but look at me today. Here I am representing the Kingdom of God and the Lord Jesus Christ." She continued, "Look, babies, stop hating whites and start loving. The Kingdom is represented by love." The next day the papers headlined, ETHEL WATERS TELLS BARBADONS TO STOP HATING AND START LOVING. She did more to bridge the racial gap than anyone else could have.

Her humor was incomparable. During a service in our Pittsburgh Crusade I noticed that her slip was showing. Judiciously I leaned over and whispered in her ear, "Ethel, I thought you'd like to know that your slip is hanging down about twelve inches too long." She drew a deep breath because "Cliffy" had already introduced her to sing. Reaching down into her dress, she tied a little knot, and I thought she was going to get the slip too short.

Whispering again I gave the message, "Ethel, there's no need to strangle yourself." Laughing, she waddled up to the pulpit. Upon arriving she kept giggling, and the audience joined her. She confessed to that crowd of 55,000: "Oh, my soul, my precious child Grade just took me by surprise, and he leaned over and whispered something in my ear. I knew for certain he was going to say,

'Ethel, I'm praying for you as you sing.' But you know what that rascal did? He told me my slip was hanging down about twelve inches too long, and I might trip myself and fall on the way to the pulpit. I began shortening my slip strap, and then he leaned over one more time, and I thought surely he was going to say, 'Ethel, I'm praying for you.' But he said, 'There's no need to strangle yourself.'" She brought the stadium down. No one could surpass her in capturing an audience.

In the late 1950s I remember Miss Ethel and I going to Washington County, Maine. A lovely lady flight attendant asked Ethel, "Aren't you Ethel Waters?" "Yes, that's right, baby," she answered.

"Tell me, Miss Waters, what in the world are you doing up here in this cold country at this time of the year?"

"I'm going to be with my children in Washington County, Maine."

The attendant blurted out, "Well, for heaven's sake!"

"That's right, baby. I'm going for heaven's sake. Everything I do now is for Jesus, heaven's sake, and eternity."

Never can I forget how God moved through Ethel to turn the tide at our Knoxville Crusade in 1970. One hundred thousand were present at Neyland Stadium on the campus of the University of Tennessee with others being turned away. President Nixon had flown down for that climactic service, and possibly 300 demonstrators were present to voice their antiwar dissent. They booed the president. They booed Dr. Ed Hill, the black minister from California, when he pronounced the invocation. They booed Billy when he introduced the president.

We had heard that the leader of that group was wearing sackcloth—and that he was going to walk down front before the entire crowd, drop that sackcloth to the turf, and stand there stark naked before President Nixon, Billy, the Team, and that throng. He would try to make fun of the gospel of Christ and the president of the United States all in one fell swoop.

He was stopped by the Secret Service men as he tried to approach the platform with a huge sign which read something like "You Dirty Yankees, Get out of Vietnam." The men took the sign away from him, and he still wanted to make a scene. Protesting, he asked, "Why don't you let me come forward? Billy Graham asks people to come forward." They replied, "We'll let you come forward, but we'll keep your signs and banners." A struggle ensued, and the man was jailed. (Later we heard that the head demonstrator had sent word he was going to remain in jail until Billy came down and apologized to him. My comment was, "Well, he's gonna stay in there a mighty long time.")

The situation was almost out of hand. When Ethel stood up to sing, the demonstrators booed her. And she chided them, "Wait a minute, children. God Almighty sent Mom Waters all the way from California to sing for you today. I want to tell you right now, you're gonna listen. If I could get back there to you young folks, I'd smack you (and she slapped her face). I'd give you that." And then she slapped her hands together. "Then I'd hug you and kiss you and pray for God to forgive you. Now, you keep quiet and let Mom sing." You could've heard a mouse walking after that. Later the president came over and kissed Ethel on the forehead. He said, "God bless you, Ethel. You did something the rest of us couldn't do."

At Soldier's Field in 1965 the heat was unbearable, and Ethel was sitting in my car behind the platform. Anita Bryant, the well-known singer, came in for the service. Seeing Ethel she said, "I've always wanted to meet Ethel Waters," so we walked down to see Ethel. With a hint of tears in her eyes, Ethel advised Anita, "God bless you, honey. I'm praying for you. Don't travel the night club road. Sing for Jesus." As they hugged, Anita broke down and wept. That was Ethel for you—always blessing and encouraging others for Christ.

When she traveled with me, many people didn't know who I was. But they knew Ethel. They mobbed her all over this land. They would run up with sheets of paper, autograph pads, and even scraps of paper, saying: "Please give me your autograph, Miss Waters. God bless you, Miss Waters." Sometimes they would simply call her Ethel or Miss Ethel.

Many people have erroneously quoted her as saying "God don't make no junk." According to Ethel that didn't originate with her. During the 1957 New York Crusade she was interviewed on the "Jinx Falkenburg and Tex McCrary Show." Tex and Jinx were asking her whether the Crusade would succeed. She declared, "I know that God's Spirit is with Billy Graham." Then came her unbeatable answer, *"God don't sponsor no flops."* That was it.

Of course, she appeared with me in most of my own Crusades almost until her death. She fell in love with Wilma and me and vice versa. She called us her "only living children." And she often declared, "My Eastern American home is in Charlotte, North Carolina. My Western American home is Bunker Hill Towers in California."

Her last visit with us lasted for seven weeks. Every moment was a pure delight, yet there was an underlying sadness because Ethel was becoming progressively weaker. While with us she had a cataract removed from one of her eyes by Dr. Reid Gaskin, a splendid Christian ophthalmologist in North Carolina. Dr. Gaskin mentioned to me, "Grady, I want to help her as much as I can after all this lady has done for the Kingdom of God."

Ethel loved to be with us and we with her. When her health was at its worst, she called and asked if she couldn't come to visit us. I answered, with hurt in my heart, "Ethel, dear, I'm afraid it would be to your detriment. We'd love to have you. Wilma would be glad to nurse you and look after you and take care of you, but I'm afraid it would be harmful for you to make the long trip."

Three weeks before God called Ethel home, Wilma and I flew out to visit her in West Los Angeles where she was being cared for in a hospital for movie stars. She had a radio going and was catching glimpses on the TV mounted high on the wall. She wanted to view her old friends on the TV, and was listening to Bev Shea on *The Hour of Decision* radio broadcast. I remember he was singing "What a Friend We Have in Jesus."

She requested, "Oh, Grade and Wilma, pray for me— but please don't pray for me to live. I don't want to live. I'm homesick to see Jesus." She continued, "Please pray for me that the Lord will release me and let me come home." Talking to Jesus she called out, "Oh, Jesus, I want to come home now." She was suffering excruciating pain in the terminal stages of cancer. Never before had I prayed this kind of prayer for anyone, but I held her hand and prayed, "Oh, Lord, please let her come home to heaven. Please let her see you face-to-face."

Toward the end of her life here, she became weaker and weaker. Even though she had trouble speaking and singing, everyone knew the Holy Spirit was moving in her.

When God called her away I flew out to conduct her funeral. I thought back on her friendship with our family, her extended visits in our home—her "Eastern American home." And I recalled her testimony about accepting

Christ at the age of twelve in the New York City ghetto and how she had backslidden for a long time, fluctuating in her devotion to God. I remembered that she had rededicated her life to Christ that first night in Manhattan. That recommitment seemed almost a conversion experience to her.

She had testified that the stage and night clubs were in the past; she totally sold out to the Master. She said to me over and over again, "I love my Savior," and she proved it by her life. Anybody capable of disliking that sweet, Spirit-filled woman of God had to be of the devil. Through Christ, Ethel Waters had become the embodiment of pure heavenly love.

At her funeral I stated publicly that her final prayer had been answered, granted by her merciful Lord. Scores of celebrities were present for the service at Forest Lawn on the top of that verdant hill in Los Angeles. I cannot recall all of them, but Pearl Bailey came by the casket and laid her head on my shoulder. In essence she said, "Dr. Wilson, this has been a great everlasting tribute to Miss Ethel whom I love dearly." Then the fabulous Miss Bailey filed out in tears.

On the outside of the chapel the press asked Miss Bailey questions about Ethel. Miss Bailey said—I don't remember the exact words—the press had misstated Miss Waters's financial condition, claiming that she had died in poverty whereas she had once lived in plenty with a net income of around a million dollars a year. She said, "Miss Ethel Waters was busy for her last twenty-two years laying up treasures in heaven where thieves cannot break through and steal, and where moths and rust cannot corrupt."

We were surrounded by a sea of Ethel's friends. Norma Zimmer, former "Champagne Lady" of the "Lawrence

Welk Show," and her husband, Randy, were on the first row of the chapel. Several moving testimonies were given at the graveside. Among those eulogizing Ethel was Mrs. Mary Crowley, who is the head of the Drake Home Interior Decorating Corporation in Dallas, Texas. Mrs. Crowley, for the last several years of Ethel's life, had helped support Ethel's ministry. Mrs. Crowley often sent one of her personal jets to transport Ethel around the country. Ethel talked incessantly about Mrs. Crowley's kindness and thoughtfulness. Never have I known a more grateful, thankful human being than Ethel.

During her last days Ethel and Mrs. Crowley were together at the San Diego Crusade. Ethel was wearing an expensive wristwatch studded with diamonds. She gave it to Mrs. Crowley, insisting that she accept it. Mrs. Crowley protested. These were Ethel's words: "Honey, where I'm going they don't need any wristwatches, and I'll never need this again. You've meant so much to me I want you to have it." How true that Ethel doesn't have to keep time. She's eternal and has a permanent home in the heavenly choir.

I praise God for Billie, Ethel, and my other friends!

14
Presidents, Princes, and Prime Ministers

The Bible is filled with examples of men and women of God who used their spiritual influence among the leaders of the world. There was Esther who became the queen of Persia (now Iran), wedded to King Ahasuerus. Daniel became a prince of Babylon under King Nebuchadnezzar and was treated like a member of the king's court.

Joseph rose to the position of second in command under the pharaoh of Egypt. Nehemiah was the most trusted confidant, the cupbearer, to Artaxerxes, the ruler of the Persian Empire.

In the New Testament, Paul related to governors and kings. He consummated his life by carrying a Christian witness into the Roman emperor's palace. In Acts 9 is recorded Paul's Damascus road experience. Ananias of Damascus was sent to minister to Saul (Paul) who was temporarily stricken blind along the road. The Lord answered Ananias's protests with:

> Go thy way: for he is a chosen vessel unto me, to bear my name before the Gentiles, and kings, and the children of Israel: For I will shew him how great things he must suffer for my name's sake (Acts 9:15-16).

I've already emphasized that Billy cares for all people—rich and poor, influential and uninfluential. He has had an unparalleled opportunity to witness for Christ to those in leadership and prominence, and he has accepted it with humility. Billy's not a deliberate name dropper, and he's never bragged about it.

Throughout Billy's ministry the press has keyed in on the "big people," the celebrities he's encountered. Of course, the press caters to the big names. Billy's taking time out for the so-called "little people" unfortunately doesn't often make news.

I repeat one observation: Billy is appreciative of the press. The media have given considerable impetus to the Crusades and to the various ministries of the BGEA. Billy has often stated that he has rarely ever been misquoted in the press, though sometimes his quotes have been taken out of context. He has a high regard for the American press and is a strong supporter of freedom of the press.

Beginning with Harry S. Truman, Billy has been a friend to every president. Some like Presidents Eisenhower, Johnson, Nixon, and Reagan have been perhaps closer than others.

Since Watergate he has been more careful to avoid any hint of partisan political involvement, though he is a longtime friend of both President and Mrs. Reagan and Vice-president and Mrs. Bush. Contrary to popular opinion, Billy has never endorsed a president.

Of course, Billy and the Team members have had their own private preferences. Billy met with President Ford several times. He and Ruth were entertained at the White House the night Queen Elizabeth and Prince Philip were the guests of honor. They also spent an unpublicized night at the White House with the Carters. Billy has visited with and talked with President Reagan a number of times. Billy and Ruth spent a night with the Reagans during their first year in the presidency. These were not widely publicized because Billy wants to avoid undue visibility.

Paul wrote the Galatian churches, declaring:

> And I went up by revelation, and communicated unto them the gospel which I preach among the Gentiles, but privately to them which were of reputation, lest by any means I should run, or had run, in vain (Gal. 2:2).

What did the apostle mean? That he carried the gospel message to prominent persons—but he related to them judiciously. In other words, he didn't want to alienate the "common man." Paul touched the lives and fortunes of many people in the courts of kings. And so has Billy visited a number of world leaders privately as well as publicly.

If the Team can reach people who have a large following, it can change thousands of lives. There are scores of living examples in the history of the Crusades. For instance, Cliff Richard, the British singing idol, sang and shared his testimony at the 1966 Greater London Crusade. Cliff has been a pop idol for more than a quarter of a century now. (He made it big as a teenager in the late 1950s—his first record even climbed to number two on the charts in Britain.) He has sold close to sixty million records and has had almost eighty British hits and three or four in the U.S., including "Dreaming," "A Little in Love," and "Suddenly" with Olivia Newton-John.

So, Cliff can do no wrong to thousands of fans in the U.S. and Great Britain. Many will comment, "Hey, if being a Christian is good for Cliff Richard, then it must be good for me." Many Christian entertainers have appeared, giving testimonies and performing at the Crusades. The list includes stars like Johnny Cash, Arthur Smith,[1] Norma Zimmer, Evie Tornquist, Bobby Richardson of New York Yankee fame, Debby Boone, Bob Dylan, and Ethel Waters. Football coaches like Tom Landry of the Dallas Cowboys and Grant Teaff and Steve Sloan (both as player and coach) have testified at Crusades, as well as many players of college and professional sports. Christian singers from country to pop to rock to classical have spoken for Christ.

Billy will never forget when Muhammad Ali and his father came to visit him and Ruth at their Montreat home. Ali later told the press how amazed he was at the Grahams' simple life-style. He expected to be met by a chauffeur-driven Rolls-Royce and transported to an ostentatious mansion, where he would be ushered into Billy who would be sitting on a throne! Ali was astonished when Billy met him and his father at the airport. Billy was driving his four-year-old Olds. Billy personally drove them to the house, which Ali found to be ordinary. The entire conversation for those five hours was about the Bible, God, Christ, and Islam. It was an intense religious conversation. Ali left saying, "I want to use the balance of my life for the glory of God."

By ministering to entertainers, presidents, kings, queens, and other well-known personages, Billy figures he can indirectly witness to thousands, maybe even millions, of people who are drawn to those personalities. Of course, Billy is aware of the danger of hero worship— that many people will be moved only emotionally. Some of them may say, "My hero or heroine has become a Christian. It must be the 'in' thing, so I'll do it, too."

But there is also that peril in the local church as well. A kid may make his "decision" because a high-school athlete has come out for Christ, or because a friend has responded, or because he heard a pro athlete's testimony. And many people may follow the "herd instinct" with no genuine commitment. But that's the chance we take.

A perfect example of hero worship gone wild is the Beatles. Their late manager, Brian Epstein, brashly commented in the 60s, "The Beatles are more popular than Jesus Christ." Many agreed with him. "Beatlemania" was the rage, and with many it's still in vogue. Consider the wave of hysteria created by the fatal shooting of John Lennon. Yes, it was a despicable act and snuffed out a brilliant talent.

One of our most embarrassing moments was the aftermath of our first visit with President Truman. We were invited through Congressman (later Speaker of the House) John McCormick of Massachusetts. We had just closed our 1950 Crusade in Boston, and Mr. McCormick was tremendously impressed with the reports emanating from that Crusade, largely from his editor friend of the *Boston Globe*.

Congressman McCormick called Billy at Winona Lake, Indiana, and asked Billy if he and the Team would visit President Truman. Billy was as nervous as I've ever seen him to meet the president of the United States! I can always tell when Billy is either fatigued or nervous—he has a tendency to bite his fingernails. Billy mused out loud, "I'm trying to think about something that might give us some rapport with the president—and also will help us to be faithful witnesses for Christ."

"Billy," I suggested, "I have exactly the idea. In every picture I've seen of President Truman he's wearing white buckskin shoes. And there's a shoe store right across the street." Billy already had a pair, but he enthusiastically answered, "That's a good idea." We—meaning Billy, Cliff,

Jerry Beavan, and I—all ended up wearing white buckskin shoes for our interview with President Truman.

We were ushered into the White House at the appointed time. We were as nervous as the proverbial cat on a hot tin roof. President Truman allowed us to spend about thirty minutes with him, and then Billy suggested, "Mr. President, before we leave, could we have prayer together?" Mr. Truman, an erstwhile Baptist who could turn the air blue when angry, cleared his throat, grunted a couple of times, and said, "Well, I don't suppose that any harm could be done."

And then Billy started praying. As I recall, Cliff gave Billy two or three amens during the prayer. I peeked while Billy prayed, squinting through my fingers which partially covered my eyes. I wanted to see President Truman's expression. To the best of my recollection, the President had his eyes wide open and he was staring at Cliff. There's no telling what he was thinking. I don't think he was raised as a shouting Baptist.

Not knowing what we were supposed to do when we departed the Oval Office, we walked into the reception room, and press members pounced on Billy. We hadn't been briefed on what to say and what not to say to the press afterwards. After a conference with the President you are never supposed to quote him.

So, the press was firing questions at Billy. Not realizing proper protocol, he began quoting President Truman. Of course, what Billy was quoting had been spoken in the privacy of the Oval Office. Billy also indicated that we'd had prayer with the President.

"Mr. Graham, would you pose for us right now, just pretending you're having prayer with the President?" Billy immediately answered, "No, gentlemen, I won't pose. I don't think it's right to pose for prayer." Billy sensed they were disappointed by his refusal. So, he relented. "On second thought, gentlemen, my Team and I had planned to have a little prayer on the outside of the White House and to give thanks to God for this great privilege and opportunity."

All of us moved out to the lawn. We four knelt on the same knee, all together, all wearing white buckskin shoes, and Billy was leading us in prayer. It was a genuine prayer of thanksgiving to God, but the press made a big display of it. The pictures were plastered all over the world.

Billy, Cliff, Jerry, and I learned soon enough that Mr. Truman was upset. He let it be known that he hadn't invited us. He emphasized that the request for the brief visit came from "the other side," meaning the House of Representatives. We had to chalk that up to experience. We realized soon how preachy and pious we looked, even though we were dead earnest and sincere. Years later Mr. Truman let bygones be bygones.

After Mr. Truman stepped down from the presidency, Billy visited him in Independence, Missouri, the Truman hometown. Mr. Truman had mellowed considerably. Don't we all? He seemed to have a grasp of our ministry and an appreciation for the Team that certainly hadn't existed when we acted like jokers years before.

On Billy's last visit to Independence, Mr. Truman was the same old war-horse and the same Democratic politician he always was. He said, "Billy, God bless you in your great work, but keep giving those Republicans h—. As long as you do, I feel like you're having a worthwhile ministry!" He was a staunch Democrat to the end.

Let me interject this. Billy, the Team members, and I have always voted for the man, not the party. We've never believed in the straight party line. I concur with voting for the person's character and principles. One of my political friends remarked years ago, "Right or wrong, the party!" I can't buy that. I think, too, that the major parties shift in their basic positions from time to time.

President Eisenhower was a deeply religious man. Quiet and unassuming, he was mostly business and didn't have time for foolishness, although he did love a tasteful joke or anecdote. He could, though, on occasions become excited.

Most of our meetings with him centered around golf— either the course or the clubhouse. Mr. Nixon, being his vice-president, followed that lead and became an inveterate golfer, too. I'll never forget the round of golf Billy and I played with Mr. Eisenhower, then former president, at the El Dorado Country Club in Palm Springs, California. The country club owners had actually built a little cottage for Mr. Eisenhower on the fourth fairway, of all places.

That day we were playing with Freeman Gosden of *Amos and Andy* fame and Randolph Scott, Hollywood star of Western movies and one of the top businessmen in Southern California. Incidentally, Randy hailed from our hometown, Charlotte. Randy and I had a tremendous amount in common. He and his wife, Pat, are two of the dearest friends that Billy and I ever had.

Our party was coming to the eighteenth hole. On number 17 I had lofted a ball so high (in baseball parlance—a pop-up) that it landed in the top of a palm tree, and we had to call an emergency confab. I asked, "Gentlemen, how do we chalk this up? What do you do when you lose a ball in the top of a palm tree?" Apparently few from that club had ever pulled a goof like that. Leave it to me. Anyway, they finally decided to penalize me two strokes. I got out easy. Billy was paired off with the president and I with Freeman.

On the last hole there was a dogleg to the left, and the green was a split-level beauty. In front of the green there were two ponds and between them an isthmus going right up to the green. But my shot from the tee landed behind—you guessed it—a palm tree. The ball was three or four feet behind the tree, but the tree was directly in line toward the pin.

Freeman pulled the golf cart up behind me and whispered, "Well, pardner, you've left yourself an impossible shot," to which I replied, "What am I going to do?" Freeman advised, "Grady, if I were you I'd twist my wrist around, follow through, and try to give that ball a strong hook so you'll miss the tree."

I rarely prayed on the golf course because I thought that would be presumptuous. I played so poorly I felt bad about asking the Lord to help a duffer like me. But this time I prayed, and I prayed hard. "Lord, in the gallery there are two or three hundred people watching me. They're on the balcony of the clubhouse and all along the fairway. And Lord, the former president of the United States is looking on, and Billy is embarrassed. Lord, if you ever helped me with a shot, do it now!"

You could hear the ooohs and aaahs as I came through with the most superb hook you ever saw. I looked like Jack Nicklaus or Arnold Palmer. That ball circled, made a perfect arc, went completely around that tree, landed between those two ponds, bounced onto the split-level green, and rolled to the back of the green almost at the feet of President Eisenhower.

As I walked by, Billy gave me a stage whisper, "Buddy, you left yourself an awfully long putt." Feeling my oats I nonchalantly answered, "Yeah."

The pin was on the front lower level of that green, and

my ball was on the back of the elongated green. The president sympathized with me: "Young man, you've left yourself an awfully long putt." Sound familiar? "I've played this course many times before, and I would suggest you'll have about a ten-foot break."

I went through all the motions of a pro. I closed one eye, squatted down, and pointed my putter toward the hole. I never understood why the pros did that, but I did it, anyhow. Every eye was on that little white ball as it scooted across that split-level green and fell right into the cup.

Mr. Eisenhower, usually not too emotional, lifted his putter high over his head and yelled, "Wow, that's the longest putt I've seen in my entire life. The next longest was by Arnold Palmer himself at Latrobe, Pennsylvania, when he sank a 39-footer." The president then stepped off the distance, and it was 55 feet.

I replied anticlimactically, "And, Mr. President, that's the longest putt I've ever sunk in my life."

Another time, which Billy would like to forget, we had played in a foursome with Mr. Nixon, then vice-president. We had finished the round at Burning Tree Golf Club in Washington and had returned to the locker room. Billy was already in the shower lathered up, and I was in my undershorts.

While Billy was in the shower, I heard a voice calling, "Oh, Dick, Dick Nixon." Lo and behold, President Eisenhower, wearing formal evening attire and en route to a state dinner that night, came into the locker room, and he was calling for Vice-president Nixon. "Mr. President," I blurted out red-facedly, "Mr. Nixon's gone to the pro shop. Could I help?" The President said, "Grady, I was really looking for Billy Graham. I was seeing if Dick could find him for me. Where is Billy?"

Flabbergasted and standing there in my skivvies, I explained, "Well, Mr. President, Billy's in here. I'll get him." I tiptoed around the corner to where Billy was showering. "Look," I nervously reported, "the president of the United States is around the corner, and he's looking for you." Billy emerged from the shower, furiously trying to dry himself. He was barely able (no pun intended) to wrap that towel around his torso before the president walked in.

There we stood: the president of the United States of America impeccably attired in formal wear; Evangelist Billy Graham barely covered in a poorly-fitting towel; and Associate Evangelist Grady Wilson dressed in his underpants! Billy was nervous, and the whole time we conversed about world conditions and spiritual awakening, Billy was popping and twisting another towel.

John F. Kennedy was highly revered before and after his monstrous assassination. I guess none of us will ever know the full truth about his life or his assassination. Unfortunately, within recent years there has been an effort to dredge up filth on many famous persons after they're gone. Many people have sought to besmirch the reputations of personalities who cannot answer back— like Kennedy, President and Mrs. (Eleanor) Franklin Delano Roosevelt, President Dwight David Eisenhower, Bobby Kennedy who was assassinated after his brother, Joan Crawford, and (horrors) even George Washington, the father of our country. It's difficult to sift the fact from the fantasy.

Billy had the privilege of playing golf with President Kennedy twice—once at the Seminole Golf Course near Palm Springs, just five days before he was elected president.

You know the awful story. When the assassination occurred, Billy, T. W., Calvin Thielman, and Lee Fisher were playing golf at Black Mountain close to Montreat. They were on the fourth or fifth fairway when Loren Bridges, manager of WFGW (the high-powered Christian radio station in Black Mountain), came driving up and blowing his horn. He ran across the fairway to give them the blood-chilling message he had picked up from the teletype. Seemingly an electric shock ran all over each of them.

Billy left the golf course and rushed to the station. There he broadcast an earnest appeal for the future of America and the world. (How ironic! As I first wrote these lines, we received word that Anwar Sadat of Egypt had been assassinated by bullets from the guns of some Egyptian soldiers.) That November day was shocking and tragic.

Who knows what would've happened if President Kennedy had heeded the warnings from his confidants and friends? They had begged him not to make the Dallas trip. They felt ominous signs were on the horizon. In 1979 the authorities exhumed and reburied the body of Lee Harvey Oswald, allegedly Kennedy's assassin. According to their findings, Oswald was indeed buried in that Fort Worth plot, and not a substitute Russian agent, as one British author had insisted. Still, we'll never grasp the full story of Kennedy's death.

I guess of all the presidents, Lyndon Baines Johnson was "the good ole boy." When it came to the craft of politics, there was none more astute. The man was a born politician; his leadership in the Senate had pushed Democratic programs for years. He first served in the House of Representatives from 1937 to 1949, even being elected by his Texas constituents while he was serving in the Navy during World War II. Sworn in as senator in 1949, he first became minority leader and then majority leader. He was canny, clever, and shrewd. I mean that in the right sense of those words. He was also a man with a sympathetic heart, and he achieved greatly on behalf of the poor, the minorities, and the disenfranchised.

Little did Vice-president Johnson sense his destiny when he was elected with President Kennedy in 1960. It took guts for him to perform as he did after John Kennedy was gunned down. Only his rich sense of humor and religious faith kept him going. Five days after he became president, he asked Billy to spend the night at the White House. Billy read the Bible with him and prayed with him. Billy saw President Johnson probably more than any other president while in the White House. It was often my privilege to go along, either to the White House or down to the LBJ Ranch. Other members of the Team often accompanied Billy.

President Johnson dearly loved to tease me, and I gave it back to him. He liked for me to come along, most of all down at the ranch on the Pedernales River where we could "let down our hair."

President Johnson had a big beer barrel installed at his ranch. He tried his hardest to entice me into taking a frosted mug of that stuff. I replied, "Mr. President, I don't drink. I don't like the mess, and I don't use it."

He answered, "Well, good gracious, Grady. It's not going to kill you!" He could use strong words when he wanted to, but that time he didn't. He went on, "You're a fanatic like a certain man down in Texas. He's such a teetotaler that he won't even sell it in his stores."

And then he said, "Grady, you're just like Marvin Watson when I appointed him Postmaster General. We had a big reception over there at the Post Office Department, and we invited guests from the Supreme Court and members of my cabinet and senators and congressmen and special leaders from Washington—from all over the country. We had hundreds of them over there.

"Would you believe," he kept on, "that ole Marvin had a whole truckload of Sprite delivered to serve those people, and most of them wanted a belt of something stronger?" He shook his head about it and lamented, "Why, Marvin was a fanatic about that!" To me that was a glowing testimony to the character of Marvin Watson, and I've reminded Marvin of that several times over the years.

President Johnson and I could become strung out on all kinds of controversial issues. In the informality of the ranch, we could lean back and laugh uproariously. Maybe those interchanges helped ease the tension of perhaps the most tension-packed leadership role on earth, the U.S. presidency.

Admittedly, Billy and the Team fellowshipped considerably with President Richard Nixon. What happened was intensely painful for us. Mr. Nixon had won a smashing electoral mandate from the populace. At the time, his diplomacy of detente was considered a success, and he had opened up the lines of communication between our country and mainland China. Objective historians will write that his achievements were immense—and so was his downfall.

There has been tremendous overplay about what President Nixon said to me one day when we were playing at Burning Tree. Mr. Nixon turned to someone and jokingly (I hope) said, "This is the poor man's Billy Graham." Exactly what he meant I've never been able to figure out.

The same day I had made a good one-iron shot from

the lengthy fairway all the way to the green. My ball landed near the pin, and Mr. Nixon's was far, far away. Nixon commented, "That's greedy." Billy replied, "No, Mr. President, that's Grady." Nixon came back, "I know. I know, but it's Greedy Grady. It's greedy of Grady to come so close to the pin with his second shot."

Over the years, though, we've been friends of Mr. Nixon. When the Watergate investigation was coming to a head, the Team was traveling up and down New Zealand. I spoke highly of Mr. Nixon. I defended him in press conferences, and I stated publicly many times that I thought he would come through with flying colors—and at the time I sincerely felt he would.

The Lord Mayor of Auckland, New Zealand, one day asked, "Mr. Wilson, why are you, an American, down here in New Zealand, trying to straighten out our people, and telling us how to live, when you have your own Watergate going on back in the United States?" I quickly answered him, "Mr. Lord Mayor, there's a little bit of Watergate in all of us, according to the Holy Bible."

He replied, "I don't understand." "The Bible declares that all of us have sinned and come short of the glory of God," I answered. "And the Word of God teaches that there is not a single perfect person on the face of the earth. Sir, that means you have a little Watergate in you. Grady Wilson has a little Watergate in him. All of us are imperfect sinners."

The Lord Mayor looked down at the floor, and a number of Christians who were present (among the 300-plus guests) were nodding their heads in agreement and smiling as though I had hit on a vitally important point.

We were appalled and shocked by the language revealed in the Watergate tapes. In the years the Team had known Mr. Nixon, we had never heard him even use a slang expression like "darn." He was under intense emotional strain and stress during the period of the Watergate break-in and thereafter. It also seemed to me and many of his confidants that there was a decided personality change in Mr. Nixon after he returned from his seemingly triumphant trip to Peking. No doubt President Nixon was exhausted. Somehow he succumbed to the relentless pressures of his high office. I cannot feel he was acting rationally, and the tapes certainly indicated he was not the same Richard Nixon we had known.

We had become friends with Gerald Ford when he was the Republican leader in the House of Representatives, and that friendship expanded when he succeeded President Nixon for an unexpired term. Ford was not at all implicated in Watergate, even though he was roundly lambasted by commentators and politicians when he pardoned the former president. From my contact with Mr. Ford I'd have to make this evaluation: he's a nice guy, a genuine All American (and he was in the 1930s for the University of Michigan football team).

By now I guess you think all I have been doing through these years is playing golf. That's simply a hobby and has given us periods of relaxation and fellowship away from the constant pressures and tensions of the Crusades. Yes, we played golf a couple of times with President Ford. Many jokes have been made about Ford, and also former Vice-president Spiro Agnew, who seemed to have a tendency to bean members of the gallery with golf balls. Yet, Mr. Ford is still remarkably agile and athletic.

Billy and Ruth spent the night at the White House with President and Mrs. Jimmy Carter, but news of it was not widespread. On another occasion T. W. sent word that President Carter asked, "T. W., are you related to Grady

Wilson?" Of course, T. W. answered that he was. Billy and I had met then-Governor Carter at the Crusade in Atlanta several years before.

President Carter popularized afresh and anew the vital phrase "born again." He was and is a man of deep and abiding faith. I was seriously ill with my heart during his term in the White House, and I regret that there was not considerable opportunity to fellowship with him and discuss spiritual matters.

We were surprised with Ronald Reagan's landslide victory over Jimmy Carter in 1980. The lopsided margin was unbelievable. One good man defeated another good man. Billy and I have known Mr. Reagan for a long time. We had met him in his movie star days and had talked with him when he was governor of California.

Our presidents deserve our prayers, not our abuse. They grapple with possibly the most difficult task in the world. Gone are the days of the nonchalant presidency a la Calvin Coolidge.

Time magazine named Winston Churchill of Great Britain the outstanding personage of the first half of the twentieth century. Number 10 Downing Street, the prime minister's address, has gone down in history as one of its most famous addresses, along with 1600 Pennsylvania Avenue, of course.

After the climactic Wembley Stadium rally in 1954, Billy had the honor of meeting and visiting with Mr. Churchill. Billy was the only member of the Team present. No word picture could do justice to the regal, supreme presence of Churchill. Sitting in front of Billy was the embodiment of history.

During their conversation of about forty minutes, Mr.

Churchill talked with Billy about, of all subjects, the Battle of Armageddon, which is supposed to be the final battle of human history—the showdown between good and evil, between God and the hosts of hell (regardless of your position on the millennium and related matters).

In essence, Mr. Churchill was concerned about the seemingly bleak future of human history. In a philosophical but pessimistic mood, the prime minister emphasized his lack of hope for civilization. He had the feeling that the world was "at the end of its tether." The prime minister stated, "Mr. Graham, I see no hope for the future of mankind now that we're living in a nuclear age."

Billy replied, "Mr. Prime Minister, I do have hope."

"Sir, what is your hope?" inquired the prime minister.

"Our only hope," answered Billy, "is in the Lord Jesus Christ and the proclamation of the gospel. I still believe it's possible to have a worldwide spiritual and moral revival."

Churchill continued, "If there is any single, remaining hope, that is perhaps the *only* hope."

The prime minister was a professing Christian, an Anglican, and often quoted from the Bible. He also once made the observation that no one could call himself educated and not be conversant with the Bible.

Years ago Billy had a remarkable visit with Chancellor Konrad Adenauer who served West Germany from 1949 to 1963. He asked, "Mr. Graham, do you believe in the resurrection of Jesus Christ?" Billy answered with an emphatic "yes."

Mr. Adenauer, in broken English, came back with a forceful, "So do I." The chancellor was firm about his purpose—"Mr. Graham, when I leave public office I want to spend all of my remaining days in defending and promoting the resurrection of Jesus Christ." Until his death in 1967 he did exactly that.

In 1955 the Team was conducting the All-Scotland Crusade headquartered in Glasgow. On Good Friday, Billy preached on nationwide BBC television at prime time. He preached the plain, unvarnished truth of the cross and its implications.

Her Majesty Queen Elizabeth was listening in Buckingham Palace. A few days later, a courier arrived at our hotel, carrying the Queen's invitation for Billy to preach at Windsor Chapel.

Billy was asleep when the courier arrived. "I must deliver this message in person," the courier insisted. Dr. Paul Maddox, then Billy's assistant, said, "You can give it to me or Mr. Wilson here, and we'll make absolutely sure that Dr. Graham receives the message as soon as he wakes up." Billy preached at Windsor Chapel, and then Ruth and he dined with the Royal Family.

People repeatedly ask, "Have the Pope and Billy ever visited together?" Billy finally had a personal meeting with Pope John Paul II in January 1981. Billy and the Team members have had occasion to fellowship with a number of cardinals and archbishops.

Archbishop Cardinali of Belgium is one of the most splendid Christians we have ever met. We had tea with him a number of times during our London visits. He was there as an apostolic delegate to Great Britain. He gave his personal testimony about being converted when he was a child. Christ's love flowed from that man.

One writer in the Vatican did a dissertation on "The Right Reverend William Franklin Graham of Montreat, North Carolina." He wrote about Billy's conversion experience as a teenager, about Billy's doctrinal preaching on the new birth (regeneration, being born again), and the like. You'd have thought you were reading a theological treatise written by one of the most conservative evangelicals in the U.S.

The refreshing breezes of revival are blowing through Catholics and Protestants alike. They are realizing, in the words of an angel, that it is "Not by might, nor by power, but by my spirit, saith the Lord of hosts" (Zech. 4:6).

The Team has had the privilege of fellowshipping with world leaders on every continent. Dr. William Tolbert of Liberia, who was brutally murdered in a coup to overthrow his presidency, was one of our gracious friends. We first met him at the Baptist World Alliance in 1955 at Rio de Janeiro.

Dr. Tolbert was an ordained Baptist minister and nearly always pastored a church while he was president. Billy flew to Liberia on the same plane with First Lady Mrs. Richard Nixon when Dr. Tolbert was inaugurated as president. Dr. Tolbert also served a term as president of the Baptist World Alliance.

Billy and I had the honor of visiting with Generalissimo Chiang Kai-shek and his gorgeous wife, the former Mei-ling Soong, in Taipei, Taiwan (Formosa). Both the generalissimo and his wife, who was educated in the U.S., were devout Christians of the Methodist faith. Their national influence led multiplied thousands of Nationalist Chinese to receive Christ.

Of course, some accused Chiang of being a cruel despot. I am averse to injecting political ideas, but I feel that in many respects we as a nation failed our staunch ally, Chiang Kai-shek.

We thank God for the many reports coming out of China to the effect that faithful Chinese Christians have led thousands to Christ during these years since the

Nationalists were driven from the mainland. The Chinese are deeply spiritual people and have a heart hunger for God.

One of our strangest encounters was our brief meeting with the Sardonna of Sokoto over two decades ago. The Sardonna was the ruler of twenty million Nigerians in the northern area of that country. He sent word that he wanted to meet with Billy.

When we arrived at his palace, out front was parked a long black Cadillac limousine. Inside sat the Sardonna in a specially prepared high-backed chair. He was elegantly clad in a big turban and a jacket with gold braid.

A graduate of Cambridge in England, he spoke in articulate English. He said rather imperiously, "Now, Mr. Graham, I hope I can convert you to our Muslim faith. We have twenty million in my domain. I must be very candid with you. I'd love to convert you and your entire Team to the way of Islam."

Billy squared up his shoulders and answered, "Sir, I would like to be very candid with you. I would love to convert you and all twenty million of your followers to faith in Jesus Christ, my Lord and Savior."

The Sardonna then folded his arms, and with a big cynical grin challenged, "Well, Mr. Graham, we shall see who wins!"

Several years later when part of the Team was vacationing, I was listening to the 50,000-watt, clear-channel station from Charlotte. I was up early as usual. "Late to bed, early to rise" was my motto until the heart attacks struck me.

On the 5 AM news there was a bulletin from Northern Nigeria. Early in the morning servants had rushed into the Sardonna's bedroom and discovered him and his wife lying in a pool of blood—another assassination of a prominent leader.

When Billy and Ruth came down for breakfast later on, I said, "The Sardonna and his wife were murdered." I was deeply grieved. At the same time his biting words rang in my brain, "We shall see who wins."

Yes, Billy and the Team have visited with presidents, princes, and prime ministers; kings, queens, members of parliaments, senators, and congressmen; leaders from every continent. Billy has done it for one overriding reason—to further the cause of Jesus Christ.

Paul wrote, "I am made all things to all men, that I might by all means save some" (1 Cor. 9:22).

15
Full Moon and . . .

Lunatic is a word coming from the Latin, *luna*, meaning "moon." A lunatic was originally a person thought to be obsessed with the moon. I do not put stock in the occult. I believe in trusting the leadership of the Holy Spirit and the power of God.

However, the moon seems to have a pull on people. It's common knowledge that the moon has an influence on the tides of the earth's bodies of water, even the smallest lake. Poets have waxed eloquently over the moon. Songwriters have written literally thousands of songs about it—"Moon Over Miami," "By the Light of the Silvery Moon," "Full Moon and Empty Arms," "Moon River," "Shine On, Harvest Moon," "Clare de Lune," "It Must've Been Moonglow," ad infinitum.

My friends and I have often discussed the effect of the full moon on people's behavior. We were not aware of it as much when most of our meetings were indoors. As we branched out to colosseums and stadiums, we became even more conscious of the situation.

As sort of a hobby I have checked with leading psychiatrists and psychologists. They all concur that unusual behavior is often a psychological reaction to the full moon. Before the day of tranquilizers, there were many patients who had to be put into straight jackets during the full moon because they would become more hysterical and irrational than usual.

One Christian psychologist from the University of Pennsylvania mentioned that he was doing a book about the effects of the full moon on animal and plant life. Many people have insisted on planting crops according to the moon—American Indians, farmers, and others.

The full moon, however, does not seem to affect the number of decisions during a Crusade. We seem to have no more, no less. Let's give credit where it's due, though. Many romances are born on full-moon nights—and many babies, too.

When we were at Madison Square Garden the first time, the manager remarked: "You'd better watch it. Tomorrow night we're going to have a full moon, and there's no telling what will happen." On the way over in a police car Billy said, "Well, we'd better be on the alert. Tonight's the full moon."

While Roger Hull, the chairman of the Crusade committee, was preparing the crowd for the offering, a drunk in the third balcony over the choir hollered, with hands cupped to his mouth, "Hey, bud, cut out all that bull and just pass those plates." Giggling and laughter rippled through the audience.

Billy whispered to me, "That guy's drunk. Get him out of here." So Leighton Ford and I went after the guy. In the process we got ourselves locked out of the Garden, and it was probably 150 feet to the sidewalk below.

Kind of skittish I said to Leighton, "Mercy, fellow, we're in a jam! How are we going to get back inside?" After we pounded on all those outside doors, a laughing usher finally let us in. At long last we reached the drunk, escorted him gently to a cab, and invited him back for the following night.

When we returned to the Garden, so help me there stood a man in the center aisle. He was clutching eight to ten Bibles under his arm. I whispered softly but urgently to one of the ushers, "Please get that man a seat." The usher said worriedly, "I've tried to, but the man refuses to sit down. He says that God sent him here tonight to preach instead of Billy Graham!"

The man stubbornly refused to sit down or leave. We feared a scene, so finally four able-bodied ushers carried him out. Billy was still praying before the message, and the man started screaming. One of the ushers slipped his hand over the man's mouth and tried to silence him. The man bit down on the usher's hand, and the usher hollered—that created a scene. We carried the man into a counseling room and Willis Haymaker, for years the dean of our setup men, calmly called the man aside, advising him to go home and come back another night.

In the middle of that, one of the ushers came in with his eyes bulging out. He almost yelled, "Look, I don't like what's going on here tonight." Willis asked, "Why, sir, what's wrong?" The irate usher shot back, "I think anybody ought to be allowed to attend this meeting, and to bodily carry this man out of the auditorium is unthinkable!"

Willis said, "Well sir, you don't believe that we should inconvenience these thousands of people and keep them from hearing Mr. Graham's message, do you?" The man answered, "No, but I just don't like it, and I want to resign as an usher." Willis reached out to accept the man's badge, and in a huff the fellow threw it on the floor.

I gave him the standard treatment. "Why don't you go

home, get a good night's rest, and maybe come back?"

Mind you, the same night while Billy was preaching a woman shouted "Shut up!" clear across the Garden to a man who kept yelling, "Hallelujah, praise the Lord, preach it, Brother Graham."

That night, when Billy started giving the invitation, I had my head partially bowed but my eyes half-open. Billy, as you know, almost without fail says, "Every head bowed and every eye closed." I often open my eyes for security reasons. Forgive me if that turns you off, but so much can happen in a huge congregation.

Oh, oh! I saw a short, "Mr. Five-by-Five" man bouncing down the center aisle. He was wearing white tennis shoes—before they were in style—and skipping along. He looked like a rubber ball with black hair. Billy saw him and started snapping his fingers behind his back. That's a signal when he wants help from the Team. He knew that one of us would rally to his aid.

So, Mel Dibble took it upon himself. (Incidentally Mel had been an evangelist and a song leader for Southern Baptists' Charles E. Matthews.) Mel came down from the platform and told the man, "Grady Wilson, Mr. Graham's associate evangelist, wants to talk with you at the side of the platform." The man became bug-eyed, "Oh, he does?" he burst forth.

Mr. Five-by-Five came tripping around to where I was and asked, "Are you Grady Wilson?" Naturally, my answer was yes. Before a packed house that man leaned over and kissed me right square on the lips. I wanted the floor to open up and swallow me. I guess half of the eyes in there were glued on that strange scene, even though they had been instructed to bow their heads and close their eyes.

"Look, brother, let's go into the Team room and have

prayer together," I said. He replied, "Oh, that's wonderful. I'd love to do that!" I reassured him with, "I don't know what's bothering you, but we're going to pray about it. Will you bow with me in prayer?" As he bowed and I prayed, I moved slowly toward the door. By the time I reached the doorknob I pronounced the "Amen." "Good night, my brother," I wished him. Guess what else? "You go home, get a good night's rest (I even stuck my neck out!) and if you're back tomorrow night, either Mr. Graham or I will talk to you again." That pleased him. We didn't see him again, even though he may have returned.

Before we started keeping up with full-moon nights, many strange incidents occurred. Looking back I feel that many bizarre happenings were on those nights during our early ministry.

During the 1950 Atlanta Crusade we were meeting at the Ponce de Leon ball park, then the home of the minor league Atlanta Crackers. During the invitation a burly, muscular man—we later found out he was a former professional fighter—came forward wearing a brand-new suit. He fell flat onto his face in the cinder path. All of a sudden he began snorting and punching like he was in a fight. People all around him were frightened. I motioned for the ushers to come, and it required six of them to deal with that fellow. He had absolutely worn the elbows out of that new suit!

At another Crusade meeting we encountered a woman who was in an anguished state, mental illness or worse. She sat on the front row of the choir the afternoon we started. All of a sudden she started trembling and screaming, "Stop them. Stop them. The Indians are coming after me!" She started quivering all over. Cliff and I led her into a side room, where she fell to the floor, started foaming at the mouth, and kicking up her heels.

She protested, "I'm going back out there and sing in that choir." "No ma'am," I came back. "You're not going back out there this afternoon."

I asked, "How often do you have these spells?" "All the time," she answered. "For that reason," I emphasized, "I'm asking you not to go back out there." Then she really had a fit. She, in no uncertain terms, told me where to go—*hades* is the Greek word. She literally glared at me and spat out, "I hate you." Then, "I hate Billy Graham. I hate Cliff Barrows. I hate Beverly Shea. All of you can go to h--- as far as I'm concerned!" And she left.

A few nights later—perhaps it was the full moon—she appeared again and tried to enter a rehearsal with the choir. Cliff recognized her and asked the chief usher to handle the situation. Four strong ushers were not able to hold her, and she bolted toward the platform to grab a front-row choir seat. As she did I threw my arms around her. She tried to bite me, and then she started kicking me in the shins.

The ushers pulled her into a locker room with her cursing and blaspheming the entire time. Of course, all of the choir members and those filing into the hall heard her. Then she lay on the floor, rolling and kicking those metal lockers as hard as she could.

What was it? Mental illness? Demon possession? I am not going to become theological here, but I recognize that the power of Satan exists. I believe that some people are possessed with demons. Of course, I've seen precious few whom I felt were possessed, and I think it's dangerous to sit in judgment on people. Yet, John wrote, "Try the spirits whether they are of God" (1 John 4:1).

One night in the Rose Bowl at Pasadena, when Dr. Carl F. H. Henry was chairman of the rally, someone was leading in prayer, and a woman began to scream at the top of her lungs in a shrill, high-pitched voice. And that happened several times during Billy's sermon. Then as he began pressing the invitation the same woman began to shriek like a banshee, "Don't go. Don't go. Don't go. Don't anyone go!"

Dr. Charles E. Fuller, host preacher of "The Old Fashioned Revival Hour" and founder of Fuller Theological Seminary, was standing by me. With tears in his eyes he said, "Grady, that woman is demon-possessed." He started praying, "Oh God, in the name of Jesus silence that woman. Jesus, I pray that you will cast the demon out of that poor woman." All of a sudden she ceased screaming.

In spite of her outbursts the remainder of the invitation went well. Dr. Fuller was one of the most biblically sound men I've ever known. And many of our most dedicated and rational missionaries have reported instances of demon possession on the mission field.

Until that first Manhattan Crusade and the London campaign, we had never stayed long enough to compare notes about people's weird behavior during the full moon. The next full moon in Manhattan a woman declared that she had come to preach. She walked down the aisle and started mounting the platform. One of the team members received her and asked, "What are you coming for?" She came back, "I'm coming to preach." He answered, "No, ma'am, not tonight but tomorrow night." Of course, he was stalling her.

She answered, "Well, then I'll certainly be back tomorrow night." She turned, walked slowly away, and left. If she came back we didn't know it, but the following night was not the full moon.

That same Crusade we had to wrestle with one fellow and the ushers had to carry him out. And the ushers also had to be called to another man.

One full-moon night in London a man jumped up and started shouting, "What about the woman at the well?" Billy answered from the platform, "Well, sir, I'm not preaching on the woman at the well." The man persisted, "I don't care, for I want to hear about the woman at the well." Protocol had it that officials were supposed to handle contingency situations. Somehow General Wilson-Haffenden, the chairman of the Crusade, was not present. Neither was Bishop Hugh Gough, the chairman of the pastor's advisory committee.

Several members of the Crusade committee put their heads together with Billy and suggested, "There's nothing we can do. Cliff Barrows will simply have to outsing the man." The audience sang "And Can It Be?"—an old Welsh song. Then "Blessed Assurance." After a number of hymns the man was still standing. Then they sang "To God Be the Glory." Billy even asked between hymns, "What about another subject, maybe the resurrection?"

Finally, an official of the meeting hall went to the deranged man and said, "When Mr. Graham gets through, you and I will tell this crowd what we think." "That sounds like a good deal to me," replied the man, who sat down smiling. There was no more trouble from him.

During the invitation a professional pickpocket in the balcony stole the wallet from a man in front of him. The man who'd had his pocket picked moved into the aisle during the singing of "Just As I Am." The pickpocket fell under conviction by the Holy Spirit, stepped out, and followed his victim into the counseling room. There the pickpocket returned the man's wallet with an apology, "Hey, sir, here's your wallet. I want to get right with God, so I'll have to give your wallet back."

On a full-moon night!

Now, I want to face up to it. The only time the full moon has gotten to me was during the London Crusade of 1954. I was so homesick that I became obsessed with "Carolina Moon."

16
Laughing All the Way to Heaven

I was tempted to call this chapter "Red Faces on the Road to Paradise."

Although over the years we have felt the pressures of our ministry, we on the Team have spent plenty of time laughing together. More often than not, Billy, Cliff, and Bev have served as my "straight men." Our personalities interacting have caused all sorts of hilarious, sometimes embarrassing, situations. Occasionally, you might even call areas of our lives "situation comedy."

In Atlanta, Billy was preaching at a Youth for Christ rally back in 1944. He was preaching away on David and Goliath. He roared out, "And David slew Goliath, and then he turned around and killed him!"

Perhaps Billy's most uproarious flub occurred at the Memphis Crusade in 1951. The police chief had asked Billy to help promote a traffic safety campaign for the city. Before 30,000-plus hearers Billy pointed to a neon sign behind him on the platform. It read: "150 Days." Billy dramatically singled out that sign and announced, "You see this sign back here? That 150 days? That means there have been 150 days without a *fertility*." There was soon a swelling tide of laughter. Dr. Robert G. Lee, world-renowned clergyman, almost fell off the platform in hysterics. Cliff Barrows cupped his hands and, in a stage whisper, blurted out, "*Fatality*, man, *fatality*!" It happens in the best of families.

God must be with us or we never would have made it. Our first city-wide Crusade in London (1954) was filled with faux pas by me and others who had never traveled to Britain as Cliff and Billy had previously. I used to think that was "fox paws" until I found out it's French for a social blunder. Boy, have I made more than my share! In London many of us had to read manuals on etiquette and protocol. The Team members were often in the company of lords and ladies, and Billy and Ruth had an audience with Queen Elizabeth.

During that Crusade I pulled my share of faux pas. The last day of the Crusade at Wembley Stadium, with 120,000 in attendance, was the largest crowd to which Billy had preached up until that time. It was the climax of three months at the Harringay Arena in London.

Even though Geoffrey Fisher, then the Archbishop of Canterbury, had not attended a single service at Harringay, he was at Wembley for the closing service. At the conclusion Billy called on the Archbishop to pronounce the benediction. He did, and it was a moving, reverent prayer of praise and thanksgiving.

The Team was worn out. I was wearily climbing the stairway going toward the Royal Box. Adjacent to the box was a reception room where we would be feted with tea for 400 dignitaries from across the British Isles. Behind me I heard this majestic voice ring out, "Young man, don't you think this is the dawning of a new day in evangelism?" Slowly I halfway turned around, thinking it was an Anglican vicar.

To my utter chagrin, I beheld the vestments—a three-quarter length coat, the fluffy sleeves, the cross. I had a mental blackout, which is about par for my course. In my best, or worst, style, I threw my arm around the Archbishop of Canterbury. I must have slapped the breath out of him, squeezing him with a bear hug. All I could think of was, "Yes sir, Brother Archbishop, yes sir." He laughed all the way to the top of the stairs. The Archbishop's wife, with her autograph book, was waiting for us up there and she was laughing, too. The team will never let me forget the day I called the Archbishop of Canterbury, "Brother Archbishop."

I could write a book (and you're probably relieved I haven't) of funny experiences from my early ministry prior to the founding of the BGEA. Anybody who has pastored a church in Hell Hole Swamp is bound to have weird happenings in his life.

When I was pastor of Friendship Baptist Church in Charleston, South Carolina, Ed Taylor was one of our deacons. One Sunday Ed called me aside and explained, "Brother Grady, I feel called of God to enter the full-time ministry. I've been fighting the call for years." Ed had been an electrician and foreman in the navy yards at Charleston.

I replied, "Ed, the best way to start preaching is just to preach. And I'm going to ask you to take the service tonight." I shouldn't have put Ed on the spot like that—I wasn't fair. He selected John 5:1-13 as his text, a passage about Jesus' healing a lame man who had laid by the pool called Bethesda. Throughout his thirty-minute sermon Ed referred to the pool as *Bathsheba*.

Don Hoke, who has become well known as an educator and missionary, once in a while would preach at Youth for Christ rallies before he went to Japan many years ago. I'll never forget when he was preaching from Luke 16 about Lazarus, the beggar, being in heaven ("Abraham's bosom") and the rich man (often called "Dives") being in hell. Only he twisted it around. He had Lazarus in hell and the rich man in heaven—and he never straightened it out.

My own embarrassments are innumerable. I doubt if the Library of Congress could contain them. I've also received many backhanded compliments. After I had preached my heart out in a revival, I was confronted with a boy around nine or ten years of age. He said, "I sure will be glad when this revival meeting is over." I said, "Fine, son, but why?" To which he answered: "I want to hear our pastor preach again!"

Another instance of being backhanded was when a dear lady came up to me after I had preached in my usual bombastic manner. She commented, "Brother Wilson, you certainly do have the gift of gab." She didn't elaborate. By the ear-to-ear smile on her face, I hope that it was a compliment. To this day I don't know for sure.

All of this reminds me of what happened to a preacher friend of mine, a man of the cloth who is rather corpulent and loud. While he was waxing eloquently from the pulpit, a six-year-old boy—bless him—yelled out loud, "Mama, mama, why doesn't that big, fat man sit down and shut up and let the pastor preach?"

Reverend John Minder has shed considerable light on Billy's early greenness as a preacher. When Billy was a student at Florida Bible Institute, Brother Minder reported, Billy forgot his Bible on one occasion. That's happened to every preacher at least once. It's a naked feeling. Bibleless, Billy tried to preach on Belshazzar's feast from Daniel 5. You've heard of "the handwriting on the wall." That expression comes directly from that chapter.

> In the same hour came forth fingers of a man's hand, and wrote over against the candlestick under the plaister of the wall of the king's palace: and the king saw the part of the hand that wrote. Then was the part of the hand sent from him; and this writing was written. And this is the writing that was written, MENE, MENE, TEKEL, UPHARSIN (Dan. 5:5,24-25).

Guess how Billy handled those last four words? MANY, MANY, TICKLE, UPJOHN. So help me! He even dragged in the name of a pharmaceutical firm.

Frankly, I have often been criticized for using humor in my sermons. If it is tasteful and clean, I see nothing wrong with it. I've found that listeners will remember your illustrations and funny stories long after they've forgotten you. Yet, many people associate religion with drabness and extreme "piosity"—not piety, my friends.

One lady—and I'm sure she was sincere—accosted me after a night service. It's strange people don't in the daytime because they're hurrying to Sunday dinner (or lunch, according to where you live). Throughout my sermon I could recognize that my humor was not clicking with her. She asked me a loaded question: "Mr. Wilson do you think Jesus ever laughed?" I answered, "Yes, ma'am, I believe he did. Because Jesus was a perfect human being, he would be bound to laugh at anything truly funny. Yes, Jesus was bearing the burdens of the whole world, but I firmly feel that he laughed at the appropriate times." The lady, rather incensed, countered with: "I just don't think it's right to disgrace the pulpit by telling a joke." The fact is: Billy's godly mother held strongly to the same view.

Years ago I was going to McComb, Mississippi, to preach for a Reverend Hedgepeth, as I recall. En route I kept asking the musicians with me, "I have to come up with a joke or funny story. Help me think of one. I want a good icebreaker for the crowd." None of us could think of anything the slightest bit funny. In the service, I stood up, announced my text, and plunged right into my sermon. My mind was devoid of humor, and that's rare.

After the sermon the preacher virtually hugged my neck. He exulted, "Brother Wilson, I'm thankful to God for a man who doesn't tell a joke from the pulpit. I know you're God's man. I just can't stand these young men who come up from the seminary in New Orleans. They get into the pulpit and tell a lot of jokes. I just tell them to go back and never show up again. I don't want any jokes, and thank God that you don't tell them!" Whew! That's one time I'm grateful my funny bone was out of commission.

As one homespun philosopher put it, "God's bound to have a sense of humor. He made us." With age and experience I have learned that humor can be used at the right time and in the right place.

When Billy first started preaching I accompanied him to a service in Charlotte. He was into his sermon, and I was sitting close to him on the platform. At the time I was hooked on Archbishop Ussher's chronology which emphatically asserted that the world was created in 4004 BC. Billy was wound up, preaching about Christmas and the first coming of Jesus. Mustering all the dynamism he could, Billy preached: "And 2,000 years rolled by, and Christ had not come. And 4,000 years, and no Christ.

And 6,000 years . . . no Jesus yet. And 8,000 . . . " That was more than enough for me. I reached over, kicked his foot with mine, and Billy blurted out, "And then Jesus came!"

There are several kinds of humor, of course. There is the deliberately planned joke or funny story. And that incidental humor which suddenly arises on the spur of the moment. There's the priceless humor created by a "blooper" in speech—*fertility*, for instance.

Or the hilarity caused by an incorrect gesture or action, like the young preacher who was preaching on the text from Revelation, "Behold, I come quickly." He became stuck on that phrase, and out of nervousness he kept leaning on the flimsy pulpit and repeating, "Behold, I come quickly." He finally toppled over the pulpit, the story goes, and fell into the lap of an amply endowed lady. Trying to scramble to his feet he begged the shocked lady's forgiveness. "Please, ma'am, oh, please forgive me. I'm so sorry." To which the lady replied, "That's all right, son. You kept telling me you were coming, and I just didn't have enough sense to get out of the way!"

Most comedians and students of humor claim that there are only seven elements to humor. All humor is based on these elements so that, in a sense, no story is really new. Clergymen are probably the best humorists in America. Many of the stories I've heard comedians use on television I have already been telling for years.

Billy has appeared on numerous comedy shows, such as with Jack Benny, on "Laugh-In," "Hee Haw," regularly with Jack Parr, and with Johnny Carson on the "Tonight Show." He has appeared on nearly all the talk shows like Merv Griffin and Phil Donahue. Until about 1974 he never missed a year appearing at least once or twice on the "Today Show" since its inception on NBC.

He has often appeared on "Good Morning, America," and he and David Hartman have become close friends. In Britain he has been the guest on many shows, including Michael Parkinson and Eamonn Andrews. He has also been interviewed many times by his longtime friend, David Frost.

Once in Australia, David Frost was interviewing him on a show similar to "Solid Gold" in this country. Billy was to appear only five minutes, but Frost became so interested he kept Billy on for the entire hour, with a little music interspersed in between. At the close he asked Billy to lead in prayer. That startled and shocked not only the viewing audience but also the studio personnel. I have rarely seen Billy appear on any of these shows that he did not give a clear witness for Christ, even though he could carry on some foolishness, tell a story about a trip, or discuss a book he had recently read.

One of Billy's close friends was Jack Benny. When Billy preached his last sermon at the Los Angeles Coliseum in 1969, Jack sat by his side. Jack sat up and jokingly asked, "Billy, are you sure they're taking pictures of this crowd? How about letting me take up the collection?" Over a period of time Jack talked Billy into coming on his show. As you may recall, Jack normally had more than one guest. Jack's producers insisted that Billy not be "too religious." I countered with the fact Billy would not appear if he could not be himself, and that meant talking about his Savior who was and is inextricably woven into his life.

Billy and Ruth carried the script to Apple Valley and almost rewrote the whole show. Ruth says to this day that listening to Billy and me in the car en route to the studio,

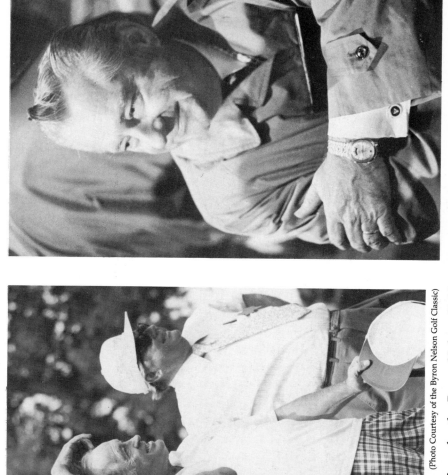

(GW)

T. W. and I joined Bob Hope for the Byron Nelson Golf Classic in 1971.

At Lenoir, NC, after preaching in the rain

Having a good time with Team and Board members in our home at Charlotte

(GW)

The Gerald Gardners in 1972—Michael standing and the twins.

Billy, Ruth, and I with the faculty of the Southern Baptist Seminary in Seoul, Korea

The crowd sitting on the ground at my Pusan, Korea, Crusade.

Speaking at commencement of Trinity College, Dunedin, FL, after receiving an honorary doctorate

Preaching at my Andalusia, AL, Crusade

I love to preach with an open Bible in my hand.

Billy and I fellowshipping with our dear friend, Ethel Waters, at "Grady Wilson Day" in 1974—Dr. Billie Hanks, Jr., "my son in the ministry," engineered that day at his ranch in Sweetwater, TX.

Dr. Sam Russell (left), Wilma (in the plaid), and I on my special day

The same day—left to right: Wilma, yours truly, Connie, Billy, Billie Hanks, Jr., and T. W.

Billie Hanks, Jr., Billy Graham, and I at the Hanks youth ranch

Out preaching in the "Lone Star State" at Sherman, TX—I'm an honorary citizen of Texas.

Jimmy Carter was honorary chairman at the Atlanta Crusade while governor of Georgia. I was behind them.

The fish I caught was that small! No, I was just making a point with the Graham Crusade television producers, Fred Dienert and Walter Bennett, along with Walter's son, Paul.

On the Crusade trail again with Steve Musto and Ted Cornell.

Dr. Walter Smyth and I visited with Prime Minister Rabin (center) of Israel in Tel-Aviv.

Wilma and I fellowshipped with Georgia Representative E. B. Toles and Governor George Busbee at my Rome, Georgia, Crusade.

Billy referring to Wilma and me at one of our BGEA Board meetings

With Randy and Norma Zimmer before a Crusade telecast

Man, was I happy that day!

Gazing at the Cairo skyline and the Nile River from a balcony

Baker James Cauthen presented me a plaque upon completion of my eight years on the Foreign Mission Board of the Southern Baptist Convention.

With my old hunting buddies, Robert Carroll (center) and Cole Means, at the Y-6 Ranch in Valentine, TX

(GW)

Wilma and I hold our two most recent grandchildren, "Lolly" and "K. C." Gardner—Lorianne and Karyn Christine.

Posing with Billy at the 1981 Houston, TX, Crusade—Johnny and June Carter Cash are on the left, and T. W.'s looking over my shoulder.

Always think of me as preaching and sharing the Good News of Jesus Christ!

ad libbing on the script and laughing it up, was ten times funnier than the script itself! She says, "Their humor was spontaneous and the laughter wasn't 'canned.'"

Some evangelicals misunderstand Billy's appearance on this type of show, but it has given him a far wider audience for his Crusades and his own telecasts.

One of Billy's funniest lines was given on the "Tonight Show." Johnny asked him, in essence, "Billy, why would you come on a show with worldly people like us?" Billy cleverly answered, "Johnny, even Jesus ate with publicans and sinners!" That brought the house down, and that was an instance of incidental humor.

Practical joking is another form of often-unappreciated humor, especially if you're on the receiving end. As I've explained, horseplay is part of being a teenage boy, but the Team had done more than its share of retrogressing to teen tactics. Shortly after we were united as a Team, Billy and I discovered aerosol shaving cream, a particular brand that was the first on the market. You not only shaved with it, but it had other juicy uses as well.

While in an early campaign we were sharing a motel room. Billy was out of the room for a while. Guess what awaited him when he returned to rest? A bed of soapy, fluffy, gooey shaving cream. In the meantime, Billy had decided on revenge. I had a favorite hat at the time, and I put it on my pate as I headed out to a local radio station for a broadcast. As I drove to the station I had to admit that there was a funny sensation on top of my head. *Nerves*, I thought.

When I began walking into the studio, the crew and guests were pointing and laughing convulsively. As the watery shaving cream began running down my face and temples, I thought of one word: *Billy!* Billy and I did our part in putting the aerosol-shaving-cream business on the map.

But the premier practical joke in my recollection was pulled by Billy? No. Cliff? No. Bev? No. Tedd? No. Give up?

Prior to our first visit to Korea in 1951, we were winding up our Albuquerque, New Mexico, Crusade. I had an upset stomach and queasiness most of the time. It was probably caused by my almost compulsive overeating. I was also nervous about flying on a plane to Hawaii and then on to war-torn Korea—taking two days and nights in those days at 190 miles per hour.

In downtown Albuquerque I asked the doctor for a mild sedative to help me rest. I lamented, "Doc, is there anything you can give me to help me sleep? I have constant indigestion, and I'm thinking about that bumpy plane flight across the Pacific." I went into hypochondriac detail. The doctor prescribed yellow capsules *which would give me comfort,* I thought.

It's unbelievable all that can happen to me in connection with radio and television stations. I left my yellow capsules in the motel room and went to a radio station to broadcast our "Prayer Time" program. Sweet, adorable, precious, lovable, diminutive, little Ruth Graham went with Billy to a drugstore and bought capsules the same size as mine—and Coleman's mustard, the kind used for mustard plasters. Uh huh. She filled the capsules with mustard plaster and substituted them for my prescription.

I started taking my "prescription" as we were leaving Los Angeles. We were traveling with Dr. Bob Pearce, the founder of World Vision International, and I remarked to him, "Bob, we're going to have time to sleep between Los

Angeles and Honolulu (in those days it took fourteen hours). We might as well take advantage of it, and besides I have this mild sedative that will help us get some rest."

In Los Angeles I had wolfed down a huge steak drowned in potent sauce. Of course, I was taking my capsules, too. After boarding the plane for Honolulu, I generously offered one to Billy and to Bob. They exchanged knowing winks of which I was not aware. "These will help you get some rest, fellows," I advised.

What I didn't know was that Billy had copped my real capsules. He took one instead of the mustard goodie and gave one to Bob. Those guys slept like the proverbial bugs in a rug. I turned. I tossed. My stomach kept burning from the steak sauce—and from the mustard plasters churning in my stomach. I belched repeatedly. Burped, too. I went to the water fountain on the plane several times during the night. I didn't have a moment's sleep.

The following day at the hotel in Honolulu there was spread before us as beautiful a buffet as I have ever laid my eyes on! And I couldn't touch a bite. I never wanted to see food again—for the moment, anyhow. All I wanted was huge quantities of water and milk to ease the burning and churning in my tum tum.

En route to Korea we stopped in Tokyo. A committee had planned a rally and banquet for over a thousand missionaries and chaplains from the U.S. military. Billy was the main speaker. In his opening remarks he turned to me and announced, "You'll notice how bedraggled and bushed Grady Wilson, my associate evangelist, looks. I apologize for his deplorable condition." Then he explained why, confessing to Ruth's practical joke, which wasn't very practical to me. Those chaplains and missionaries must've taken out all of their pent-up emotions on me, laughing tumultuously, as though none of them had ever before heard a joke. All the while I felt like shaking my fist at Billy.

T. W., my older brother and manager of the Montreat office, figures into one of the most uproariously funny incidents in the history of the BGEA. Let me set the stage.

In the late 50s the Team was preparing for the Manila, Philippines, Crusade. I had just concluded a Crusade in the Southern Philippines at Ilo City, where the University of the Philippines is located. I was tuckered out. Billy and part of the team had arrived at Honolulu on the first leg of their journey to Manila. And Billy had come down with a severe case of pneumonia and had to enter the hospital for two weeks. It had become impossible for him to meet his commitment in Manila and I was already there. The Crusade committee called me from Manila. Dr. Grover Tyner, president of the Baptist Seminary in Baguio, had encouraged us about the Crusade.

The committee expressed distress about Billy's not being able to make it. The chairman explained, "Brother Wilson, we've prayed and worked for this Crusade for months—even years. We've spent multiplied thousands of pesos in promotion and preparation; we've promoted the Crusade all over the islands. We're at our wits' end. We don't know what to do. Would you come and conduct the Crusade?" What could I do but answer *yes*?

I traveled on to Manila, and I, along with Cliff, Bev, and Tedd Smith, our pianist, began the Crusade in Rizal Stadium, where the response was tremendous. We were averaging abuot 15,000 in attendance each night and hundreds were stepping out for Christ.

In the meantime . . . after he had partially recovered from the pneumonia and contrary to the doctors' advice, Billy decided he was going home. When he arrived in Los Angeles, a doctor friend urged him to enter the hospital because Billy's fever was 101°, but Billy was determined. "No, I'm going back home to Montreat. My father-in-law, Nelson Bell, is the best doctor around. I want him to look after me." As Billy arrived in Atlanta from the West Coast, Stan Mooneyham from our office there met him and T. W. at the airport. There were tornadoes all over the area with pouring rain and bad visibility, so Billy insisted T. W. rent a car, put pillows in the back seat for him, and drive straight on through to Montreat. Billy was terribly fatigued and sick. His clothes were rumpled and he was a mess. But when you're that sick, you don't care what you look like.

T. W. set out in that rental car with Billy lying in the back seat. It was before the completion of modern I-85, so T. W. had to drive up and down hills and through valleys and around hairpin turns. It was enough to make T. W. sick. He drove as far as he could and came to the town of Commerce, Georgia. It was pouring rain, so he stopped at a country cafe-service station. He went into the service station for directions, also asking the distance to Greenville, South Carolina. Out in the car Billy raised up on one elbow, wiped the sleep from his eyes, spied the rest room, and groggily staggered to it.

Meanwhile, T. W. strode out into the early-evening pouring rain. He climbed into the car and quietly as possible, not wanting to disturb Billy, drove off into the darkness. Faithful chauffeur!

About midnight T. W. was nearly out of gas. He stopped in Oteen, North Carolina, about eighteen miles from Billy's home, to refuel. He decided to wake Billy up, and to his absolute amazement, there was no Billy! He scratched his head in consternation. Frightened, he called Ruth on the phone and nervously asked, "Ruth, have you heard from Billy?"

She replied, "No, I thought he was with you."

While driving from Oteen to Montreat, T. W. began to think that maybe the Rapture had occurred and left Ruth and him behind! As he drove up into the Grahams' front yard, Ruth and her daughter, Anne, were there. Anne was in tears. By this time the police had been informed and were out looking for Billy. Ruth later said that when T. W. called from Oteen he sounded "incoherent."

What had happened? Poor Billy was in the rest room when he heard T. W. rev up the rental car. Desperately he tried to yell but couldn't because of the laryngitis. And in his weakened and embarrassing condition, he couldn't run after the car.

Billy was in a fix. He stumbled into the cafe. His appearance was less than impeccable, and I guess the proprietor was used to all kinds of transients coming through. He inquired, "Is there any way of getting a taxicab to carry me to Greenville? I've been stranded." The man at the cafe gave him the name of an elderly gent who drove a ramshackle cab. Billy tried to call Montreat, but he didn't have the number. It was a new unlisted number that had been in service only a few days, and Billy had handed the number over to T. W.—and T. W. was on the road to Montreat!

Billy reached the long distance operator and whispered into the phone, "Hello, I'm Reverend Billy Graham, and I'm trying to call my home in Montreat, North Carolina, but I don't know my number." The operator answered, "I'm sorry, sir, that's an unlisted number." "I know it's an unlisted number," Billy said. "But it's my phone number. It's my home I want to call. I'm Reverend Billy Graham!" The operator, growing impatient, came back with: "I've heard that line before. Can't you think up a new one?"

"Lady, I'm sick," moaned Billy. "I'm serious. I need to

talk with my wife. I *am* Billy Graham, and my home is in Montreat, North Carolina." The operator did her duty and adamantly stuck to her guns. No phone number. No contact with Ruth and home.

The cabbie arrived. His vehicle did run. Billy introduced himself, "Sir, I'm Billy Graham, and I want a ride to Greenville, South Carolina. How much will it cost?" Fortunately Billy did have his billfold. That in itself seemed a miracle after the previous night's turn of events.

The old cab driver scanned Billy up and down and from side to side. He snapped back, "Yeah, I'm George Washington. Listen, whoever you are, I'll take you there for twenty dollars—cash on the barrelhead, in advance!" Believe it or not, Billy had twenty dollars.

As Billy weakly crawled into the cab, the cabbie began an interrogation. "You a man on the run? A fugitive? The law after you? Have you robbed a bank or something? Huh?" Billy said, "If you can just get me to a certain Holiday Inn in Greenville, you'll find out."

When Billy and the cabbie reached the motel, it was into the wee hours. Fortunately, Bob Green, the manager and our friend, was behind the desk. "Thank goodness, you're here, Mr. Green," Billy sighed. Bob exclaimed, "Billy Graham, what on earth has happened to you? Where'd you come from?" The cabbie almost dropped his teeth. He finally drove off, scratching his head and rubbing his eyes. Sick though he was Billy rented a car and drove on to Montreat.

It wasn't funny then, but the Team still chuckles about that night. There was Billy Graham stranded in a rest room by the side of the road in Commerce, Georgia.

The author of Proverbs was indeed wise when he wrote:

> A merry heart maketh a cheerful countenance: but by sorrow of the heart the spirit is broken. All the days of the afflicted are evil: but he that is of a merry heart hath a continual feast. A merry heart doeth good like a medicine: but a broken spirit drieth the bones (Prov. 15:13,15; 17:22).

And the psalmist sang:

> Then was our mouth filled with laughter, and our tongue with singing: then said they among the heathen, The Lord hath done great things for them (Ps. 126:2).

The Christian who's against laughter should reexamine his heart. After all, Christians are going to rejoice throughout eternity. In one sense they're the only people who have a legitimate reason to laugh for the sheer joy of it.

I've always advised young preachers to cultivate a sense of humor and to look for humorous things along the way. I don't understand how a conscientious preacher—with all of the pressures on him in our neurotic society—can keep his sanity without a sense of humor. Billy, Cliff, Bev, T. W., I, and the Team members have had the knack of laughing at our own foibles and mistakes. Without "comic relief" life would hardly be worth living.

I remember the words to that old poem, "Laugh, and the world laughs with you; weep, and you weep alone." That's partially true. People gravitate to the joyful people and joyful places. That's why, by and large, the fastest-growing churches are those with a joy-filled atmosphere. Most everybody would rather hear "The Hallelujah Chorus" than "The Funeral March."

Yes, "a funny thing happened to me on the way to the Promised Land!"

17
One More Time

Believe it or not, the account of Elijah's challenging the prophets of Baal in 1 Kings 18 had humorous irony to it. Honestly, everytime I read it I laugh out loud because the prophet of God, on that occasion, was sort of a Don Rickles. When the prophets of Baal were howling and screaming for their false god to answer, Elijah gave a chiding side commentary, "Maybe your God is dead. Why don't you shout a little louder?" And those prophets prayed all the louder.

Then Elijah said, "Hey, maybe he's gone for a walk." And those prophets wailed and even cut themselves with knives, the blood flowing out. Still no answer from Baal. The prophet of God was sarcastically laughing, I'm sure. One paraphrase has him asking the question, "Maybe he's gone to answer the call of nature?"

And even the story of little David and the giant Goliath had its humor. Can't you see David trying to put on Saul's heavy armor? It was weighting him down. The helmet probably fell down over his eyes and ears. David couldn't fight for God with impediments on him. If he had worn that armor, the outcome might've been different. And

David put that little slingshot in his hand. Goliath thought the scene was funny—for a while. Goliath taunted and laughed. Goliath chortled, "Look at this little character coming after me with staves!"

When I was five years old Daddy carried me to hear Billy Sunday. Billy Sunday seemed to know that Bible backwards and forwards. One night I was sitting on the front row with my Daddy and Billy Sunday was reading away from the Word, and I saw his Bible was turned upside down. Sunday was quoting from memory but acting like he was reading. So I began to look for the ludicrous early in life.

One of the funniest experiences we've ever had was when Billy Graham and I were coming back from New York City where Billy had appeared on several nationwide telecasts. He was tired and a bit self-conscious of his facial image.

We boarded the plane about 7 in the evening at Newark, New Jersey. Billy was trying to be inconspicuous but he wasn't doing too well at it. He had his hat pulled down low over his eyes, and he was wearing sunglasses, of all things, at night.

Immediately, I recognized John Belk from Charlotte, the president of the Belk's Department Stores in the Southland. They have around 500 stores. I had grown up with John Belk and we are about the same age. John and I had been in the same church and Sunday School class and had been members of Boy Scout Troop 11 at Caldwell Memorial Presbyterian Church.

I grabbed Billy by the coat sleeve. "Just a minute, Billy. You want to speak with John Belk here, the mayor of Charlotte and the president of the Belk Stores." Billy turned around momentarily and said, "Oh yes, how are you, John? It's good to see you."

Across the aisle was a rather portly—actually huge—drunk man. The flight attendant had removed the middle armrest so the man could fill two seats. I found out he was from South Carolina. He reached up tipsily and grabbed me by the hand. He said, "Hello, there, Mayor Belk. I've been one of your admirers for years. Just call me a friend." And he kept pumping my hand and talking loudly.

As passengers were snickering and giggling all over the plane, he didn't stop at that. He leaned across the aisle and slapped Mayor Belk on the shoulder and said, "Hey Buddy, reach over here and shake hands with one of my longtime friends and admirers, John Belk." Mayor Belk looked over and realized that the man was inebriated. Belk went ahead and shook hands with me.

Then the drunk started to sing. The attendant warned him that he was disturbing the people around him with that noise. Sounded like he was in a hog-calling contest. Then after we were airborne he got up and started staggering down the aisle, falling over into the laps of several female passengers back there. The attendant pleaded, "Please sir, return to your seat. You're annoying these ladies." Then he began pounding on the door to the cabin up front. The co-pilot came out and reprimanded the man, asking him to return to his seat. Then Belk said to the man, "Incidentally, the well-known radio and television preacher, Billy Graham, is seated right behind you."

"You don't say?" He turned around, blearily looked Billy in the eye, and asked, "Are you Billy? Are you the Reverend Billy?" Billy was now self-conscious. Billy quietly answered with a nod of the head. And the guy stuck out his hand, "Boy, put her here and shake my hand. Billy, I've been listening to you preach for years and I want to tell you this. Boy, your sermons sure have done me a whole lot of good!" And the man kept mumbling to himself, "Billy Graham, Billy Graham."

When we were somewhere over Philadelphia or Washington, D.C., I leaned over to Billy and whispered, "Wonder what he was before you did him so much good?"

Cliff Barrows has done more than his share to embarrass himself. One time we had conducted a service in McCormick Place in Chicago and we were about to dismiss. Cliff climbed up on the platform and announced, "Now, ladies and gentlemen, drive carefully tonight when you leave. We had a fatal accident that almost happened out there last night." And the crowd roared. A fatal accident that almost happened!

One of the first times we were on nationwide TV Cliff was emceeing the program from Washington, D.C. Cliff was distraught and nervous about being on TV. It was live, and videotape hadn't come into its own. There were three directors in the studio. And each one of them gave Cliff a different signal as to the time he had left. One director held up two fingers, another three, and another one, and Cliff didn't know whether they meant it was one, two, or three fingers—er, minutes—until time to start signing off to end the program.

But when he began to sign off he said, "Now ladies and gentlemen, hope you enjoyed this program. I'm sure we have." And then he said, "I want to speak for the whole *Cliff Barrows* Team." Then he gulped, realizing what he had done. He laughed and said, "Ha, friends," and then he pointed his thumb toward his chest and said, "*I* am Cliff Barrows. What I meant to say was for the entire Billy

Graham Team we're going to wish you well and may God bless you and write us at our headquarters in Minneapolis, Minnesota." And he repeated, "I'm Cliff Barrows—I meant to say for the Billy Graham Team and Billy Graham Evangelistic Association, we wish you good night and God bless you."

Howard Butt, Jr., the well-known Christian businessman from Texas, and others of us were up in the control room. We were convulsed over Cliff's foot-in-the-mouth disease. Each of us was pointing to himself and saying, "I'm Grady Wilson. I'm Bev Shea. I'm Howard Butt."

One evening Bev Shea stood up to sing in a Crusade. He forgot to bring along his little notebook. He keeps the words in the notebook. He got up to sing an old-time favorite. Suddenly he had a mental block, forgot the words, and tried to make up some words. Nearly every professional singer has had to do that at least once. Bev pulled words like these out of the sky somewhere: "God made the birds and the bees and the flowers everywhere." Billy, Cliff, and I couldn't help from laughing—stifled laughing, of course. The people in the audience were enraptured. They didn't seem to notice the difference. Since then Bev seldom goes before a crowd or the cameras without his little notebook, even though he rarely looks at it.

Bev's home was in Western Springs, Illinois, for years (now he has his residence in nearby Glen Ellyn). On Mother's Day in the church at Western Springs—after Billy had moved from the church—the new pastor called on Bev to come out of the congregation and sing a certain hymn. The pastor announced, "Mr. Shea is going to sing this next hymn for us. It's hymn number _____," and the pastor announced the number. "We're going to dedicate this one to all of the expectant mothers." Bev came, the pastor handed him the hymnbook already open to the place, and the hymn was "Our God Is Able to Deliver Thee." Bev sang it reluctantly. As he sang it, the congregation rippled with laughter. When Bev finished the first stanza he left the platform and sat down.

One night in London, a young fellow came up to Bev after the service and commented, "You Yanks sure have a great sense of bigotry and conceit." And Bev asked, "Young man, what do you mean?" The young chap had misunderstood the words of a song Bev had been singing, "It took a miracle to put the stars in place." The kid thought he was singing, "It took America to put the stars in place." Then the young man requested, "I would much prefer that you sing 'How Great *I* Am.' "

Another time in Britain, a kid came looking for Bev to give him an autograph. He had heard somebody call the name of Jerry Beaven, who at the time was one of Billy's top assistants. The kid looked up at Jerry and said, "Bev, can I have your autograph, please?" Beaven paid little attention to the kid and scribbled "Jerry Beaven." That kid looked at the pad and back up to Jerry, "Are you not Bev Shea?" he innocently asked. "No, son, I'm not Bev Shea." The kid immediately handed the pad and pencil back to Jerry and demanded, "Well, then, rub it out, please." In other words, erase it!

In the Republic of Panama we had a Crusade many years ago. A kid from far back in the audience approached me after the benediction. He said, "Mr. Tedd Smith, I sure enjoyed your playing." I didn't want to hurt the kid's feelings, so I just smiled and said, "You're mighty kind." And he asked, "Tedd, could I have your autograph?" Tedd was near me and heard the kid talking. Not to offend the kid, I signed Tedd's name on the piece of paper. I asked,

"Would you also like to have Grady Wilson's autograph?" He would. I handed the pad to Tedd and said, "Grady, give this young man your autograph." Tedd signed "Grady Wilson." Reckon they could get us for forgery?

In London during the 1954 Crusade, we were staying in a hotel near Oxford Street. Paul and Josephine Mickelson were in a room on the top floor. The room had a slanted roof. Paul called the desk and politely explained, "We're too crowded in this room. We need another closet here," not knowing that closet meant "bathroom" in England. The front desk clerk said, "We'll send the hotel engineer up there immediately."

The engineer arrived and asked, "What's the problem?" Josephine said, "We just can't get along with one closet." The engineer was perplexed and replied, "Well, ma'am, it's going to be rather difficult to install another closet in here." Josephine remonstrated, "Sir, we simply cannot get along with one closet." "Madam," he explained, "this is an old building, and we'd have to tear out some bricks and all. We can't install another closet."

He went down the hall and came back with one of those old-fashioned chamber pots, similar to what we used to call "slop jars" in the country. He asked, "Madam, would this accommodate you temporarily?" Paul and Josephine turned all the colors of the rainbow when they found out they wanted a *wardrobe*, not a bathroom.

It wasn't funny at the time, but I remember one evening years ago that Billy was going to introduce a well-known personality. Usually Cliff or I hand Billy the microphone so he can fasten it to his belt and attach it to his lapel or the front of his tie. That night I goofed; Billy limply dropped the mike down to his side. "Ker plunk." The mike fell into the glass of water on the side of the pulpit. I quickly pulled it out, but the mike was dead. All of those people were sitting out there. Fortunately, we had a standby mike. Billy is terribly restricted unless he has a portable mike which enables him to move around and face different areas of the audience, and even turn around and look at the choir behind him.

Humor isn't always in the form of a joke or a ludicrous situation. There is verbal and visible humor—and also unintentional humor in the form of writing. The Billy Graham Evangelistic Association receives several million letters a year. Some heartwarming. Some tragic. Some intimate. Some impersonal. Some downright funny.

One letter was labeled to "Bily Gram, Many Apples, Many Soda." Not bad for phonetics, eh? Years ago we had a letter addressed to "Billy Graham, Oiltown, USA." It was sent to Houston and then finally to the office in Minneapolis.

Through the years Billy or Cliff have signed off with, "Address your letters to Billy Graham, Minneapolis, Minnesota (in recent years the zip has been added). That's all the address you need. Just Billy Graham, Minneapolis, Minnesota." One letter came in from overseas addressed to "Billy Graham. Jest (sic) Billy Graham. That's all the address you need." And bless your heart, Billy got the letter!

Without the gift of humor, I think the entire team would have been less effective in the work of evangelism.

18
If You Can't Stand the Heat

Billy conducted his first revival meeting at the East Palatka Baptist Church, Palatka, Florida, in 1939. He has been holding evangelistic meetings ever since.

The beginning of the Team, according to Billy, was in the fall of 1943 when he and the Western Springs Church began "Songs in the Night" over a 50,000-watt station in Chicago and he invited Bev Shea to become the soloist. Bev actually was the first one to join what has now become known as the Billy Graham Evangelistic Team. Then Billy met Cliff Barrows in 1945, and he and Cliff have been partners ever since. As a matter of fact, in the earlier years of the campaigns they were known as the Billy Graham-Cliff Barrows Campaigns. They were advertised as such, along the lines of Sunday-Rodeheaver or Moody-Sankey campaigns of years past.

Even though T. W. and I had known Billy since 1934, we did not join the Team until later. Billy invited me to the Charlotte evangelistic campaign in 1947, and our evangelistic relationship became permanent with the founding of the Billy Graham Evangelistic Association in 1950.

The Team has always lived under intense pressure. In

the pastorate the minister lives in a fishbowl, especially in a smaller church. The members and the community tend to watch what he and his family do. But that's even more the case with us, since the press hangs on every word—and thousands, even millions, of souls are at stake.

It required several years for the organization to run smoothly. And the public doesn't understand what's going on behind the scenes. I've lived with a nervous stomach. Yes, I believe in the providence of God, and I have faith in the promises of God, but there are periods when I've been shaky about myself, especially the times I've had to step in for Billy at the last minute and preach or appear on the program. After each time I've pinch-hit for him, I've told him, "I never realized what you go through night after night standing before large crowds in these great auditoriums and stadiums. I'm a nervous and physical wreck after each time I've had to substitute for you!"

Here I'm not trying to sound melodramatic, but we've undergone many harrowing experiences and narrow escapes. Most of these were not even reported. It's only because of God's canopy of protection that we're still alive today.

One of the most frightening occurrences was in the famous copper belt of Northern Rhodesia. I had stood at my mother's grave only a few weeks before. When I had prayer with Mother on her death bed, she whispered, "Son, you and Billy and the Team are going to Africa in a few weeks." Mother gasped, "Grady, I'm going home soon, but my prayers will go with you to Africa. I'll no longer be alive, but my prayers will follow you."

Several weeks later I was preaching in the town of Chingola where the soccer stadium was located. The stadium was in the middle of 60,000 natives who lived in little thatched huts. For days terrorists had been circulating information that Billy Graham was a foreign devil there to deceive them. They proclaimed, "Billy Graham represents white American imperialism and capitalism. He doesn't represent the kingdom of God and he has no religious motives for coming here."

Dr. Erasmus, a Baptist minister and pastor in the area, drove me to the stadium at Chingola. When we arrived, over 100 uniformed soldiers had surrounded the facility. They were armed with rifles and bayonets. That's the first time I've ever preached the gospel with six uniformed soldiers on the platform to protect me.

Naturally, I preached a rather short sermon that night, but I had to speak through an interpreter, and that took longer than I would've liked. As I preached I remembered that was the day Prince Charles of Great Britain was born.

As I preached all I could think of was my last visit to Mother: "Son, my prayers will go with you to Africa." I had a strange awareness that the angels of heaven, not merely the soldiers, had surrounded that stadium.

In the middle of my sermon, rocks began to rattle against the bleachers on the far side of the stadium, and the crowd became hysterical with panic. I calmed them, "My friends, the devil is trying to disturb this service, but don't let it bother you. God is here tonight, and he is speaking to our hearts." Then I quickly presented the invitation, and there was a glowing response.

Suddenly red flares burst into the air. Crazy me. I made a statement that the flares were probably a tribute to the birth of Prince Charles. That was a monstrous goof. The populace had intense anti-British sentiment at the time. They thought Britain was trying to force a certain type of rule down their throats through the Central African Federation.

After the service I was told the flares were fired by the military, trying to drive the people back into their villages. Seventeen people were killed that night trying to enter the stadium to assassinate me and our associates. At least that was my impression then.

At the time Billy was in Southern Rhodesia, and the following morning he heard over BBC news from London that those people were killed at the stadium the night before. He was concerned and called me at my hotel. He said, "Thank God, Grady, you're still alive!" I replied, "Yes, brother, by the grace of God. Billy, pray for us tonight because we're going to Bancroft, then tomorrow night down to Lusaka (now Zambia). We've had some threats. In the last couple of days two European women were assaulted and murdered on the highways by guerrillas."

This terrorism has now become a pattern around the world. It makes you realize that the second coming of Christ must be around the corner.

About a week later Billy came to Kitwe for a giant, climactic rally. Hearing from me about all the bloodshed and threats, Billy entered the stadium realizing there was danger. But danger is often exhilarating to Billy. I've seen him and our Team members go places and do things which required a tremendous amount of faith and courage. There was no incident whatsoever. Billy smiled and commented, "Grady, you're pulling my leg. There's no trouble here. The people are friendly and warm." The Lord, I feel, had simply calmed down the people for Billy, but it had been a close call for me.

Another incident comes to mind that happened in Kano, Nigeria, in the northernmost section on the fringes of the Sahara Desert. To this day I guess a big army of camels haul pyramid-shaped bags of peanuts on their backs through Kano. Kano, for that reason, is called "The City of Pyramids."

At that particular time, when the people were trying to gain their freedom from colonial power, there was a strong anti-European feeling. Of course, since I was white they didn't know whether I was an American or a Britisher. In Kano the motel management put me far out on the back row of rooms. It was a long, rambling type of motel. The doors were easily opened there. The porter led me to the rooms right next to the forest. I conjured up visions from old movies I had seen—about the "leopard men" and strange creatures coming out of the night to attack "Bwana."

Kind of shakily I mentioned to the porter that I had read about a murder that occurred in that very motel the night before. A European was murdered.

"What room was he in?" I nervously asked.

"That room, sir," he explained, pointing. "The room right next to yours."

"Really," I commented, endeavoring to appear casual. "Next door to me, eh?"

I turned my light on. I propped two or three chairs against the door. Then I pulled the foot of the bed up against that flimsy door. I tried to sleep that night—but fitfully. The overhead light was on, and there were neither shade nor blind on the window. I later found out that the guerrillas were murdering a white person every third night.

Another time I had a Crusade in Maracaibo, Venezuela, while Joe Blinco of England had one in Caracas. Billy had gone to Caracas to help Joe out. Thirty minutes after Billy left the hotel, terrorists dynamited one whole end of the hotel. Then Billy flew over to be with me in Maracaibo.

One night I was preaching and heard trouble going on outside. When the service was over I heard that the terrorists had gone clear around the parking lot of the stadium and dropped roofing tacks, so all the missionaries who came to the meeting would have to drive over those tacks to leave. The missionaries had parked as close to the stadium as possible because they feared vandalism.

One Southern Baptist missionary found all four of her tires flat. Many other missionaries had flats that night. Fortunately, none of them were harmed.

Billy arrived the following day, and he had accepted an invitation to address a radical political party. They had a Christian leader who believed in evangelism. Billy has often declared that he would go anywhere to preach the gospel if there were no strings attached to his message. Billy and several of our Team members entered the ramshackle building by the back door.

The Christian leader spoke to Billy: "Dr. Graham, excuse me if I take a few minutes for preliminaries. Then I want you to address us." He turned to the group and announced, "Gentlemen, you will pull back your jackets." As they did I noticed that each had a pistol, presumably loaded, in a shoulder holster. The leader then sort of sighed and remarked, "I merely wanted to make sure all of you had your firearms with you. We're expecting trouble soon."

He continued, "Therefore, I'm going to introduce Dr. Graham and his Team and ask Dr. Graham to speak quickly. After that I'm going to ask you, Dr. Graham, and your party to leave by this door." He pointed to a back door. "Get out of here just as soon as you can when I give the signal."

Billy expressed appreciation for being allowed to proclaim the good news of Christ. He began to speak on John 3:16. About that time soldiers pulled up outside in three trucks and began to surround the building. They began to fire rifles and pistols into the building, and the bullets were riddling the front of the building. The leader stood up and apologetically announced, "I'm sorry, Dr. Graham, I must interrupt. Leave now by that door."

Newsweek later carried an account of this incident and reported that Billy was under the table praying the Lord's Prayer when this happened. I can assure you he was not. He was trying to evacuate the building as fast as he could along with the rest of us. Guess who was the first getting to that door? Not Billy Graham, but Grady Wilson himself. I was leading the pack running for the car. Billy was right behind me. About three hours later we drove by the building and it was pock-marked with bullet holes and flak. Every window was shot out. We had gotten out in the nick of time.

I'm not going to dwell on this, but you recognize that we're living in a day of mentally and emotionally disturbed people. Many nondescript people are filled with rage. They take out their pent-up emotions of hatred and disgust by becoming violent—child abusers, rapists, gangsters, and terrorists. No place on earth is safe from violence.

I hate to pick up the newspaper, even though I want to be informed. Hardly a day goes by that we are not faced with gruesome, grisly headlines. People shot, brutally tortured and murdered, blown to bits with bombs or hand grenades.

If only we Christians had imported the love of Christ with an urgency. Even Leon Trotsky, one of the founders of Russian Communism, might have become a Christian. At one time he had lived in New York to work as a tailor.

He once wrote that his neighbors dressed up on Sunday morning, walked out of their houses and apartments with their big, black Bibles to attend church, but none of them ever invited him.

Joseph Stalin once studied for the Russian Orthodox priesthood. I often think of how close Mahatma Gandhi came to becoming a Christian while he was still in South Africa. Because of the color of his skin he was turned away at the door of a church. He never got over that incident. It makes you sick at your stomach to realize the opportunities Christians have squandered.

I'm not dramatizing it, but throughout our ministry we have faced the threat of serious injury or death. That's why Billy can't get around as freely as he once did. He's received numerous threats on his life. He is constantly being informed by police or the FBI, or receiving letters that are immediately turned over to the FBI and the local police.

Billy and the Team members have received more than our share of hate mail and malicious phone calls. One minister in particular hated me with a passion. He confronted me at a Crusade and coldly declared, "Mr. Wilson, I have hated you for years. I simply hate the mention of your name." From his acquaintances and even members of his congregation I had tried to find out why.

So, I asked imploringly, "Now why is it you have hated me over these years?" He answered, "I don't know. I can't put my hands on it. And I can't point out any particular reason." Finally I asked him to forgive me if I had ever offended him. And he requested my forgiveness, and I pray that he no longer hates me.

We could fill a mail room with letters that have told us where to go (even though we're not going there!).

Once in Philadelphia a fellow came to the house phone

at the hotel and called Billy. When Billy answered, the man spat out, "Drop dead!" Then the spiteful guy hung up. In a few seconds he called back and yelled into the receiver, "Mr. Graham, you go to h—!" He called again and threatened, "Mr. Graham, some of us are going to kill you before midnight tonight." The hotel management moved Billy to an unregistered room, and T. W. and I got rooms nearby. The police warned us not to leave him unattended and not to let him travel by himself. They had a lengthy list of subversive groups who could cause considerable trouble.

Our board of directors felt that we ought to have every precaution to protect the lives of Billy and his family. Ruth told Billy, "Bill, the Bible unmistakably teaches that the angels of the Lord encamp 'round about those who trust in and fear him. I don't believe any person on earth can ever harm even one hair of your head without God's permission." Anyhow, our board adopted precautionary measures to protect the Graham's safety and well-being.

Ruth has the courage of a modern-day Daniel. One deranged man drove his Cadillac up to Billy's home and literally broke the door down before Ruth had a chance to answer his knocks. There stood Ruth with the girls.

The man announced, "I'm the Messiah, and I've come here to talk with your husband." Without flinching Ruth replied, "Well, sir, if you're the Messiah, why did you break down my door? Why didn't you just walk right through the wall?"

Disarmed by Ruth's cool, the man said, "I guess you've made a point there, Mrs. Graham. But if I can't see your husband now, I'm going to end my life." Ruth tried to counsel with him. She quoted comforting passages from the Word of God. The man became huffy and drove away with a screech of tires. He pulled up to the lake at

Montreat, put the car in gear, threw his wristwatch and billfold into the lake, and then removed the brake. He watched his expensive car sink. The authorities picked him up, and Ruth never filed charges. To the best of our knowledge the man never committed suicide.

I remember when Billy received from the San Diego area a deranged and vicious letter. In macabre language the letter described what that person intended to do to Ruth and the children. I cannot repeat the details here, for they are too gruesome. The Post Office Department and the FBI somehow traced that letter to an extremely mentally deranged person. I have no idea what happened in that person's case.

The BGEA receives several million letters each year, most of them good, thanking Billy for preaching the gospel and ministering, along with Cliff and Bev and the others. Each letter is carefully answered.

Everyday perils exist for every human being. People are killed slipping on a wet floor in the bathroom. They trip and fall and hit their heads. They are often involved in freak accidents.

Years ago in South America we were coming in on a DC-7. While landing the plane blew a tire, and the plane spun completely around in a circle before coming to a stop. They ushered us off in a hurry.

We have flown in all types of aircraft night and day— from old-fashioned prop planes to the giant 747s. And in the old days, before modern radar equipment, there was always the danger of unexpected thunderstorms. Most of the planes back then were DC-3s which sometimes had to plow right through those thunderstorms. Today, even though the cabins of jets are pressurized, people with circulatory problems are sometimes bothered.

Billy once had to undergo a forced landing in an open

field at four in the morning during a snowstorm. It happened in Western Canada back in the 40s. The plane practically ran out of fuel. It was a miracle he survived. That is a long story within itself.

Years ago when we used to cross the Atlantic by ship we had a number of interesting experiences. Once our ship was caught in a perilous hurricane while in the North Atlantic. We were returning from Europe, and the crew had to bolt, screw, chain, nail, or tie down all of the furnishings. You would've thought we were on a battleship. The winds at sea were over 100 MPH. Wilma was sick nearly unto death and falling all over the place. Wilma had always been afraid of the water and boats, and that hurricane certainly didn't help matters.

I have already mentioned the isolation and loneliness of being thousands of miles away from your family. Even though you're surrounded by the Team and leaders in the Crusades, there's still no place like home. Yet, those periods of isolation in a hotel room give me time for meditation, reading the Scriptures, and prayer, even though I am lonely for my family. Of course, now that I'm not traveling far away as much, Wilma is often with me in Billy's Crusades and my own campaigns. That's why I'm so sympathetic with people who are lonely.

Loneliness can sometimes be a bereft feeling, even though you know the Lord is there with you in the hotel room. There is an indescribable loneliness, even though you are aware the Lord's will is being done. If God hadn't called me to this ministry, I never would've become a traveling man.

I remember being in Perth, Australia, for three weeks. If you'll pinpoint Charlotte, North Carolina, and Perth on the map, you'll discover that they're 10,000 miles apart—almost halfway around the world from each other. We have always had family devotions with Bible reading and prayer, and I'd try to conduct my devotions with Wilma and the girls, even though those miles separated us.

I'd use my little tape recorder. I'd record our devotions and then send them to the family. "Girls, gather by Mother now. I'm going to read The Twenty-third Psalm. Then let's all kneel and have prayer together." Fortunately, by special air mail it would reach them within three or four days.

That loneliness and being away are probably the worst difficulties we have suffered. Many people see only the so-called glamour of the Crusade, the excitement, the attention from the press and the public, and the hundreds of inquirers streaming down the aisles. But being an itinerant evangelist such as I, especially when I am away from the main Team conducting my own meetings, has proven lonely at times.

Billy admits that I make friends easily and quickly, many of them lasting, lifelong friends. All across the world God has given me prayerful, loving, supportive friends—genuine friends who truly care about Wilma, Nancy Carol, Connie, and me. I mention a number of them in the pages of this book. For fear of hurting feelings I must be careful in giving names. If it were possible I would publish a roll call of friends here, but then I could leave out a dear soul who has blessed me personally and ministry-wise . . . and that would hurt.

Praise the Lord that Wilma and Connie Jane often accompany me on the Crusades in which I'm involved.

Throughout these pages I have referred to the misunderstandings by the media—magazines, newspapers, radio, television. I'll never forget when Billy and the Team were making the New England Tour, and Billy woke up one morning with a sore throat. He said, "Grady, I can't take the press conference this morning. You'll have to go down and meet the press for me. Be sure to be brief and be sure to be careful. Tell them I have a sore throat, and I'm going to rest up today on doctor's orders, hoping to preach tonight."

Determined to be brief and to be careful, I went down to the conference. "Gentlemen," I announced, "I'm sorry Mr. Graham can't be here this morning. He has a sore throat."

One of the reporters inquired, "Mr. Wilson, have any doctors ever advised him to slow down?" To which I *briefly* answered, "Yes sir." He continued, "Well, do you think he can continue to carry on at this rapid pace? He's been speaking seven or eight times a day." My answer: "No sir, not forever." *Brief and cautious,* I thought.

Can you imagine the headlines that came out that afternoon in big, bold, boxcar letters? BILLY GRAHAM CARRIES ON IN SPITE OF DEATH PERILS. I never mentioned death, not even the threat of death. I merely stated that he could not continually carry on at that pace. I declared, "He has a sore throat and must rest today."

When Billy saw the paper he asked me, "What did you say to those reporters?" I told him. Fortunately, I had a recording of it. For years now we have recorded every press conference. I guess a certain politician wishes he'd never seen a recording machine. It's easy to be misquoted, misunderstood, or misrepresented.

By the way, it is certainly not always the fault of the press. Interestingly, Billy has rarely been misquoted in the American press. He has a high regard for the American media and press. He feels that our ministry would have

been greatly limited had it not been for the press' help—
and he is eternally grateful to them. He is also a strong
believer in freedom of the press.

To show how you can be misrepresented, I offer this
example. Before we left for England in 1954 a friendly
Anglican bishop had come to New York and was interviewed. One of the reporters asked, "Bishop, by the way,
do you plan to visit any night clubs while you're in New
York City?" Not wanting to provoke the American press
the Bishop inquired, "Are there any night clubs in New
York?" The press corps answered, "Yes, there are many."
The following morning the papers reported, "One of the
first questions asked by the Bishop was, 'Are there any
night clubs here?'"

As I record in another chapter, we were met by a few
sensation-hunting reporters when we reached England.
They had caught wind of the Bishop's question which was
quoted out of context.

A noted British columnist was Cassandra (William
Conner). He was renowned for his acid and caustic, but
clever, writing. He wrote about a group of "American
circus performers" having arrived in England. He warned
the populace to beware of us, those American circus
performers and entertainers. He even surmised that
George Beverly Shea was a girl because of the name
Beverly, which is common in the U.S. There are also
males named Joyce, Shirley, and even one named Sue,
according to Johnny Cash. Cassandra referred to Cliff
Barrows as having a glorified plumbing arsenal with him,
because Cliff played the trombone at the time. He rarely
plays it now. In fact he used to lead singing with that
trombone in hand.

A number of sharp English columnists wrote critical
articles about us. All across the Isles other journalists

joined in the cacophony of criticism.

After we had been in London's Harringay Arena for only three weeks, Cassandra called Billy and posed the question, "How would you like to meet a sinner on his own grounds?" Billy met Cassandra in a London pub where Billy drank a glass of orange juice and Cassandra had a beer. Cassandra became our friend and wrote about it; the news was plastered all over the globe.

Cassandra wrote that Billy was simple, down-to-earth, unvarnished, and dedicated. He further opined, "I went away from that pub with a lump in my throat and a prayer in my heart that I might have a portion of what Billy possessed."

Another problem we have always faced is the time bind. There is the constant demand for your appearance. Go here. Go there. Rush. Hurry. Expedite. Meet the deadline. Catch the plane. Hurry for the cab.

All of the Team members have had to cut out many appearances which have little to do with evangelism. Billy has had his share of ribbon cuttings, the dedication of buildings, and the like, events which are commendable in themselves. Many of these have opened the doors for evangelism later.

Billy still accepts a number of major conventions each year, like the Real Estate Convention, the Bankers Association, the legal profession's organization, the Young Presidents Organization, the National Chamber of Commerce, and others. In recent years, however, he and the Team have accepted such only rarely. I guess Billy has turned down ten honorary degrees, awards, and honors for every one he's ever accepted. Even if I filled all of my invitations, I would still have to clone nine other Grady B. Wilsons.

There have been periods in my ministry when I've had

a feeling of sheer pressure. In those early days I had as many as eight or nine engagements in a day. I've addressed as many as four breakfasts in one morning. It's a problem traffic-wise and transportation-wise. I don't know whether I could make permanent residence in New York, Los Angeles, or another metropolis. I've traveled in tight situations by almost every conceivable means of transportation—subway, car, bus, train, ski lift, private plane, rickshaw, wagon, cart, walking, sometimes running (prior to my heart attacks). All of that builds up your nervous tension. No, I've never jumped over luggage like O. J. Simpson used to on those commercials, but it's a wonder.

Then there's the menace of health problems, but they're more severe when you operate under pressurized conditions. For years the doctors had warned me about my health, but I wouldn't listen. And I was about to let all of that pressure and strain catch up with me.

19
The Valley of the Shadow

Steaks with plenty of fat. Copious amounts of gravy. Macaroni and cheese running with butter. Sour cream on my baked potatoes. Rich dressings on my salads. Ample amounts of peanuts and pecans. Layer cakes thick with calory-laden icings and frostings. A constant round of snack foods, washed down with soft drinks. I was invited to thousands of meals in homes where the lady of the house insisted I eat.

No, I wasn't really living to eat, but you'd have thought it. Through the never-ending round of demands on my time, most of which I was trying to fill, I eventually became a compulsive eater of sorts. I excused myself by alibiing that, amid a killing schedule, I had to "keep up my strength." In my younger days I was thin, and some of my skinny pictures are in this book.

It was in the late 1970s, and for at least seven or eight years the doctors had warned me about my health. My Christian friend, Dr. Carl Morelock of the Mayo Clinic, had counseled me, "Grady, you're committing suicide day by day. You're heading toward a stroke or a coronary. Your weight is up to 235 pounds. On your five-foot-nine-inch frame you're carrying around sixty-five or seventy extra pounds. You're going to have to slow down, eat sensibly, exercise, and lose that weight!" I heard those medical homilies, but I didn't heed them.

Dr. Morelock discovered that I had already developed borderline diabetes. Some doctors didn't call it that, but they did at Mayo. Later on, I was to develop a more serious form of diabetes.

Since I was experiencing periodic pains in my chest, shortness of breath, and a general tiredness, some of my friends had begged me to enter the Joslin Clinic in Boston. I had just come back from one of my own meetings and was preparing to leave for the Las Vegas Crusade. I talked with Billy on the phone and commented, "I'm suffering these pains in my chest. And I think I'm having more diabetic problems."

Concerned as always, Billy advised, "Grady, don't come out here to Las Vegas. Go either to the Joslin Clinic or Mayo Clinic." Billy was beginning to suspect that my main problem was with my heart. For the first time, he wasn't so sure that I should enter Joslin Clinic because it specializes in diabetes. My good friend, Jim Roberts, had wanted me to check in there. Jim had been a leading executive with the New England Life Insurance Company.

My doctors knew the effects of unattended diabetes, which can cause gangrene in the lower body because of poor circulation. Many diabetics have lost feet, even legs, and eventually died. If left unchecked it can blind a person.

Finally, I checked into Joslin but didn't stay long enough. They asked me to remain another week, but I left there for Miami where I was to lead a tour of Christian friends to the Caribbean. Dr. Roy Gustafson and I would conduct the services.

I felt duty-bound to make that cruise. Rather than relaxing me, it became an extra strain. All of the time I was having heart problems, and I didn't recognize them, even though the clinicians diagnosed me as having an enlarged heart.

Almost daily, I was having pains in my chest. I was having shortness of breath. I had never smoked except for a few cigarettes when I was a teenager. Like most people with impending heart failure, I didn't want to recognize the signs—or wanted to push them into the back of my mind, telling myself, *It's OK. It's merely the overwork and a strain.* I thought perhaps it was the recurrence of a stomach ulcer.

So, I was back at my retreat on the Santee-Cooper. Like a moron, I was breaking down a cord and a half of wood that I had cut with a chain saw. I was vigorously cutting the wood into smaller pieces, using a godevil, a combination ax and sledge hammer. I hadn't done that kind of exercise in years. It was enough to make even Paul Bunyan faint. I split up all of that wood, and the next morning a friend of mine, Red Pendergrass, came by and asked me to go bird hunting with him. We walked for at least five miles while we hunted. Finally, I was pooped. Gasping for breath, I leaned against a tree.

Red commented, "Grady, you'll have to set your own pace if I'm going too fast for you." Now Red is a physical giant who's in good shape the year round. I came in that night downright sick. Red invited me over to his house for dinner (they call it supper down there), and I declined apologetically. Can you imagine Grady Wilson turning down a scrumptious, free meal?

No sooner had I reached the cabin that a friend from

Manning called. His wife was in the hospital at Charleston, over a sixty-mile drive. He asked, "Grady, please go to the Roper Hospital there. They gave us word that she's dying with cancer." Even though I felt terrible, I visited her in Charleston.

I read the Scriptures, had prayer with her, and she began to give me a radiant testimony about what Christ meant to her. She testified, "Grady, it may be sooner than I think that I'll be face to face with Christ."

While in the room I felt stabbing chest pains. I asked her if she had any indigestion medicine. So, I headed home with those pains, and no amount of indigestion medicine seemed to help. The pains were fierce, and the next morning John Richburg came over with a crew of men to burn my leaves. We had to watch carefully for fear that the fire would spread.

I hadn't had breakfast—didn't feel like it. I came into the cabin and fell flat on the floor. I was out like a light, and when I woke up I crawled into the bedroom.

I was praying all the while, "Lord, I don't know what's happening, but my life's in your hands. Help me, Lord. See me through this if it's your plan."

Then John came around to the bedroom window and hollered, "Grady, I've got to leave for another job." He was walking to his pickup truck. He was going off and leaving his crew behind. Weak as a kitten, I tried to yell through an open window, "John, come here quick. John, I'm deathly sick. I'd better go to the hospital immediately." He hastily called Dr. A. C. Bozard in Manning.

Fortunately, I had those little nitroglycerin tablets handy. I had taken six of those, and they hadn't helped. Richburg—and I hope they won't give him a ticket after the fact—drove into Manning at 100 miles an hour. Both of us were scared, too, because the gas gauge was on empty.

He screeched right up to the emergency entrance. Dr. Bozard and the emergency crew met us at the entrance. They carried me from the car to the stretcher and rolled me in. I blacked out about that time. For many hours I lost awareness of anything, and I didn't wake up until that night.

Wilma had arrived about three or four that afternoon. Billy rushed straight from Montreat with T. W., my brother. When I woke up that night, I looked through foggy vision and saw Billy. He was holding my hand in his. I remembered nothing after it happened, but Billy later reported that I blubbered, "Billy, turn loose of my hand so I can hold Wilma's." Of course, I've always felt that Wilma was prettier than Billy! I kept trying to reach out and hold somebody's hand. I also kept knocking the tubes out of my nostrils.

Twice, Dr. Bozard told Wilma out in the hall, "There's no human way possible for Grady to pull through. There's a possibility that he's not going to make it. We're going to do everything we can to pull him through, but we've had many men who've come here and haven't made it, and they were in far better condition than your husband." My, he certainly believed in being candid and honest!

In careful examination later on, they found that 30 percent of my heart muscles were dead from my attack.

The doctors repeatedly commented that my living was a "miracle." I now realize it was. My recuperation period was long. The doctors almost scared me to death, explaining my regimen—diet, less pressure, less excitement, and light exercise later on.

October 12, 1978: I had a second massive attack. It was in the wee hours of the morning. Once again, the pains in my chest were excruciating. Wilma gave me the first nitroglycerin tablet—and then I took five more to no avail. I finally fell asleep for about fifteen minutes, but the intense spasms woke me up. We arrived by ambulance at the Manning Hospital. Dr. Roberts, an intern from the University of South Carolina Med School, was there. Dr. Bozard had died three weeks after he had released me from the hospital. He had a cottage out near my cabin. On Saturday morning he was out working in his garden and keeled over with a cerebral hemorrhage. A few days later, he was gone. In a real sense, he was the doctor responsible for pulling me through in March of 1977.

Incidentally, another doctor that had assisted Dr. Bozard, Dr. Jackson, was tragically killed while piloting his private plane en route to a medical aviators' convention.

Dr. Roberts rode with me to the Roper Hospital in Charleston. Dr. Peter Hairston from Johns Hopkins, who had established himself as one of the expert cardiovascular surgeons in the Southeast, was standing by. Many friends wondered why I didn't go somewhere else, but time was of the essence.

First, they had to give me an angiogram, where they shoot iodine dye into the circulatory system. One of my doctors, Dr. Grossman, remarked, "I hate to lose one of my patients at the beginning of the Jewish New Year. It's dangerous for you to undergo this angiogram, because you're allergic to penicillin, iodine, shrimp, and lobster."

He used rather strong language and burst out with, "This scares the devil out of me!" I retorted with, "Well, doctor, I'm kind of glad that something scares the devil out of you, 'cause I don't want anyone working on me if he has the devil in him!"

He momentarily smiled, but then became grim. "If you

pull through this test, you'll have to have some help from upstairs." I commented, "Dr. Grossman, see all those cards, letters, and cablegrams over there. They represent the prayers of thousands of my Christian friends from all over the world. I believe that help'll come through."

If you've never experienced an angiogram, there's more to it than a simple test. You feel the heat from the dye spreading from the bottom on up to the top of your body. As the test moved along, Dr. Grossman commented, "I think we've found all of the blockage, Reverend. But do you want to go all the way into the arteries of your neck and brain?" (He called it an arteriogram.) "Shoot the works, Doc," I answered.

As Dr. Grossman prepared to send the dye clear into my brain, I thought about my concern before submitting to these procedures. I had previously called Dr. Jim Cain from Texas, a devout Christian, who had served as President Lyndon Johnson's physician at the White House. Dr. Cain advised me to go ahead with these tests, along with bypass surgery if necessary.

Billy had called Dr. Cain from Warsaw, Poland, that very morning. Even though nervous from the tests and the prospect of surgery, I was praying for the Polish Crusades as I lay on that table.

These were Dr. Cain's reassuring words, "Grady, go ahead with everything. My wife, Ida May, and I will be praying for you." All of a sudden the sweet peace of God had flooded over my soul. I had felt contentment, complete release, and relief.

As I lay there, I told Dr. Grossman, "I'm ready to stay. I'm ready to go. The good Lord will see me through, or else he'll call me home." And I meditated on Paul's prison testimony to the Philippians:

> For me to live is Christ, and to die is gain. . . . For I am
> in a strait betwixt two, having desire to depart, and to be
> with Christ; which is far better (Phil. 1:21,23).

Praise the Lord! No blockage was found in my brain. My friends would have argued otherwise! For years they thought I had a block of concrete between my ears!

There was a seventy-five-year-old man across the hall. He balked about having these dye tests, but when he found that Brother Grady was going through with it, he consented.

There were no side-effects from the tests, and I was immediately prepped for surgery. And I was "prayed up," as the expression goes. *Ready to go or ready to stay.* I thought of that old hymn, "Ready." I mused, *And that has to be the everyday attitude of the Christian. Ready for any contingency, emergency, or eventuality.*

I lay on that operating table for many hours. Dr. Hairston, the surgeon in charge, was supposed to get married that night at 7 o'clock. He was able to arrive at the church by 8:30, and he postponed his departure for the honeymoon to check back with me.

The following morning, Dr. Hairston removed the balloon they had inserted into my heart in order to perform the four-way bypass. I was perfectly conscious, and they didn't give me any sedative as they removed that balloon from my throat. I've heard about people who have swallowed fire and swords—but a balloon?

Surprisingly, they kept me in the hospital only one week as I recuperated. All of the doctors testified that: (1) It was a miracle I survived the first attack in March of 1977. (2) It was a miracle that I lived through the second one in October of 1978. (3) It was a miracle that I pulled through the four-way bypass, spending about nine hours in surgery.

It was miraculous. Why did I live? Was it because I'm a servant of the Lord? Servants of the Lord die every day. Was it because I was deserving? Certainly not.

I thought about all of those hymns and songs of the faith:

> Naught of good that I have done,
> Nothing but the blood of Jesus.

> Amazing grace, how sweet the sound,
> That saved a wretch like me.

> Alas! and did my Saviour bleed?
> And did my Sovereign die?
> Would He devote that sacred head
> For such a worm as I?

They've changed it to "sinners such as I," but I prefer the old-fashioned version.

> In my hand no price I bring,
> Simply to thy cross I cling.

Why did I survive? It was simply that the Heavenly Father still had a work for me to do.

So, I was going home after a week. Wilma was advised by the doctors to stop every few miles and let me walk around the car to stir up my circulation. The doctors laid down the law—down to the minutest detail including, "Don't cross your legs."

They advised me to restrain myself. I was used to doing everything "whole hog"—whether it was preaching, playing golf, driving my car, eating, or sleeping. Now, when I preach it's in a lower key. I used to rear back and scream from time to time. You've heard the story about the preacher's sermon notes where they found scribbled in his own handwriting: "Weak point. Scream like the mischief." I can't fortify those weak points anymore, so that probably makes for better preaching. Also, I can't preach lengthy messages anymore—thirty minutes is about my limit. The great Southern Baptist pulpiteer, Dr. Herschel H. Hobbs, found that out after his heart attack. He declared that he could preach more effective sermons in twenty minutes than he previously could in forty.

Since my surgery, I must have a built-in alarm system. If I preach beyond thirty minutes, my head starts beating like a trip hammer and I become faint. That doesn't bother me if I'm teaching a Sunday School class or leading a discussion in a small group. It's the pressure of speaking to a large crowd.

As my health has improved, I have gradually stepped up my pace. I have trimmed off the excess weight, even though I still have slight "love handles" around my waist. Now I'm in no more than five or six of Billy's Crusades a year, and I accept a few Crusades of my own. But there is tremendous tension merely sitting on the platform at a Crusade where God is doing such a mighty work. It does pump blood; it does accelerate the heart; it causes excitement to rush through your entire being, physically, emotionally, and spiritually.

The doctors have also warned me against taking too many long jet flights where there is "jet lag" involved. I have a rigid diet program, and I'll have to stay with it the rest of my life. Except during bad weather, I walk at least two miles or more a day.

Until my heart surgery I didn't think it wise for a clergyman to have an unlisted phone, but because of my health I've had to install unlisted numbers for Charlotte and the Santee-Cooper cabin.

"Darling," I said to Wilma, "I just can't subject you to this any longer." Of course, many people must have my number—members of the Team, long-time friends, and members of the Board of the BGEA. Now I average around twenty to thirty calls a day. Most of the time Wilma or Connie answer, and they help manage the calls. When I'm down at the cabin, which is about 100 miles south of Charlotte, I have about that many, but I normally go there without undue publicity.

People often ask me, "What are your plans for your remaining years?" I'm aware that some people may live thirty or forty years after a heart attack. I'd like to do that if God is willing. I guess you could sum it up with these words of Redd Harper's song, "Each Step of the Way."

> I'm following Jesus One step at a time,
> I live for the moment In His love divine.
> Why think of tomorrow? Just live for today,
> I'm following Jesus each step of the way.[1]

Upon waking up I thank God every morning, more so than ever before. I thank him for the light of a new day and another night's rest. I remember those heart attacks and the postoperative feelings. I knew what it was to spend anxious, sleepless nights because of the pain and the shortness of breath, feeling like you're smothering or strangling to death.

I am painfully aware that people are sinning if they take God's ordinary blessings for granted. Have you ever thanked God for being able to breath without choking? Yes, this is indelicate, but have you ever thanked him for being able to use the bathroom? That's no joking matter to those who've had their health but are now losing it. Thank God. Praise him for the little things, for they look large when you lose them.

Now that I have stared death squarely in the face on two occasions, life means more to me than ever: blades of grass; the fall of a golden leaf; a sparrow outside the window; a warm summer breeze; the glory of a snowflake or the smiling face of a child. Every second is of eternal significance and magnitude. I recognize that every person I come in contact with is a candidate for the kingdom of God—busboys, deliverymen, secretaries, people from all walks of life.

And I do what I can to influence each person for Jesus Christ. Maybe it's easier for me than some, because I have that "gift of gab"—that's the expression the lady used many years ago.

And I'm more urgent in personal evangelism, winning people to Christ. I have to do it low-key, of course. Many of my friends, since I've had my heart condition, have been buried. I've conducted their funerals. I've consoled their families. When I was released from the hospital the last time, I called the doctor and asked him if it were wise for me to conduct the funerals of close friends. He advised me not to do it because it would cause extra emotional strain.

I still attend funerals—sometimes preach them—but I'll never forget what the late President Lyndon Johnson told me: "I attended Tennessee Governor Buford Ellington's funeral, and that set off another heart attack for me. I'll never attend another man's funeral but my own." And he didn't. As far as I know, that was the last funeral Johnson ever attended—but his own. Johnson had a sense of death. His father, I understand, had died around the age of 62 or 63. Johnson died at 65, as he had predicted. Now I'm not going to predict my decease. I'm going to live as long as the Lord will let me.

I've had tremendous joy contacting my dear friends all over the country. I am in many of the Billy Graham Crusades. From time to time I conduct Crusades of my own.

So I have an expanded ministry now, not as fast-paced, but fully as meaningful. During my illnesses—no exaggeration—I have received thousands of letters from people who have undergone the same problems. I have tried to answer those letters with the help of my secretary (and daughter), Connie, and some other secretarial assistance from BGEA.

These people have phlebitis, heart trouble, diabetes, and cardiovascular diseases. They've heard of my bout with diabetes and heart disease. They realize that I've pulled through only through the grace of God. Many have written to say, "I'm shaky, Brother Wilson. I'm facing the prospects of open heart surgery." I can help them by saying, "Maybe all is not lost. You can pull through, God willing, and you may have a fairly normal life." I now have the ministry of comfort and encouragement. I can be a "Barnabas" (meaning "encourager") to them.

When I was younger and healthier I tried to sympathize—and emphathize—with the ill. I couldn't do it like I can today. I've been there. I'm a walking miracle, because I walked twice through the "valley of the shadow of death." I could almost feel the death angel's presence.

That's why I can now read the Twenty-third Psalm with more joy and exuberance.

> Yea, though I walk through the valley of the shadow of death, I will fear no evil: for thou art with me; thy rod and thy staff, they comfort me.

Listen, I can also caution younger people, especially in the service of God, to take care of their health. Even though I preached that our bodies are the "temples" of the Holy Spirit, I failed to put that into practice. I explain to people who'll listen, "I was on the college weightlifting team. I was in excellent condition. But I stopped my weightlifting and started *pushing my weight around*. For a long time, about the only thing I lifted was a barbecued rib or a chocolate eclair.

I've always loved that old song, "Sweeter Than the Day Before" by Robert C. Loveless. It partly goes:

> Every day with Jesus
>   Is sweeter than the day before.
> Every day with Jesus,
>   I love Him more and more.
> Jesus saves and keeps me,
>   And He's the one I'm living for.
> Every day with Jesus
>   Is sweeter than the day before.[2]

And every precious day is sweeter. All of us should have zest for life. The Christian should exult in every new day.

Now I love life far more than I can put into words— because I have walked through the valley of the shadow of death, and God has allowed me to return to the land of the living!

> Only one life, 'Twill soon be past;
> Only what's done for Christ will last!

20
The Real Billy Graham

Most of you remember the top-rated TV show of several years ago, "The Tell the Truth." After the panel tried to guess which of the three guests was the real whoever, Emcee Bud Collier would dramatically announce, "Will the real (and he used the name) please stand up?"

Interviewers have probably asked me one question more than all others. "What kind of person is Billy Graham?" And they have branched out to similar questions: "What makes him tick? Is he easy to work with? What are his faults? Why have you stuck with him, and vice versa, all these years? Do you ever disagree with each other? What do the other Team members think of him?"

In other words, they actually want to learn who Billy Graham is away from the Crusade crowds, the klieg lights, the interviews with the press, the public appearances.

The fact is: Billy Graham is the same person all the time. There is no coverup or facade. Billy is Billy wherever he is, preaching to multiplied thousands, jogging on a path near his home in Montreat, riding horseback, playing golf, swimming, preparing a sermon, or eating lunch with his lovely wife, Ruth.

Earlier in this book I have written about how the media has sometime salivated for even a hint of scandal in Billy's life or the lives of his Team members. Those days of intense probing are now virtually gone.

Out of fairness I have referred to a few of Billy's peculiarities and dislikes. When we first started out we had to learn the hard way. Most of us have to learn that way, if we learn at all—right? In those early days, when the BGEA was being launched, we made a number of goofs. They were largely due to lack of experience and planning, or downright inefficient methods.

Outside of sins against God and man, Billy often becomes irritated at inefficiency. He also has a phobia of tardiness. If he has an appointment he always tries to arrive a few minutes ahead of time, but he doesn't mind having to wait on the other person as much as having that person wait on him. Billy wants efficiency because he works for the most efficient Employer of them all. Now most of the hiring for the Association is done out of the home office in Minneapolis, and efficiency has high priority throughout. Only a few people have been released from the Association. There had to be serious reasons like repeated inefficiency.

When Billy was sixteen and selling Fuller Brushes in South Carolina, we were eating in a boarding house where room and board cost one dollar a day. The waitress served Billy a biscuit with a burnt place in the crust. Billy kidded the waitress and remarked, "This looks like a fly!" The waitress had been a little flirtatious. Laughingly, Billy picked up the biscuit and threw it back into the kitchen toward the waitress.

Today Billy does have a few peculiarities. When at home he likes to live in blue jeans (not actually that peculiar now). Instead of having a good meal that perhaps Ruth has planned for him, he often goes to the pantry and grabs a can of vienna sausages and a can of pork and beans. I suppose that comes from eating in hotels and restaurants most of the time. He likes pick-up meals where he can choose impromptu from the refrigerator or pantry.

Outside he has always been a more conservative dresser than most of the Team. He favors dark clothes. For example, he never wears brown. I think this may be because he would then have to carry brown shoes, ties, and the like to coordinate with the suit—and he likes to travel lighter than that. He does carry too many bags with him when he goes, which are usually full of books he has every good intention of reading and studying—but he doesn't always get around to it.

In earlier days I was a careless dresser, but in recent years I have probably become more fashionable in my tastes than Billy and some of the other Team members.

I have also referred to several of Billy's characteristics— the fact that he is a loyal and trusted friend and that he never forgets a friend or a good deed. Every associate of his, every close friend would have to admit that Billy is an inspiration to others. Being with him is an uplifting experience. Some people low-rate you. They pull you down. You become downtrodden and depressed in their presence. Billy is exactly the opposite. The radiance of Christ exudes from his person, and being with him is a blessing. Admittedly, there are times when it is best not to be together. All of us have our quiet times and periods of withdrawal. Jesus himself did.

For long periods of time I would see Billy almost every morning, especially when we were engaged in Crusades nearly all year. On the road other Team members, including Bev, Cliff, T. W., and I would join him for his morning devotions when we would read God's Word, share prayer objects, and pray, oftentimes on our knees.

Even now he reads five psalms, one chapter of Proverbs, a portion from the Old Testament, and part of the New Testament every day in the week! He goes through the Book of Psalms and the Book of Proverbs once a month. You might inquire, "Why does he? He's gone through the Bible several times. He's preached to millions of people. Why does he, perhaps the outstanding religious leader in the world, have to read the Bible like that?" Because Billy, as Jesus did, feels the need of spiritual sustenance which includes Bible reading and study, meditation, prayer, and communing with God.

Believe it or not, Billy has always felt inadequate in Bible knowledge. Ruth, he testifies, is far deeper in the Bible than he. She has committed vast amounts of Scripture to memory and probably recalls far more passages and verses than her husband. So, Billy is a constant student.

Speaking about the Bible, Ruth has often stated publicly that she has reared their children by the Bible. She's said, in essence, "If the children misbehaved, if they did wrong, it was the Bible that guided me—differently with each child."

Ruth and Billy's devotional lives have prodded me in my own. Without cultivating meditation and prayer, the Christian will begin to take his spiritual walk for granted. It helps to remember those truths you've learned over the years.

> Thy word have I hid in mine heart, that I might not sin against thee . . . Thy word is a lamp unto my feet, and a light unto my path (Ps. 119:11,105).

> All scripture is given by inspiration of God, and is profitable for doctrine, for reproof, for correction, for instruction in righteousness: That the man of God may be perfect [spiritually mature], throughly furnished unto all good works (2 Tim. 3:16-17).

> And take the helmet of salvation, and the sword of the Spirit, which is the word of God (Eph. 6:17).

> Study to shew thyself approved unto God; a workman that needeth not to be ashamed, rightly dividing the word of truth (2 Tim. 2:15).

I doubt if there is a seminary professor who reads and studies more than Billy. He has, as should every committed Christian, a planned program of going deeper in the Bible, the inspired Word of God which is "quick [living] and powerful, and sharper than any two-edged sword . . . " (Heb. 4:12). He has memorized many portions of Scripture (especially when he was young), a technique which he has urged on those who have received Christ in the Crusades. "Thy word have I hid in mine heart, that I might not sin against thee" is as beneficial today as it was during David's reign. Today Billy finds it more difficult to memorize Scripture. One of the problems with Scripture memorization now is the many translations. You can take a passage and misquote it, and people think you are using another translation.

Billy, of course, likes many of the new translations, but he basically sticks with the King James Version because of its classic beauty and because he has done most of his memory work from it. There is no substitute, he feels, for "hiding" the Word of God in one's heart. Sometimes a person might not have a Bible or Testament with him, but he can draw on the memorized treasures of the Word from his memory bank.

Reader, I would encourage you to commit at least a verse a day to memory. Use the Scripture cards similar to those distributed by the Navigators. Carry the card with you. Look it over and study it throughout the day. It will surprise you what memorization will do for your life as a Christian. Our own Lord Jesus Christ answered the temptations of Satan from the Old Testament Scriptures. In the wilderness trial he parried every thrust of the devil by combating him from the Book of Deuteronomy (see Matt. 4).

We are headed toward the "retirement" age—but Billy denies it! I doubt if many Team members will ever officially retire. Like "ole man river," we'll just keep on rollin' along. Some of our number are already having health problems, but most people our age do, especially when they have lived in the pressure cooker as we have.

There is not a lazy bone in Billy's body. Ideas of withdrawing have crossed his mind, of course—as they have most of the older Team members: *rest more; retire; quit the Crusades; teach in a college or seminary; train young preachers.* From time to time rumors about Billy's "retirement" have spread through the media, but Billy keeps on. Because of my health I have been forced to conduct far fewer Crusades, yet the Team continues to conduct Crusades all over the world. I participate in all I can. Our Crusades are reaching millions of people by television, more than we ever dreamed possible a few years ago. Thousands of people are also coming to Christ through the television counseling service we initiated in 1981. We hope to be evangelizing when Jesus comes back to receive us unto himself in the Rapture.

Billy seems to have an endless reservoir of energy. Cautious doctors have warned him to slow down—and even to drop out of his hectic pace. He'll rest a while, but then he'll be in the Crusades again.

I've lost track of how many times doctors have called

me aside and urgently requested that I dissuade Billy from continuing. "He's killing himself," they've often observed. "Nobody can continue that pace and survive," they've cautioned. The doctors from Mayo Clinic, where Billy goes at least once a year, have often advised me about Billy's limitations.

While we were en route to Australia in 1959, Billy developed a severe blood-vessel ailment in his left eye. The doctors called it angiospastic edema of the macula. It could have caused blindness if it had moved in the wrong direction. The doctors warned me, "Please, please don't let him take any press conferences or ministerial meetings during the day. Limit him to one service at night, and even that's risky." They realized that as soon as Billy reached "The Land Down Under," the bigness of his heart would emerge, and in order to be with his brothers and sisters in Christ, he might violate medical advice. In the earlier years of our Crusades he would accept a staggering schedule, going all day long and late into the night.

One doctor at the Mayo Clinic—I won't call his name—said, "Look, Mr. Wilson, it would be far better if you'd take a two-by-four and hit him over the head with it than to let him go through all these pressures—the endless string of meetings, conferences, the Crusade services. He'll live much longer if you'll just go ahead and immobilize Billy for a while!"

Through the years I have sort of served as his guardian. I'd have to remind him, often against his protests, "Billy, you have to consider the long haul. You'll have to cut back now in order to prolong your health, your ministry, and your life." Most of the time he'd listen. Then, again, I should have paid more attention to my own physical condition, but that was in a previous chapter.

It is interesting to note that great evangelists like

Whitefield, Moody, and Sunday had given up their large evangelistic meetings by the time they were in their late fifties or early sixties and had turned more to smaller church meetings. Whitefield died at fifty-eight. So far as I know, no one has continued this long in big stadium Crusades. However, there has never been an evangelist with the kind of back-up team Billy has had. Neither has there ever been an evangelist with such technological devices at his disposal as Billy has—radio, television, satellite, and the like. All of this has helped preserve him physically.

Although Billy enjoys relaxation, he has an underlying restlessness. He has repeatedly confessed to Cliff, Bev, T. W., and me, "There's so much to do, so many books to write, so many invitations to preach all over the globe (that's why he gave up golf a few years ago), so many lost people, and not enough time." He is consumed with the tragic fact that multiplied millions will go to a Christless grave. And it haunts him, even when he's taking a much-needed and deserved rest.

Before and after Crusades the Team has often made little side trips for R & R (as the military calls it). One of the most memorable was a month-long retreat in Hawaii prior to the aforementioned Australian Crusade. The Team invited the venerable Dr. V. Raymond Edman, long-time president of Wheaton College, our alma mater. Dr. Edman, a spiritual and humble giant of the faith, became our pastor-Bible teacher-Christian counselor for that retreat. Every morning Billy, Ruth, Wilma, and I would meet with Dr. Edman under the palm trees on the hotel lawn. Dr. Edman would probe perceptively into the Word. Each of us would have a different translation, and Dr. Edman would do an exposition of the Scriptures verse by verse and chapter by chapter. That was one of the most enriching periods of my life.

Billy is still energetic and vibrant, but he can't go at breakneck speed as he once did. Yet, he has practically no "down time." Now he's writing more than ever, and he seems to write best away from the telephone and other responsibilities. He and Ruth often go to another country as the guests of friends in order to write. Now I'm finding more time for study and writing. Until this book I had written sermons, which have appeared in *Decision* magazine and in BGEA booklets—but no books. I have two or three more books on the drawing board, God willing.

Every Christian has the fruit of the Spirit in his life. Paul the apostle listed them:

> But the fruit of the Spirit is love, joy, peace, longsuffering, gentleness, goodness, faith, meekness, temperance: against such there is no law (Gal. 5:22-23).

Every believer in Christ will manifest these fruit in varying degrees. So, when I write about "The Real Billy Graham," I indicate that his character contains all of the fruit—love, joy, peace, longsuffering . . . .

Yet in every person's life certain qualities rise to the top. Billy is a devoted friend, a loyal supporter, an energetic activist for Christ, an efficient administrator and manager of his energy and time, a loving father and husband—all of these and more.

Those who are not close to Billy have never seen all of his facets. They conjure up an image based solely on his Crusade and television appearances. They are mesmerized by his flashing, steely blue eyes, the authoritative ring to his commanding baritone voice, and his control of the situation. According to where they're coming from, they view Billy differently. Because of his preaching the whole counsel of God, and his emphasis on judgment and hell, some may think of him as stern, even harsh. Because of his equal emphasis on grace and God's redeeming love, others may think of him as too lenient. It's all according to where the person is positioned.

In my lengthy ministry I have known thousands of Christians from every walk of life. All of them have had Christ in common. They have shared *koinonia* (fellowship) with one another. They are imbued with the same Holy Spirit. But I can candidly make the statement that Billy Graham is the kindest, most compassionate person I have ever known.

Back in the late 1950s the team was conducting a series of meetings in Kaduna, Nigeria. We were meeting the public in the open air. During that meeting we were contacted by Dr. Farrell Runyan, a Southern Baptist missionary.

Dr. Runyan invited us to visit a leprosarium outside of town. The mention of leper or leprosarium sends most people up the wall. They are reminded of the biblical examples of leprosy, its horror and devastation. As we were driving out to the lepers' compound Dr. Runyan explained, "Now, Billy, there are a number of Christians out here at the leprosarium. They've never seen your face before, but they've been looking forward for many months to your coming. They've built a temporary shelter out of limbs and straw (we used to call them "brush arbors" back in the country). We'll have services there."

When we arrived there, the lepers were in a spirit of joyful expectation. There they were, marred and scarred for life—many of them without noses, fingers, toes, hands. But they were ready to grasp the gospel with spiritual fingers and hands.

Billy preached passionately through Dr. Runyan as interpreter. The entire congregation was visibly moved and shaken. When Billy gave the invitation, many leprous stubs were raised high to signify that those lepers were coming to Jesus Christ.

After the service was over, and we were preparing to leave, a little lady, whose hands were eaten away by the hideous disease, meekly approached Dr. Runyan and Billy. Runyan interpreted for her:

"Mr. Graham, before today we had never seen you. But since your London Crusade in 1954 we Christians have been praying for you. Here in our little leprosarium we have been keeping up with your ministry."

Then, she reached out her little nubs and handed Billy an envelope. Through Runyan she said, "This is just a little love gift for you and your Team for your worldwide ministry." Humbly, Billy shook hands with the little lady's nubs.

As she left, Runyan read her note which was inside the envelope. "Wherever you go from now on, we want you to know we have invested in some small way in your ministry and given, in a sense, our widow's mite. We send our love and prayers with you around the world."

Inside the note were two Nigerian pounds, then the equivalent of $5.60 in U.S. money. Billy looked out at the handless woman—a saint of God who had the radiance of Christ—and wept. He turned his face out toward the bush country which stretched in every direction. Hardly able to speak, Billy said to Cliff Barrows and me, "Boys, that's the secret of our ministry." He was speechless for several minutes.

I shall never forget one of our tenderest moments several years ago. As you realize Billy has often visited our military personnel, whether in peacetime or during the Korean and Vietnam conflicts. In 1951 we were visiting the troops in Korea. On Christmas Day it was arranged for us to have dinner with Major John Eisenhower, the son of the president-elect. Billy had become friends with General Eisenhower in France and later had worked with him on several projects. Billy had telephoned Mr. Eisenhower before our leaving for Korea. The president-elect said, "I've got a son over there. If you see him, give him my love." During that trip I used my little Rollieflex camera to make a picture of Major John Eisenhower and Billy on Christmas Day. When I returned home I had the picture blown up and sent a copy to President-elect Eisenhower. He wrote me a gracious note of thanks.

On Christmas Eve right behind the front lines, Lt. General Jenkins had arranged for us to have dinner with him in the mess hall which was actually a tent. It was bone-chilling cold, probably below zero. Before going to eat, the General and Billy were escorted by the chaplain to the hospital where they greeted the patients and shook hands. Billy would pray with every wounded soldier. I remember that they had helicoptered in a young soldier who had been machine-gunned in the back. He was lying facedown in a MASH unit of the Tenth Corps. Billy fell down on his hands and knees so he could have eye contact with the badly wounded GI. Billy wished him a Merry Christmas.

Gasping for breath the GI testified, "Mr. Graham, I heard your message, even though I can't move. I want to tell you—it's worth coming all the way to Korea, it's worth being machine-gunned down, to open my heart to Jesus Christ. Mr. Graham, this day I have accepted Jesus Christ as my Savior."

The young GI was crying, and one of his tears fell, hitting Billy right in the eye. And their tears mingled together. It was an unforgettable Christmas Eve for me.

There was no peace on earth, but there was peace in that tent!

That's one of the tenderest moments I can recall. Billy said that it was one of his most meaningful Christmases.

In contrast the real Billy Graham can gain maximum mileage from a clean joke. However, he admits that he's not a comedian. His incidental humor is funniest, and he's also made some gigantic boo boos in the pulpit. In his early days as a preacher he could twist his tongue. He didn't know how to use the object of preposition. He'd say "to you and *I*," for instance.

Let's put it like this: Billy loves humor, but he's not a humorist. Most of the time, if he tries to be funny, he bombs. He still likes to tease with me and Team members like my brother, T. W.

Billy is a well-balanced person. His number-one preoccupation is preaching the gospel, but he doesn't talk religion all the time. Some people think you have to be yelling "Praise the Lord" or "Hallelujah" incessantly. That's marvelous if you're sincere. Billy's entire life is caught up in Christ, so anything he does is actually "Christian." And that's true for any believer who has captured the essence of discipleship.

Billy admits that he is not always the best judge of character. After all, he picked me as his first associate evangelist! Yes, with people he tends to be naïve. He wants to believe in people and trust them. It's easy to work with Billy, and has been through the years, because he does believe in people. He trusts you to do what you're supposed to do. He doesn't have to look over your shoulder. He's the opposite from paranoid. He's not a suspicious person.

But certain happenings of recent years have caused him to become far more cautious. He doesn't visit Washington to see politicians as much as he used to, especially during election years. Throughout his ministry he has tried to avoid partisan politics, still being friends of political leaders in both major parties. I believe his primary purpose has been to witness for Christ. Friendship with certain political leaders has opened many doors for him, of course. For example, when he has gone abroad, the fact that his friendship with a president or prime minister was known, has helped his witness in many ways. Though he does not agree with their political ideology, he also has friends in Eastern Europe. He has friends at the Vatican and many other places. These contacts have been invaluable in opening doors of witness which many other evangelists might never receive.

Billy once stated, even under the severest criticism for his broadmindedness and tolerance toward other cultures and traditions, "I will go anywhere, whether it is Moscow, Peking, or the Vatican, if I am allowed to preach the gospel."

At many press conferences, some of the reporters will try to pressure him into some sort of political statement. In the past he has put his foot in his mouth several times. These experiences have taught him to be extremely careful in answering these questions so as not to reflect a political bias.

I well remember one Crusade in El Paso, Texas. We had for years been friends with John Connally. He was running for governor of Texas for the first time. That particular night he was campaigning in El Paso. Billy said from the platform without thinking, "If I were a Texan I would vote for John Connally." Unfortunately, Billy's innocent statement was front-page news throughout

Texas the following day. As far as I can remember, this was the only time he ever publicly endorsed a candidate. Many people thought he had endorsed either President Johnson in 1964 or President Nixon in 1968. While he was close friends with both, and his name was often linked in the press with them, he did not openly endorse them. In fact, in 1960 when Mr. Nixon was running against Senator Kennedy, Billy came close to endorsing Nixon at the request of his friend, Henry Luce, publisher of *Time* and *Life*. Mr. Nixon called Billy on the phone and said, "Billy, your ministry is more important than my election. Don't get involved in this campaign." All of us will be forever grateful to Mr. Nixon for his gracious gesture. Later, President-elect Kennedy invited Billy to Florida to play golf with him. They became friends.

As a world citizen Billy feels a burden not only for Americans but for everyone. At the moment he is caught up in the cause of peace. While he is not a pacifist or for unilateral disarmament, he is for the destruction of all nuclear and biochemical weapons. He feels that permanent peace will only come when the Prince of Peace returns. But in the meantime we Christians have a responsibility to work toward the total elimination of these terrible weapons that could destroy civilization.

Certain writers have claimed that Billy is a complex personality. Not to me. He is transparent. He is God's man, but so is every person called to a particular task by the Lord. To Billy the task has been awesome and humbling. Even now, after all these years, he is amazed that God has called and used him.

In spite of all the attention paid to Billy, he is unspoiled. I have known of certain "Christian personalities" who have become stuck on themselves. They have become prime examples of the proverbial statement, "Pride goeth before destruction, and a haughty look before the fall (Prov. 16:18). I've seen "religious professionals" insult waiters, snap at busboys, and hurt the feelings of hotel maids. Never have I seen Billy resort to that kind of uncharitable behavior. He is a gentleman through and through. He recognizes people are judging his Savior by his attitudes and actions.

I live in awe of no one but God. Billy has always disliked people making over him, fawning over him. He is minute-by-minute aware that he is merely a vessel through which the message of God flows. The only time it *appears* that he asks for special attention is when he must have privacy and rest to prepare him for preaching and serving mankind. The pastor of the smallest mission likewise deserves that consideration.

Through some periods of his life, I have spent more time with Billy than even his own family, especially in the late 40s, 50s, and 60s. In more recent years I have conducted many Crusades of my own, and my brother, T. W., and others have traveled with him more than I have. But I feel that I really *know* Billy Graham. If Billy were less than genuine I would have parted company with him decades ago.

Yes, Billy Graham embodies the fruit of the Spirit, the attributes that every Christian should cultivate through the agency of the indwelling Holy Spirit. He is a people person. If he could, he would sit down and pray with every human being on the face of this globe. But he's one man. He is limited, even though millions have responded to the Christ he preaches and represents—and that's not counting those converted from reading his books and the Association's literature and from far-reaching radio and television broadcasts, including *The Hour of Decision*.

Billy is truly humble. His humility is refreshing, not a

mock, self-deprecating humility. He realizes from day to day that his life and ministry are totally dependent on Christ. Even though his salvation is secure—and every believer's is—he never takes his ministry for granted. He never assumes that God will continue to empower him if he drifts and becomes careless in his Christian walk.

Paul's words to the Philippians best sum up Billy's feelings at this point:

> Brethren, I count not myself to have apprehended [arrived, reached all my goals]: but this one thing I do, forgetting those things which are behind, and reaching forth unto those things which are before, I press toward the mark for the prize of the high calling of God in Christ Jesus (Phil. 3:13-14).

21
Where Do We Go from Here?

It is my fervent prayer that no readers will interpret me as bragging about our ministry. We realize that if God turned us loose we'd disintegrate. What has been accomplished has been done by the amazing grace of God. Billy has often said that if God took his hand off his lips, they would turn to clay. I've heard him repeat again and again, "God will not share his glory with another."

Many have commented, "Well, why doesn't the Team branch out into something else? You've done it all in evangelism. You've been on every continent of the globe. You've traveled thousands—maybe millions—of miles. You've seen several million people walking the aisles for Christ. There have been other millions by television, radio, and through the efforts of various Team members. Aren't you jaded about it all?"

By satellite there's no telling how many hundreds of millions have watched Billy Graham on television. And there are the videotapes and radio tapes translated into scores of languages.

Let's face it. We're human. Many people have tried to sidetrack Billy. They've tried that on me and the other

Team members, too. They've remarked to me, "You can make money as an entertaining speaker, as a motivational speaker, as a humorist." (That's what they call 'em instead of comics or comedians!)

Not long ago Billy was offered big money to go on a speaking circuit. They would pay him $15,000 to $20,000 per speech, and they would expect him to give two or three speeches a month. Of course, he gave them the answer he gave Y. Frank Freeman in Hollywood back in 1949. Freeman had a luncheon for him at Paramount and they offered him a movie contract. Billy always answers, "God has called me to preach the gospel, and I do not intend to do anything else as long as I live."

The major political parties, at least certain leaders in them, have tried to interest Billy in the presidency. Some people feel that he might have won, at least fifteen to twenty years ago. One day Billy was swimming with President Johnson at Camp David. Suddenly President Johnson, in front of several other people, suggested, "Billy, I think you ought to run for president when I'm finished with my term. If you do, I'll put my entire organization behind you, and I'll be your campaign manager." Billy laughed and answered, "Mr. President, I don't think I could do your job." The President then said, "Billy, I know you think I'm joking, but I'm really serious. You're the one man who might turn this country around."

Around thirty years ago one of the major networks called Billy, Walter Bennett, and Fred Dienert into their headquarters in New York City. They offered Billy a million dollars a year to sign a contract for nationwide television with an hour and a half program opposite the highly popular Arthur Godfrey. Out of courtesy to the network officials Billy did take a few weeks before giving them a definite reply, because in the offer they had stipulated that he could continue with his Crusades, and that they would happily originate his program in whatever city he was in. They felt the Crusades would even add interest to the program. They explained, "We can't find anybody who can give Arthur Godfrey any competition. He has the ratings locked up."

Later Billy told them he was flattered and that he appreciated the offer. He had given it thought and prayer but had decided to decline. Those TV executives were amazed and flabbergasted. Billy said once again, "Gentlemen, God has called me to preach, and I'd be afraid to do anything else. My life is the gospel of Jesus Christ." Through the years it has made my blood boil in my veins when I hear his critics falsely accuse him of being interested in money because such talk is a satanic lie.

Several years ago one of the big networks offered him a quarter of a million dollars merely to sit on their board and serve as a consultant. He declined, saying, "When I have time I'll give you my counsel, but it won't cost you a dime." Imagine it—turning down an offer like that—meet now and then with the board of directors, give advice, and pocket a quarter of a million dollars a year. He testified to them, "I believe God has called me to do what I'm doing, and I can't mix my motives. My ministry is proclaiming the gospel of Jesus Christ."

Billy and the great movie producer, Cecil B. DeMille, were close friends. Billy had also met him at the aforementioned luncheon hosted by Y. Frank Freeman. DeMille had become fascinated with the way Billy had turned down Freeman's offer for a Paramount contract. He asked Billy if he would serve as one of the consultants in making the epic film, *The Ten Commandments*. Billy would never forget the expression on Mr. DeMille's face and the sparkle in his eyes as he later confessed, "Billy, I was hoping secretly in my heart that you would turn Frank down. I am now thoroughly convinced of your integrity and sincerity as a preacher of the gospel." Mr. DeMille, himself a professing Christian, encouraged Billy with these words: "I wish you Godspeed and God's blessings."

When the filming of *The Ten Commandments* was completed, Mr. DeMille gave Billy a private showing. Then he and Charlton Heston, the star of the film, presented to Billy The Ten Commandments written in stone that had been used in the filming of the picture.

We've been asked to do commercials and to put our stamp of approval on all kinds of products. Firms have made the Team members all types of offers, especially Billy. A number of years ago I found myself in a bind. A certain insurance company was headed up by a Christian friend of mine. His company was brand-new and offered a special type of insurance at low rates. I thought it was a good idea and endorsed it. They carried my picture in Christian magazines and secular publications throughout the country. Dr. L. Nelson Bell, Billy's father-in-law, also appeared, along with Dr. Palmer Muntz, the general director of the Winona Lake Bible Conference.

However, to many people this company had the endorsement of the Billy Graham Association. At that time Billy's name was on the front pages of newspapers across the country. They never paid the BGEA a cent; neither did they pay Dr. Bell or me. Yet that company was built at least in part on those early endorsements and has gone on to make millions of dollars. The founder and now the foundation have been most generous in helping Christian causes. I have rejoiced. Yet, I have been a little puzzled why they have never given a dollar to the BGEA, as far as I know, when they did not hesitate to use the reputation of the BGEA in the early years.

I am sure that Billy is going to keep on with the Crusades because they have become television Crusades. We are now reaching more millions of people in one Crusade than the Apostle Paul did in his entire lifetime. We will continue as long as the Lord gives us health and strength. I'm sure that Billy will continue writing; he loves to write as much as he loves to preach. And God has used his writings as thousands of people have been converted through the tracts, books, and articles he has written.

The Association has built and paid for "The Billy Graham Center" located on the campus of Wheaton College at Wheaton, Illinois. This Center already has the largest library on evangelism in the world. It has a graduate school of over 500 students at present. We feel that the Graduate School is one of the best of its kind in the world, where students can earn their master's degrees in communications, biblical studies, psychological counseling, and related subjects. All of the Association's archives eventually will be there.

There students can study the history of evangelism. Also, hundreds of evangelical organizations are housing their archives there, as well as many clergymen. It would be difficult for a person to write a definitive thesis on evangelism and missions without consulting the Center. The archives of all Billy's memoirs, writings, recordings, tapes, and books of the Team members—plus everything Billy has written, and virtually everything that has been written about him—will be there.

In all of our Crusades we have Billy Graham Schools of

Evangelism. The faculty is largely made up of prominent pastors and seminary professors from across the nation. Of course, we have many people coming to these, and they might not have had the opportunity to attend a college or seminary. We do try to line up outstanding evangelical professors, preachers, and scholars to teach and preach at these pre-Crusade events. This also has an appeal to many top Christian laypersons who want to lay hold of the rudiments of Christ.

We will continue to pull out all the stops to send the gospel to the ends of the earth. Our organization is spending much time in helping nationals from the Third World to receive proper training in Bible schools, colleges, or seminaries so they can return to their countries as indigenous workers.

Some groups, of course, have accused the BGEA of doing things "the American way" wherever we go. We know better than that, and we realize our methods must be contextualized. The message is always the same, though. This same message of Jesus Christ has been interpreted into many different languages, and it always works when it is preached in the power of the Holy Spirit.

There are many ministries of the BGEA that have never been generally known. For example, there is a student scholarship fund, and hundreds of students, especially from the Third World, have been trained as a result of this fund. They have received training, not only in their own countries, but in seminaries and Bible colleges in the United States, Great Britain, and elsewhere.

There is also an emergency relief fund through which millions of dollars have been given for relief in many parts of the world.

World and regional congresses of evangelism have been organized and financed by the BGEA.

For instance, the Berlin Congress of 1966 which made such an impact on the evangelical world was the vision of Billy Graham. The Association organized and paid for the Congress. Billy had decided to let *Christianity Today* officially sponsor the Berlin Congress because he felt that would give far more of an intellectual respectability to it. He asked Dr. Carl F. H. Henry if he would serve as chairman. Dr. Henry at that time was editor of *Christianity Today*.

The magazine itself had been founded by Billy. With the help of his father-in-law, L. Nelson Bell, it was launched in 1956. Before that it seemed that *The Christian Century* had the field to itself. Billy felt there ought to be an evangelical theological journal. When he first began to organize *Christianity Today*, we thought it would be owned and operated by the BGEA. It took Billy eighteen months to convince those around him that the journal was needed and to receive pledges of financial support to launch it.

Billy eventually decided it would be a mistake for the magazine to be run by the BGEA, so a separate board was set up, chaired by Dr. Harold John Ockenga of Boston. The first editor was Dr. Wilbur M. Smith. Dr. Smith accepted and then backed down about six months later, feeling he could not make the move from the west coast. Upon the recommendation of Dr. Harold Lindsell, Billy asked Dr. Henry to become the first editor. Dr. Henry served ably for about eleven years.

Then when *Christianity Today* was looking for a new editor, Ruth suggested her old boyfriend at Wheaton—Harold Lindsell, so Billy called him. After considerable thought and prayer Dr. Lindsell accepted the invitation to come as editor and performed an able work for several years. Billy now serves as the chairman of the Board of *Christianity Today*. The current editor is Dr. Kenneth Kantzer.

The Lausanne Conference of 1974 was also a vision of Billy's. It was also largely organized and financed by the BGEA. The Lausanne Covenant, which came from that conference, was written first by Jim Douglas of Scotland, revised later with the help of Leighton Ford, and then the entire planning committee went over it line by line and phrase by phrase, almost everyone having a part in it. Then at the end John Stott was asked to put together the suggestions recommended by the committee. The Lausanne Covenant was actually a composite of many people's thinking. It is almost another Nicene Creed and is used as a platform for evangelical thinking throughout the world today. Without the BGEA there would never have been a Berlin Congress or a Lausanne Conference.

There are other congresses that the Association has organized and financed, the European Congress on Evangelism held in Amsterdam, the Singapore Congress, and others. We have scrupulously managed money designated for such use with evangelical conferences and pastors' conferences throughout the world.

Billy has always felt that the BGEA should be kept in the background, for fear that people would think we were trying to dominate the evangelical world. As a matter of fact, the headlines of a Toronto paper in 1974 read, BILLY GRAHAM THE NEW EVANGELICAL POPE. Such misunderstandings as that have caused Billy often to withdraw from leadership roles he perhaps should have accepted. Dr. Carl Henry has strongly chided Billy for not accepting the leadership of the evangelical movement in the 60s. Dr. Henry felt that the evangelical world missed an unparalleled opportunity. At that time, perhaps Billy was in a position to lead the evangelical world as no one else was, but Billy felt—and still does—that God has called him primarily to Crusade evangelism and nothing was going to deter him from that ministry.

Strange, though, giving money is sometimes far more difficult than raising it. Let me give you an example of an unusual problem. When we left Albuquerque in 1950, we had $7,500 left over, and we had no idea what to do with it. Those involved in the Crusade there suggested, "Since you're now going to Korea, take the money and give it to the various missionaries over there. We know that you're going to minister to the troops on the front lines, but we want to send this to the people of South Korea." One of the biggest problems Billy and I ever had was trying to give away that money. We didn't want to make anybody mad. We gave several hundred dollars to the Southern Baptist Hospital in Pusan. Some other denominational workers and missionaries heard about it and wanted us to give them the same amount. And it was difficult handling that money, which was small by today's standards.

Billy and those of the BGEA have agonized and prayed that God would help us be proper stewards and trustees of all the funds with which he has entrusted us, because every week we receive requests from scores of established institutions to educate students, feed the hungry, and help many Christian causes.

Some people have the idea that the Billy Graham Evangelistic Association is always affluent and in no need of funds. That is not the case. In 1981 it looked as though the BGEA was going deeply into the red, and we had no surplus funds. But somehow God laid the matter upon the hearts of God's people and we ended the year in the black. The Association is faced with the tremendous task of helping Wheaton College raise enough money to keep the doors of the Wheaton Center open. It costs almost a million and a half dollars a year to support that vast enterprise alone.

Personally, Billy and the older Team members become more tired than when younger. The schedule is constantly being made up by younger men who don't understand that Billy's strength is limited. In the last two or three years Billy seems to be doing more than ever. It is simply a fact of life that we are getting older. What we are going to do in the future remains in the hands of the Lord. I might live thirty more years, but that's with divine providence. We're living one day at a time, one step at a time.

We don't know what the future holds for the Crusades. Unfortunately, a few years ago one of our associates accidentally misrepresented to the press in Dallas, indicating that we were going to change our approach. The reporter thought that "we" referred to Billy and the rest of the Team, but the associate was speaking of his own particular ministry with the Team. As you realize we have several associate evangelists who often carry on their own independent Crusades. That associate said, "We're no longer going to these big open-air Crusades. We're just going to the campuses of the universities. Private homes. We're going to have more coffee breaks. Teas. Places where we can share ideas in an informal atmosphere. And talk with people as they did in the early church."

When he found out about that statement, Billy had to call another press conference and deny the report that was spreading across the nation. Some damage had been done. People to this day are still asking me, "Is it true that Mr. Graham is giving up the Crusades?" I have to answer in the negative. Billy plans to die with his preaching,

Crusade boots on. He wants to preach the gospel to as many people as possible until his last fleeting breath.

What happened to us through the years is that we'd come in both exhausted and thankful, and we still couldn't sleep because we were keyed up and had to "wind down." Any preacher relates to the feeling, especially at the end of a taxing day on Sunday—preaching two or more sermons, visiting in the afternoon, counseling, meeting with people, trying to collect your wits to face people with your messages. Whew!

But the overriding thought that seizes the concerned preacher of the gospel is thousands and millions of people without Christ and tremendous multitudes who have never once heard the message.

In the New York Crusade of 1957, for example, I found myself lying awake in my hotel room, wondering how many thousands out there in those seats were fighting the invitation that particular night, tightening their fists. How sad that thousands were going out into midtown Manhattan without Christ—and out into Picadilly Circus in London, or down Broad Street in Nashville, or out into the surrounding areas of Tokyo. You try to leave that in the hands of God, but it still haunts you. You think about the thousands who were under conviction but answered, "Almost thou persuadest me to be a Christian." And they say within their hearts, *Not now. I'll call for you at some more convenient season.* "Not now" often turns into "never." No matter how prayed up you are, that gnaws at your vitals. People without Christ going out into the never-ending night of eternity—without Christ, without hope in this life, or in the world to come.

One of the greatest lessons I've learned in the ministry is not to take God Almighty or the Scriptures for granted. It's easy to read a portion of Scripture one time, then put your Bible down, and sort of forget about it. I have read the Word of God through again and again during my ministry. I've lost track of how many times. Billy has read it through many times. For a while he was trying to read clear through the Bible at least once a year.

Every time I read the Bible something new and exciting leaps out at me. "Beyond the sacred page, I seek thee, Lord, my spirit pants for thee, oh living Word."[1] One of my daughters said to me several years ago, "Hi Daddy So and So." I think it was "Warbucks" or "Daddy-O." She hesitated for a moment and said, "How does that grab you?" I answered, "Well, honey, I never heard that expression before. That grabs me the wrong way." But I understood what she meant, and now it's becoming daily language for people all over.

Maybe that's far-fetched, but that's what happens about certain portions of the Bible as they grab me and finally become a part of my life. You could read the Bible through a thousand times, but there will always be something cleansing and exciting about the Word. That's why I plead with all preachers, whether in conferences, schools of evangelism, or whatever, to read the Word of God. Get into the Word and study it daily and systematically. I served on the Foreign Mission Board of the Southern Baptist Convention for eight years. I always interviewed that would-be missionary by asking him/her: "Do you have any systematic form of daily devotional life?" And too often I have seen those missionaries shamefacedly admit that they had no form of daily, systematic prayer and Bible study. And that has shocked me. I never recommended turning a candidate down on those grounds, but that is a serious lack.

A leader of one of the great missionary organizations told me many years ago that in a private questionnaire he found out that 92 percent of seminary students for that organization had no daily program of devotion. I answered, "Dear Lord, help us. No wonder the world's about to blow itself to bits. No wonder we're living in a nuclear, divisive world. If missionaries of the cross go to farflung fields without a daily devotional walk, what will we do?"

The devotional life with God is the key source of one's spiritual sustenance day by day—all under the power of the Holy Spirit, of course. God has promised to bless his Word. He has commissioned us to pray and not to faint. He wants us to commune with him. And I have learned that a Christian needs to be instant (ready) in season and out of season to share Christ with others and to become soul-winners and maintain the soul-winning life.

And I could've excused myself and rationalized, "Lord, I'm with Billy in mass evangelism, and thousand of people are coming to Christ through the contacts of others and Billy's preaching. I've sometimes had to stand in for Billy. And I have my own Crusades and revival meetings, as many as I can arrange. Lord, surely I don't need to be out there doing that business of personal soul-winning." The devil wants me to alibi and excuse myself with, "I'm so busy I don't have time to be a soul-winner."

God doesn't look upon numbers as such. Every soul is priceless in his sight. That's why I pray God will give me the energy to share Christ with people all around me, wherever I go—on planes, in restaurants, in motels and hotels, on the streets, in stores, at resort areas, waiting for cabs and limousines to and from the airport. Everywhere!

Several years ago a young preacher from Maine wrote me a terribly caustic letter. He was pastor of a very small church. He wrote, "I'm sick and tired of hearing about

Billy Graham and all of those huge crowds. I don't read about Billy talking to individuals."

I wrote him back that Billy constantly witnesses one on one, but that never makes the press. I wrote, "God has called you to a small parish, but God has called all of us to faithfulness. You are to be faithful to that small church; you are to love and win every person in that community to Jesus Christ. God is going to hold you responsible for how faithful you were to that little flock and not how many you had. 'To whom much is given, of him much shall be required.' Someday Billy Graham will have to give account to God Almighty for the millions of people to whom he preaches, and you will have to give account of those forty or fifty people to whom you preach."

And I've learned, through bitter experience, to take care of the temple of the Holy Spirit, my body. Every Christian ought to make this a priority. I've already talked about my heart trouble. Yes, there was a constant activity in the ministry (and still is)—and tension, also a building up of nervous energy. And all of these took their toll on "this old house" that Stuart Hamblen wrote about.

Every Christian should spend time on his body and not merely his soul. The two are interrelated, and the Bible speaks about "to wit, the redemption of our body" (Rom. 8:23). We misunderstand Paul when he writes: "For bodily exercise profiteth little" (1 Tim. 4:8). He wasn't teaching that it doesn't profit. Rather, he was speaking relatively. Granted, bodily exercise is not more important than spiritual, but why separate the two? The dedicated Christian should be aware that his body is the temple of the Holy Spirit. Both kinds of exercise are essential to health.

I urge people to have an exercise program. All I can

handle is walking a couple of miles a day. The doctor advised *me* never to jog. I've been the prime target of Billy's preaching when he has dealt with gluttony from the pulpit, and it used to be embarrassing when he'd turn around, looking almost directly at me, and say, "There are certain people on this Team who need to go on a diet— and stay there." It got a laugh, but it also used to get my goat because I was under conviction. Good grief, I've had people all over the world approach me and say, "Grady, don't feel bad about it, since Dr. Graham is saying it in love. Don't be offended by it."

When dear Ethel Waters was with the Team we used to kid her. At one time she weighed around 375 pounds, but in the few years she regularly sang at the Crusades, she lost around 200 pounds, which was amazing. Ethel realized that fat was bad for her, and she prayed that the Holy Spirit would help her to exercise discipline. There was a certain brand of fried chicken she adored. Oftentimes during a Crusade she would request of me, "Babe, go out and get me a bucket of that stuff. I don't mean a slice—get me a bucket." And she would nibble on that chicken for three or four days. We need to learn about proper nutrition and proper food.

Through the years the Team members have learned a great deal about the control of their time and energy. We lead far more disciplined lives than we used to. In the early days we tried to do everything and be everywhere at the same time. In many ways I burnt myself out in my early ministry. Yes, it was (and still is) thrilling and humbling to realize that multiplied thousands of people are coming out to hear Billy preach and members of the Team participate. And it's an ecstatic thrill to watch those flood down those aisles for Jesus Christ. That never grows old.

In our early ministry there were times when I would speak seven, eight, nine, ten times a day. That's too much. When a man spreads himself out too thin, the effectiveness of his ministry will lessen. I am fully persuaded that's why many men are sometimes dull and flat in the pulpit. Maybe sitting up all night studying. Making a long trip back from an evangelistic meeting when one should've stopped somewhere along the road and spent the night instead of driving straight through. Sometimes a person will speak halfheartedly to a group, and it's often only an indication that he's merely worn-out. And even your reasoning power begins to leave you a bit. Charles Haddon Spurgeon, the great English Baptist preacher, testified that he always took a short nap before preaching on Sunday night.

I did a heap of thinking while I was in the hospital recuperating from surgery. It's kind of corny, but I've stopped to smell the roses. I have also learned the value of true friendship. I never minimized that, but I didn't do enough to stay in touch. For years Wilma and I have sent out many Christmas cards, even though I know many people have quit that practice. Sometimes we would enclose a picture of the family. That's one form of keeping in touch. I'm not making a commercial for the phone company, but I've more and more gone to the phone to encourage my friends, to share with them, and just to talk, since the miles separate us. I'm not a letter writer, and it's taken me many years to write this book. I have depended on the telephone.

People need to know of your compassion, sympathy, love, and prayers. And I make mine known, but until my worst heart attack I'd never done enough of that.

And I want to spend my remaining years imparting to

young ministerial students and clergymen the value of tender, friendly compassion for their parishioners and other friends. Many of us need to spend more time being compassionate and loving and not jocular and backslapping, and you realize nobody on earth enjoys a joke more than I do!

Billy has repeatedly bared his soul to me, "Grady," he has mused out loud, "I pray that we can preach the gospel until Jesus returns in his second coming." If God wills it that is our dream, a dream that quietly began almost a half-century ago when a short kid from Charlotte met a tall, gangling guy from the country.

John Pollock wrote about me:

> His most vital contribution lay behind the scenes. In his company Billy could relax. Beneath jollity and buffoonery Grady hides a rapier mind, and if his gift of seeing the absurd could relieve tensions induced by awkward committees or sudden adversity, he could also, as Billy's closest friend, help him to retain his balance. "If the Lord keeps Billy anointed, I'll keep him humble."[1]

By the grace of God I've had a hand in that!

Epilogue

In the Preface I began with James 1:2 which encourages the reader to "count it all joy." I have often used this phrase (and sometimes the entirety of James 1:2-4) as a parting thought to my friends.

My dear friend and hunting buddy, Dr. Sam Russell, likes that admonition so well he printed up a batch of stationery for me which reads, "Count It All Joy." In spite of numerous trials and oftentimes difficult circumstances, one can "count it all joy."

Supremely joyful are the memories which I have reviewed. I am thankful for literally thousands of fond and sacred recollections. The Bible says, "The joy of the Lord is your strength."

The past seven years of my life have been the most difficult, and yet praise be to God for the unspeakable joy through it all.

*   *   *   *

My friend, this is my closing word to you: if you have never known joy, real joy, and peace of heart, mind, soul, and body, you can find it only in a personal saving and keeping faith in the Lord Jesus Christ. Since our earliest meetings we have given away multiplied thousands of little gospel booklets entitled "Four Things God Wants You to Know." In essence, here are the four things:

1. *You are a sinner and need a Savior.* Romans 3:23 tells us: "For all have sinned, and come short of the glory of God." Romans 6:23 says, "For the wages of sin is death; but the gift of God is eternal life through Jesus Christ our Lord."

2. *You cannot save yourself, no matter how hard you try.* You can work your fingers to the bone for some good and worthy causes or the church. You may pray and pray and pray until all of the breath and strength have departed from your body. You may read the Bible many times or memorize great portions of Scripture and still not become a Christian. You see, the Bible says, "For by grace are ye saved through faith; and that not of yourselves: it is the gift of God: not of works, lest any man should boast" (Eph. 2:8-9).

3. *You must repent of your sin.* Jesus said, "I tell you, nay: but except ye repent, ye shall all likewise perish" (Luke 13:5).

4. *You must be born again.* John 3:7 (in Jesus' words): "Marvel not that I said unto thee, Ye must be born again." In John 3:3 Jesus said, "Except a man be born again, he cannot see the kingdom of God." All the way through the New Testament, repentance is clearly taught. Without true repentance of sin, no person can enter into God's kingdom and no one can go to heaven. Being "born again" literally means being "born anew" or "being born from above" which is borne out by the original Greek text.

God loves us and made it possible for us to have this new life. "For God so loved the world, that he gave his only begotten Son, that whosoever believeth in him should not perish, but have everlasting life. For God sent not his Son into the world to condemn the world; but that the world through him might be saved. He that believeth on him is not condemned: but he that believeth not is condemned already, because he hath not believed in the name of the only begotten Son of God" (John 3:16-18).

Jesus declared, "I am come that they might have life, and that they might have it more abundantly" (John 10:10). Second Corinthians 5:17 emphasizes, "Therefore, if any man be in Christ, he is a new creature: old things are passed away; behold, all things are become new." Now that means anyone, any person.

Wherever you are right now, this very moment, you can pray in your heart, asking God to be merciful to you, a sinner, and asking him to save you for Jesus' sake. In your own words and in your own way, you can pray: "O God, I'm a sinner, and I'm sorry that I've sinned. I confess my sin to you now. I repent of my sin; I turn from my sin. Right this moment, as well as I know how, I receive Christ as my Savior and Lord."

The Bible says in Romans 10:9: "That if thou shalt confess with thy mouth the Lord Jesus, and shalt believe in thine heart that God hath raised him from the dead, thou shalt be saved." God will save you.

Then launch into your life for Christ. Read the Bible, God's inspired Word. Read *and* study it every day. Pray. Pray throughout the day. It's not essential that you pray out loud or on your knees, even though there may be times you'll want to do that. Align yourself with a Bible-believing, gospel-preaching church where the fundamentals of the Christian faith are believed, taught, and preached. Determine that you are going to be faithful and loyal to the kingdom of God. (See Ps. 119:11,105; 2 Tim. 3: 16-17; 2 Tim 2:15; 1 Thess. 5:17; Matt. 6:9-13; Matt. 21:22; Luke 18:1; Matt. 10:32-33; Eph. 5:25; Col. 1:18; Heb. 10:25; 2 Pet. 3:18; Matt. 6:33.)

This is the secret, the only *key* to real *joy* and peace. The Bible says, "The joy of the Lord is your strength" (Neh. 8:10). Therefore, "count it all joy" when you truly know Christ and experience the joyful life he alone can give you!

AMEN!

NOTES

Preface

1. Billy Graham asked Dr. Wirt, then a pastor in California, to become the first editor of *Decision* in 1958. Actually, the first issue came out in November of 1960, and the popular magazine has been a success since its inception. A superb author and editor, Dr. Wirt spearheaded the Schools of Christian Writing which continue to inspire and help train multitudes of Christian communicators. Upon his retirement in April of 1976, Dr. Wirt was succeeded by Roger Palms.

Introduction

1. Copyright, 1936, by Percy B. Crawford.
2. Words by Stuart K. Hine © Copyright 1953, 1955, Renewed 1981 by Manna Music, Inc. Used by permission.

Chapter 2

1. John Pollock, *Crusades: 20 Years with Billy Graham*, Special Billy Graham Crusade Edition (Minneapolis: World Wide Publications, 1969), p. 6. Copyright © 1966, 1969 by John Pollock. All rights reserved.
2. Lyrics and music by P. P. Bliss.

Chapter 5

1. Originally published by McGraw-Hill, Copyright © 1966 by John Pollock—later published as *Crusades: 20 Years with Billy Graham*, Special Billy Graham Crusade Edition, Copyright © 1966, 1969 by John Pollock.
2. Copyright © 1979 by John Pollock, published by Harper & Row Publishers, San Francisco.
3. "It Is No Secret" by Stuart Hamblen © Copyright 1950 by Duchess Music Corporation. Used by permission. All Rights reserved.

Chapter 8

1. *Pollock, Crusades: 20 Years with Billy Graham*, p. 171.

Chapter 9

1. From "I'd Rather Have Jesus," © Copyright 1939 by George

Beverly Shea. Assigned to Chancel Music Company, 1966. Reassigned to Rodeheaver Company, 1982. Used by permission.

Chapter 12

1. The five were Nate Saint, Jim Elliot, Ed McCully, Roger Youderian, and Pete Fleming. Nate was Rachel Saint's brother; Jim was Elisabeth Elliot's husband.

2. By B. B. McKinney, 1949. Copyright 1949 Broadman Press. All rights reserved.

Chapter 14

1. Songwriter-singer-instrumentalist Arthur Smith is one of my good neighbors in Charlotte. He is best-known for his "Dueling Banjos" instrumental number. Several years ago he and I collaborated on a Christian record album, "The Finger of God," featuring his music and my reading of the Scriptures.

Chapter 19

1. © Copyright 1951, Renewal 1979 by Redd Harper. Assigned to Zondervan Fiesta Corporation. All rights reserved. Used by permission.

2. Copyright, 1936, by Percy B. Crawford.

Chapter 21

1. Pollock, *Crusades: 20 Years with Billy Graham,* p. 85.

INDEX